Urban Architectures in Interwar Yugoslavia

Resulting from a twenty-year period of research, this book seeks to challenge contradictions between the concepts of national and modern architectures promoted among the most pronounced national groups of Yugoslavia: Serbs, Croats and Slovenes. It spans from the beginning of their nation-building programs in the mid-nineteenth century until the collapse of unified South Slavic ideology and the outbreak of the Second World War.

Organized into two parts, it sheds new light onto the question of how two conflicting political agendas – on one side the quest for integral Yugoslavism and, on the other, the fight for strictly separate national identities – were acknowledged through the architecture and urbanism of Belgrade, Zagreb and Ljubljana. Drawing wider conclusions, author Tanja D. Conley investigates boundaries between two opposing yet interrelated tendencies characterizing the architectural professional in the age of modernity: the search for authenticity versus the strive towards globalization.

Urban Architectures in Interwar Yugoslavia will appeal to researchers, academics and students interested in Central and Eastern European architectural history.

Tanja D. Conley is Associate Professor of Architecture at Massachusetts College of Art and Design, USA.

Routledge Research in Architectural History
Series Editor: Nicholas Temple

Books in this series look in detail at aspects of architectural history from an academic viewpoint. Written by international experts, the volumes cover a range of topics from the origins of building types, the relationship of architectural designs to their sites, explorations of the works of specific architects, to the development of tools and design processes, and beyond. Written for the researcher and scholar, we are looking for innovative research to join our publications in architectural history.
www.routledge.com/architecture/series/RRAHIST

Time, History and Architecture
Essays on Critical Historiography
Gevork Hartoonian

The Rise of Academic Architectural Education
The Origins and Enduring Influence of the Académie d'Architecture
Alexander Griffin

Finding San Carlino
Collected Perspectives on the Geometry of the Baroque
Adil Mansure and Skender Luarasi

Architecture and the Language Debate
Artistic and Linguistic Exchanges in Early Modern Italy
Nicholas Temple

Urban Architectures in Interwar Yugoslavia
Tanja D. Conley

Urban Architectures in Interwar Yugoslavia

Tanja D. Conley

LONDON AND NEW YORK

First published 2020
by Routledge
2 Park Square, Milton Park, Abingdon, Oxon OX14 4RN

and by Routledge
605 Third Avenue, New York, NY 10017

Routledge is an imprint of the Taylor & Francis Group, an informa business

First issued in paperback 2021

© 2020 Tanja D. Conley

The right of Tanja D. Conley to be identified as author of this work has been asserted by her in accordance with sections 77 and 78 of the Copyright, Designs and Patents Act 1988.

All rights reserved. No part of this book may be reprinted or reproduced or utilized in any form or by any electronic, mechanical, or other means, now known or hereafter invented, including photocopying and recording, or in any information storage or retrieval system, without permission in writing from the publishers.

Trademark notice: Product or corporate names may be trademarks or registered trademarks, and are used only for identification and explanation without intent to infringe.

Publisher's Note
The publisher has gone to great lengths to ensure the quality of this reprint but points out that some imperfections in the original copies may be apparent.

British Library Cataloguing-in-Publication Data
A catalogue record for this book is available from the British Library

Library of Congress Cataloging-in-Publication Data
Names: Damljanovic, Tanja, 1963– author.
Title: Urban architectures in interwar Yugoslavia / Tanja D. Conley.
Description: New York : Routledge, 2020. |
Series: Routledge research in architectural history |
Includes bibliographical references and index.
Identifiers: LCCN 2019048711 (print) | LCCN 2019048712 (ebook) |
ISBN 9781138393646 (hardback) | ISBN 9780429401640 (ebook)
Subjects: LCSH: Nationalism and architecture–Yugloslavia. |
Identity (Psychology) in architecture–Yugloslavia.
Classification: LCC NA2543.N38 D36 2020 (print) |
LCC NA2543.N38 (ebook) | DDC 720.9497–dc23
LC record available at https://lccn.loc.gov/2019048711
LC ebook record available at https://lccn.loc.gov/2019048712

ISBN 13: 978-1-138-39364-6 (hbk)
ISBN 13: 978-1-03-223823-4 (pbk)
ISBN 13: 978-0-429-40164-0 (ebk)

DOI: 10.4324/9780429401640

Typeset in Sabon
by Newgen Publishing UK

To Carlton and Ella

Contents

Introduction: historical outline of a Yugoslav nation and its appearance through urban architecture of the capital cities   1

PART I
The birth of national architectures   15

1   De-Ottomanized Belgrade   17

2   Croationed Zagreb   41

3   Architectural affirmation of the Yugoslav idea   65

PART II
National architectures in the unified nation   87

4   Imperial Belgrade   89

5   Avant-garde Zagreb   127

6   National Ljubljana   166

Conclusion: national and urban architectures within the Yugoslav cultural space: the role of architectural historiography   205

Index   *218*

Introduction
Historical outline of a Yugoslav nation and its appearance through urban architecture of the capital cities

Yugoslavs or South Slavs were gathered into one state in 1918 after the end of World War I. This was considered the fulfillment of their century-old romantic aspiration to create a national state until the dissolution of the country in the 1990s.[1] The formation of the Kingdom of the Serbs, Croats and Slovenes resulted from a new political order in post-war Europe when the "South Slavic question," initially discussed among German politicians and thinkers, was answered by the winners of the war: France and Britain.[2] With the fall of the Berlin Wall and the reunification of Germany, both multi-ethnic Slavic nation-states created out of the territories of the disintegrated Habsburg Monarchy – the North Slavic Czechoslovakia and South Slavic Yugoslavia – split into multiple national units. While the northern counterpart, entirely under the Habsburg rule prior to WWI, was divided peacefully, Yugoslavia suffered through a sequence of military conflicts run by the army associated with Serbian leadership – the successor of military formations which had initially gained Serbs autonomy from the Ottomans.

The first, short-lived South Slav state was formed from lands of today's Slovenia and Croatia during Napoleon's reshaping of Europe after the war with Austria, when he gained control over the region that had for centuries been controlled by the Habsburgs. Named Illyria, after the ancient Roman Illyricum, with its seat in today's capital of Slovenia, Ljubljana, the province was considered "the safeguard in front of the Viennese door" securing the Napoleon's victory. As part of the French Empire, Illyria was run under the Napoleon Codex, asserting equal human rights and equal status regardless of religion, which was publicly declared to citizens of Ljubljana in 1811. The foundation of the modern school system, along with the first attempts at creating a unified South Slavic language were made at the same time. Establishing Napoleon's rule and putting civic laws in effect in the Illyrian Province inspired the First Serbian Uprising against the Ottomans, considered the earliest bourgeois revolution in Southeastern Europe. Although it ended in failure, the uprising inspired further fights for national freedom, which resulted in the autonomy of the Serbian principality in 1830. While Napoleon's Illyria was returned to the Habsburgs at first as the Kingdom of Illyria and later, after the 1848 Revolution, subordinated to the reorganized administrative hierarchy of Austria-Hungary, the Serbian principality took advantage of the slower pace of modernization in the Ottoman Empire and finally reached the status of an independent state at the Berlin Congress of 1878.

Although the first South Slavic nation-state was created by France, the concept of a modern nation was imported and adopted from the Romantic thought flourishing in German lands in the nineteenth century. The national movements of Central Europe, which culminated with the Revolution of 1848, have been associated with the creation of democratic societies based on principles of equal rights for all citizens regardless of their status at birth, defined by the French Revolution. However, the transformation from traditional to modern societies took a slightly different direction in Central Europe and especially in its peripheral zones. In contrast to France and the Anglo-Saxon countries, the concept of *Kulturnation*, insisting on the cultural authenticity of the nation embedded not only in language but also in history, folk myths, arts and poetry predominated here over the idea of nation based on constitutional law. As it had been discussed by Hans Kohn,[3] and later elaborated by Liah Greenfeld,[4] the types of nationalism have varied between the Anglo-Saxon and French versus German and Russian models, of which the first two fostered individualism and civil rights while the latter insisted on collectivism and common ethnic roots, thereby providing fruitful ground for the constitution of authoritarian democracies. The process of modern nation-building among the Slavs of Central and Southeastern Europe followed the second pattern recognized in recent literature as ethnic nationalism, the initial concept of which dated back to Johann Gottlieb Fichte's writings promoting the language as means of binding the nation together and the educational system as a tool for her awakening and remembering her origins.[5]

The creation of modern societies assumed the power of the city as a place of trade and production, but also as a place of generating an enlightened culture opposed to the narrow-minded rural world. However, in Central Europe and especially in its peripheral zones, where peasants drastically outnumbered city dwellers, the ruralness was blessed as an intrinsic deposit of the national body. The enthusiasm about the Romantic notion of *Volksgeist* – the people's spirit – was projected on a special attitude toward the rural population. Therefore, the modern dichotomy between the progressive urbanity and backward ruralness occurred here in a more ambiguous form than in the Western world. Differently from the Western trend of rapid industrialization associated with urban life, the modernization of Central Europe assumed that the majority of the rural population were involved in cultural and educational programs without being affected by substantial economic transformations. Accordingly, Ernest Gellner's argument about nationalism as a force of social entropy arising in response to the needs of social communication in industrial society was not quite applicable onto the Central European context.[6] By means of cultural exchange which had been embedded in pre-industrial societies mainly through church canons in old-Slavic alphabet and unwritten, orally conveyed historical narratives, the Slavic population maintained a sense of national affiliation despite the slow pace of transformation into a bourgeois society, and further developed a Romantic kind of nationalism focused on folklore as a source of identification. As the South Slavs accepted and adopted the Romantic type of nationalism based on the concept of *Kulturnation* with the rural population being the carrier of the spirit of the people, the accelerating urbanization was not a precondition for generating modern nationhood. Lacking the component of early industrialization, the age of modernity was first announced here as the strive for national affirmation not necessarily conjoined with the homogenizing forces of modernization.

Attempts at creating modernized grammars and scripts for specific South Slavic languages or, even more, unified linguistic templates, defined more profoundly the programs of national unification. The South Slavic distinctness was noticed and praised in the West, after Herder's writings on the exceptional character of Slavs. Herder's view of a nation defined by language and folklore inspired a generation of Slavic intellectuals[7] to show to the rest of the world that Slavic people share equal status among Europeans. Many of them, such as Slovenian polyglot, scholar and librarian of the Habsburg court Jernej Kopitar, prompted Slavic intellectuals to study the language and poetry of their people and introduce the collections of national epics and poems to Western Europeans. Kopitar's disciple, Serbian-born Vuk Stefanović Karadžić, who learned how to read and write in a remote Orthodox monastery, was fortunate to meet Kopitar in Vienna, where he emigrated after the failure of the First Serbian Uprising in which he had participated. Following Kopitar's advice, Karadžić collected and published volumes of Serbian folk songs, tales and riddles, but also created the first dictionary of vernacular language and the first grammar. Karadžić developed a modern alphabet to serve a unified language in both Latin and Cyrillic scripts, for which he was praised by the advocates of a unified South Slavic ideology, but also heavily criticized by opponents who attacked him for either Catholicizing Serbs or Serbianizing Croats. In addition to collecting and publishing medieval literature, the establishment of newspapers, reading rooms, theater groups and intellectual societies in towns of the Habsburg Monarchy populated by large sections of Slavic population, was instrumental in formulating the national programs. However, the intention of Habsburg authorities was to adjust to the new political realities inspired by the French Revolution and convey the idea of Slavic national awakening subjected to the existing imperial hierarchies. Therefore, the creation of nation-states out of territories controlled for centuries by the Habsburgs was not anticipated as part of the same plan.

On the other hand, the idea of statehood had existed among the South Slavs since the constitution of medieval kingdoms. Slavic tribes inhabited the region during the great migrations in the fifth century, while the evidence about the later arrival of Croats and Serbs dates to the rule of the

4　*Introduction*

Byzantine Emperor Heraclius, who invited them to settle in his territories in fear of the penetrating Avars. Croats and Serbs were, as most Slavs, Christianized during the ninth century, when Greek missionaries Cyril and Methodius translated the Bible to the Old Slavonic language by using the newly invented Glagolitic alphabet adjusted to the vernacular language of Slavs. The emergence of the first early medieval Slavic Kingdom has been linked to the still disputable coronation of Croatian King Tomislav in 925 CE. Tomislav's title of king, probably gained from Byzantium, was recorded in Ljetopis Popa Dukljanina [Chronicle of the Priest of Dioclea] or Regnum Sclavorum,[8] a precious medieval manuscript serving as the starting point for all later historical interpretations in service of a national ideology. Nineteenth-century scholars – such as Ivan Kukuljević-Sakcinski, the founder of Croatian archeology and Franjo Rački, a prominent historian and politician supporting the Yugoslav idea – paid tribute to Tomislav's coronation as the pivotal event for the rebirth of the statehood. The event was also celebrated by nineteenth-century Croatian painters, as well as a younger generation of Yugoslav artists during the millennial celebration of the event in Zagreb in 1925. Another event also keenly celebrated during the revival of Croatian national ideology in the nineteenth century was the coronation of Dmitar Zvonimir as the king of Croatia and Dalmatia in 1076 by Pope Gregory VII, who saw advantage in granting the titles to the Slavic kings for their loyalty. Prior to the coronation, Zvonimir served as the Ban of Slavonia, a title that would in later Croatian history play a significant role in building the self-esteem of Croatians as a historically self-governed nation.

　The same chronicle speaks about the acknowledgment of the Kingdom of Duklja [Dioclea], the Serbian counterpart to the Croatian kingdom, on the territory of today's Montenegro, Kosovo, the western portion of Serbia and the eastern of Bosnia-Herzegovina, reached by King Mihailo [Michael] who skillfully balanced between Rome and Constantinople and was finally address as king by the same pope in 1077. Mihailo's son Constantine Bodin allegedly incorporated the northern Serbian principality of Raška [Rascia] into the boundaries of Dioclea, thereby for the first time unifying all Serbian-settled territories under the same crown.[9] However, the coronation of Serbian King Stefan Prvovenčani [Stephan the First Crowned] with the crown sent from Pope Honorius III in 1217 would become honored as the pivotal event attributed to the Serbian statehood. Prvovenčani was a son of Duke Nemanja of Raška, the founder of the Nemanjić dynasty whose later fourteenth- and fifteenth-century successors, Milutin and Dušan, managed to take control over large areas of today's Serbia, Montenegro, Macedonia, Albania, Bulgaria and Greece. While Prvovenčani gained the crown from the pope, his brother Rastko Nemanjić, later to be canonized as St. Sava, took advantage of the unsecure position of the Ecumenical Patriarchate, at that time it was moved to Nicaea due to the crusaders' conquest of Constantinople, and reached the autocephaly for the Serbian

Orthodox Church in 1219. The most ambitious among the Nemanjićs was Dušan, the self-proclaimed tsar of Serbs and Romans who ruled like a Byzantine emperor and accordingly raised the Serbian Orthodox Church to the level of patriarchy. However, Dušan's glory was short-lived; after his sudden death, the vast territory was divided into five principalities, among which Prince Lazar's portion approximately corresponded to the modern-day central Serbia. Prince Lazar lead the Serbian Army in the battle against the Ottomans at the Kosovo Plain in 1389, the central national tragedy causing the collapse of the medieval state and thereby inspiring efforts at revenge and recuperation until the Serbs recaptured Kosovo in the Balkan Wars of 1912–1913. Dušan's empire played a special role in the genesis of the modern idea of a supranational Slavic state under the shield of the reborn Serbian crown – the idea which could be understood as accomplished after the formation of Royal Yugoslavia, with the Serbian dynasty of Karađorđević being its sovereign.

After the collapse of the medieval states, the South Slavs lived for centuries in territories belonging to two multiethnic empires: the Habsburg and the Ottoman. While Croatian lands at first became a part of the Hungarian kingdom and were later incorporated into the Habsburg's boundaries, the Serbs were conquered by the Turks and remained in the Ottoman Empire until the beginning of her withdrawal from Europe after the Berlin Congress of 1878. The border between the Habsburgs and the Ottomans almost coincided with the previously established division between the Catholic and the Orthodox realms from 1054, originally rooted in the split of the Roman Empire into the Western and the Eastern, with the capital being moved from Rome to Constantinople – the seat of the first Christian emperor. After the loss of the medieval independent state, Croats along with Slovenians, who had already obeyed the hierarchy of Catholic bishop seats, continued living under the Habsburgs, the holders of the crown of the Holy Roman Empire. On the other hand, Orthodox Serbs, like most ethnicities oriented toward the Ecumenical Patriarchy in Constantinople, were conquered by the Ottomans, who did not explicitly prosecute the Christians, yet did not allow any social advancement without converting to Islam.

The further Ottoman penetrations into the European continent lasted until their defeat in the Battle of Vienna of 1683, followed by the Karlowitz Treaty of 1699, after which sentiments toward the Christians radically changed. The Great Migration of Serbs of 1699 from Kosovo to the Habsburg-controlled territories resulted from the Ottoman revenge following the unsuccessful rebellion after the treaty. With the promise of better life and privileges than under Ottoman rule, more than 36,000 Serbian families moved from Kosovo under the leadership of Arsenije III Čarnojević, the Serbian patriarch with the original seat in Peć [Albanian Pejë] to the region of today's Vojvodina, which had been settled by a significant percentage of Slavs mainly subordinated to the Catholic Church. They had received an invitation from the Habsburg Emperor Leopold I to settle on territories north of the Sava and the Danube and the military frontier originally controlled by the Croatian ban. At first forced to obey the Catholic authorities, Čarnojević and his followers managed to maintain the political autonomy of the Serbian church, while the Patriarchate of Peć came under the jurisdiction of Ohrid archbishops. The church's autonomy was the leading factor for maintaining a specific Serbian identity both under the Ottomans as well as the Habsburgs, yet its power was not limited only to maintaining a cultural identity. The political aspirations of the Serbian church lead to the proclamation of the Serbian Duchy of Vojvodina during the 1848 Revolution.[10]

The different religious affiliations and political and economic circumstances in the Habsburg and Ottoman Empires were the major factor in generating distinct modern national identities of Serbs and Croats. Most Slavic populations in both cases consisted of poor peasants. However, in the Habsburg regions there was still a noticeable number of Croatian and Slovenian aristocrats with some political rights, which was not the case with Serbs, neither those who emigrated during the Great Migrations nor those who remained in the Ottoman Empire and did not convert to Islam. The ethnic policies of the Habsburg court granting different rights to certain South Slavic groups – such as the religious concessions to Serbian communities and limited political rights only to Croat nobility, but also the different status to solders of different ethnic origins – played an important role in splitting Serbs and Croats into two modern nations.

While individual medieval states and different affiliations to Christianity traced the future identities of Croats and Serbs, the Slovenian modern identity was rooted in the linguistic movement spread with the rise of Reformation. As early as 1550, the first book in the Slovenian language was printed by Martin Luther's follower and protestant reformer Primož Trubar, who gave birth to what would later develop into the Slovenian alphabet, and shortly thereafter, in 1584, the Bible was rendered into Slovenian as one of the earliest compilations from Latin and Greek by Trubar's disciple Juraj Dalmatin. Although entirely suppressed by the Counter-Reformation, the spread of Jesuits and their teachings in the following century, the short-lived excitement about the Reformation has remained celebrated as a herald of modern Slovenian nationhood – October 31, the day when Martin Luther nailed up the Ninety-five Theses has been acknowledged as a national holiday in the recently recognized state of Slovenia. Although ideas about the formation of the independent state of Slovenia have existed since the 1848 Revolution, the fact that the Slovenian population was not numerous usually led to the belief that Slovenians could only survive as a separate group with specific cultural and political rights within a larger nation-state. Many leading Slovenian intellectuals saw Catholic Austria as the best natural protector of Slovenian rights in a multinational framework, while the others hoped for the end of German influence and unification with other South Slavs. Nevertheless, both options were burdened with a threat of potential assimilation, the reason why Slovenian intellectual leaders reached a consensus about preserving the uniqueness of Slovenian language despite the attempts at integration with the other South Slavic languages. The enthusiasm about the Yugoslav idea was somewhat present among Slovenians in the nineteenth century, yet it certainly grew into the mainstream after the Austrian annexation of Bosnia-Herzegovina, as in other parts of the future Yugoslavia. Although Slovenians had political rights under the Habsburgs and were elected in the Carnolian Diet,[11] which led many to believe that their political place was within Austria, it was not before the creation of Yugoslavia following World War I that they gained recognition and power as a political nation.

When Zagreb grew into the center of the Slavic linguistic movement in the early nineteenth century, behind the fight for a reformed language stood a broader ambition for national emancipation. The reformer of the Croatian language and admirer of Vuk Stefanović Karadžić's work, Ljudevit Gaj, accompanied by a group of Croatian intellectuals and young patriots, established the Illyrian Circle with the aim of promoting a broad concept of pan-South Slavic unity rooted in the belief that their origins reached as far as to the ancient Illyrians, as Napoleon had promoted by the short-lived Province of Illyria. The acme of the Illyrian project was reached when the Yugoslav Academy of Science and Arts was established in Zagreb in 1868 to make Zagreb a focal point of the South Slavic arts, humanistic studies, scientific research and education. The academy was funded and financially supported by the principal proponent of Yugoslavism in Croatia, Bishop Josip Juraj Strossmayer, and headed by his collaborator, a leading politician and historian, Viennese-trained Catholic theologian Franjo Rački. The foundation of the Croatian University and the Philological Circle in Zagreb as well as a variety of publications, schools and cultural institutions in smaller cities received financial support from Strossmayer and Rački. Although Strossmayer and Rački's Yugoslavism, promoted under the name of Illyrism, applied to all South Slavic ethnicities within and beyond the existing boundaries of the monarchy, their ideology of unification has been more recently understood as being at odds with the similar ideas coming from Serbs from the Ottoman Empire, who at the time of the Illyrian Movement had already reached a certain level of political autonomy. The forerunner of an idea of the political emancipation of South Slavic people under the Croatian name, however, dated back to the earlier times coincident with the Ottoman pushback after the Treaty of Karlowitz. Pavao Ritter Vitezović, a Croatian chronicler educated in the Jesuit school of Zagreb, who developed a keen interest in printing and cartography, and accordingly established the first Croatian Printing House in 1694[12] after inheriting a printing machine from the bishop, brought to Zagreb via Ljubljana. The key contribution to a modern view of the place of Croats in the context of Yugoslav ideology were his publications *Croatia Rediviva* [*Reborn Croatia*] from 1700, accompanied by the *Mappa generalis regni Croatiae totius* [*Map of the Entire*

Croatian Kingdom] and *De aris et focis Illyriorum* [*About Illyrian Alters and Hearths*], through which he promoted a belief that all South Slavs were Croats.

It was in 1830, after the Second Serbian Uprising under the leadership of Miloš Obrenović, when the principality of Serbia was acknowledged by the Ottoman Porte, and only five years later the first modern constitution based on the French models, thereby considered the easternmost offspring of the French predecessors at the time, named Sretenjski ustav [Candlemass Constitution], was put in effect. Although short-lived, it defined the roles of the prince and later the king, the State Council – consisting of departments for internal and foreign affairs, defense, education and legislature – and the National Assembly in a way that would have a strong impact on its later longer-lasting versions. Since the final collapse of Yugoslavia and the proclamation of the Republic of Serbia in 2006, the Candlemass has been celebrated as the Day of Serbian Statehood in observance of the first constitution. Its author, Dimitrije Davidović, born to the family of an Orthodox priest from Zemun, was educated in Vienna where he founded and edited a Serbian newspaper *Novine serbske iz carstvujuščeg grada Viene* [*Serbian Newspaper from the Imperial City of Vienna*] "to enlighten and entertain over four million Serbs living under the Habsburg yoke at the time." Recognized for his diplomatic skills, Davidović was appointed Miloš's secretary as well as the Minister of Education, yet his main role in defining a political role for Serbia in the context of South Slavic ideology was the publication of a *History of Serbian People* in Vienna in 1821 – including a map with territories inhabited by Serbs, a big portion of which would later become Yugoslavia. Yet, a clearly elaborated idea about a South Slavic state, with Serbia being its unifying power, was inaugurated by a politician of Czech origins, František Zach, who believed that Serbian leadership would support a broader pan-Slavic reciprocity, namely the Polish efforts to suppress both German and Russian domination over their territory. Zach believed that once Yugoslavia was formed out of a strong Serbian core, the rest of the Slavs would be able to resist foreign intrusions. This idea was further elaborated by Ilija Garašanin, the Serbian Ministry of Interior Affairs in Prince Miloš's government in the essay *Načertanije* [*Outline*] written in 1844 as a close replica of Zach's original text with the same title. Despite the close analogies to Zach's template, Garašanin's *Načertanije* has been discussed through the lens of the Great Serbian ideology, since Garašanin used the word "Serbian" instead of "Yugoslav," as it had appeared in Zach's version. On one side considered as a Slavic Bismarck[13] and on the other as an advocate of Serbian expansion and assimilation,[14] Garašanin and his *Načertanije* inspired the nineteenth-century Yugoslavian euphoria as much among the protagonists of the Illyrian Movement as it did among Serbian politicians. Despite a more recent interpretation about the Serbian politics of unification amounting to a quasi-South Slavic ideology that only covered the Great Serbian agenda, young intellectuals from all over the future country accepted Belgrade as the unifying center at the turn of the century. They did so believing in Serbian political power as the prerequisite for an independent Slavic state, a single nation fused from different ethnicities to be able to cope with the aspirations of Austria, as well as Russia, to dominate the region. Thus, the leading Croatian artist Ivan Meštrović, the dramatist Ivo Vojnović and many others accepted and promoted Belgrade as the center of Yugoslavism and emphasized Serbian superiority while using the Serbian history, myths and folk epics as the main source of inspiration for their politically engaged art projects.

The battle for supremacy between the two potential South Slavic capitals, Belgrade and Zagreb,[15] along with the concepts of centralism versus federalism, were the poles of inescapable tension during and after the creation of Yugoslavia in 1918. The involvement of the Slavic population in Austria-Hungary on one side and of Serbs from the Kingdom of Serbia as the ally of France, Britain and the USA on the opposite during the Great War, was an additional factor that produced tensions and separate identities among ethnic groups within the future state. The creation of Yugoslavia came after intensive diplomatic consultations among different political groups in the region, but also as an agreement among the big powers.[16] The first South Slavic state to appear after the collapse of the Habsburg Empire was announced in Zagreb on October 29, 1918 by the National Council of Slovenes, Croats and Serbs, which met in the Croatian Assembly and proclaimed itself as the new supreme organ of the state of South Slavs in Austria-Hungary.[17] It was named the State of Slovenes, Croats and Serbs, with Zagreb as its capital. The same political body announced the unification of the state with the kingdoms of Serbia and Montenegro, so that the new state named the Kingdom of Serbs, Croats and Slovenes was proclaimed in Belgrade on December 1, 1918, with Belgrade as the capital city.[18] Not only did the Serbian capital become the capital of all South Slavs, but the Serbian royal dynasty became their ruler. The discontent about the supremacy of Serbia in the newly formed state was best expressed by the activity of Croatian opposition parties, which ended tragically when their leader Stjepan Radić was murdered inside the parliament. Claiming that the stability of the country was jeopardized by the disorderly conduct of the parliament, King Aleksandar established a dictatorship in 1929. The revolt caused by the king's authoritative decision culminated in his assassination in Marseilles in 1934. The final collapse of the Kingdom of Yugoslavia occurred during the Second World War, when the eastern territories – Serbia, Macedonia and Montenegro – were occupied by Germans, while the western lands – Croatia and Bosnia – became the Independent Kingdom of Croatia under the protection of the Third Reich. In the last years of the war, the Allies helped the partisan army lead by Marshal Tito defeat the German army, but also supported the official army of the kingdom in its fight against the Germans. After the capitulation of Germany, the Socialist Federative Republic of Yugoslavia was formed and was led by Tito and the communist party until his death. The dissolution of

10 Introduction

Socialist or Second Yugoslavia, which could be traced back to the 1970s, finally occurred during the 1990s.

The aim of this study is to link the urban and architectural identities of the three capital cities of the so-called First Yugoslavia, the Kingdom of Serbs, Croats and Slovenes with national identities of its three constitutive nations. The search for the occurrence of the ideas of nation in urban architecture is of fundamental importance in the region throughout which the nation has been identified with the *Volksgeist*, and consequently the ruralness and vernacular traditions provide the essence of a national soul. The ideas of national identity and architecture have been most often discussed through the concept of national style and to some extent in regard to the architectural programs in service of the nationhood. What has been missing until this publication is analysis of the urban fabric of the three Yugoslav capital cities, emerging since the modern national awakening of the South Slavs in the nineteenth century and lasting until the collapse of the Yugoslav nation rooted in the bourgeois values, after the victory of communism.

The construction of national monuments and shrines among Yugoslavs was similar to the endeavors of other European nations that had accomplished national unification and the constitution of nation-state prior to WWI. Programmatically, those structures aimed to add a new layer of spirituality to the existing congregational monuments and memorials by the power of historical narrative or simply by the aesthetic experience separate from prayer and commemoration. The modern nations-in-making worked hard on establishing their images through the foundation of new institutions and programs run by the power of reason, whose architecture was swayed by the sublime of aesthetic judgment. The intentional monuments to the nation reached the level of collective identification mostly indirectly, being introduced to the broad national body through educational systems and mass media. The new secular architectural monuments primarily relied on the quality of architectural and art works by the members of an imagined community. Thereby, the question of art and architectural education became the leading force in conceptualizing a national identity.

The invention of a national style, inspired by archaic art and indigenous folklore, was common among the nations that fought against the domination of Western European empires – the colonization powers. The interest of the young nations' architects in pre-Gothic layers of architectural history were attempts at digging deeper from the period considered the evidence of nation's birth by the colonizing powers. While the nineteenth-century architects from the leading nations fostered the academic, either neo-Classical or neo-medieval sources, their turn of the century followers, mainly from the periphery, switched toward more remote references, both in terms of timeline and geography. The search for an expression of a national spirit stylistically differed in those nations that still searched for a national cohesion in the first decades of the twentieth century. This trend was clearly shown among the nations created after the dissolution of the Habsburg Empire, whose architects were educated under Otto Wagner and art historians influenced by Josef Strzygowski. The preoccupation with primordial forces deeply hidden in national origins waiting to be revealed by unique national genii, occurred not only in works by direct disciples of Vienna Secession, such as Ivan Meštrović and Jože Plečnik, but also among the next generation of more radical avant-garde artists and thinkers, indirectly tied to the Wagner legacy. Despite the attempts of the young and rebellious, most of the architectural development around Europe, including its periphery, would end up relying on the trusted academic models, inherited and perpetually transformed in the architectural institutions since their establishment in the 1600s. Once the nation was affirmed and the initial passion evaporated, the architectural radicalism would be altered with the universal Classicism, or the later Classical reiterations – the Renaissance and the Baroque. This was the case even when the Modern Movement penetrated; after the initial phase of avant-garde breakthrough, the Modernist realizations on a broader scope turned both compositionally and formally towards the certified Classical schemes.

Architecture of the capital cities in interwar Yugoslavia was attuned to the widespread programmatic and stylistic models of their European counterparts, yet the way these broadly conceived ideas were applied to each urban situation was what made them particularly Yugoslav – Serbian, Croatian or Slovenian. This book is based on a premise that the analysis of urbanistic and architectural designs from the past still matter as the means for improving the contemporary design methods and the built environment in general. Although not concerned with the idea of a national style in the romantic sense, the question of style is being addressed through the lens of most popular, predominating formal modes, making the cities visually coherent and distinctive. Thus, the interwar architecture of Belgrade has been discussed from the standpoint of monumentality, achieved either by the means of Historicist styles or Modernist experimentation with new forms and materials, relevant to its status as the main capital of the three-tribal kingdom pushing toward a coherent national identity. On the other hand, Zagreb's interwar identity has been explored through the fact that the city remained the leading economic center of the country, open toward the international leftist movements and the ideology of classless society, after it had failed in becoming the prime capital of the South Slavdom. Ljubljana was, differently from Belgrade and Zagreb, building its image of a national capital for the first time after the constitution of the Kingdom of Serbs, Croats and Slovenes; luckily for the city, one of the world's most ingenious architects, Jože Plečnik, took a pivotal role in shaping the city as well as a program for the newly formed school of architecture.

Nevertheless, the prevalent stylistic tones and the typical programs would not be relevant for the discussion about the link between the national and urban identities if they were not contextualized within the ambitious urban transformations and reshaped micro-spaces – the

12 Introduction

polygons of immediate identification of citizens with the abstract concept of nationhood. Bonding the citizen with the civic identify depends on a vast range of social groups and their activities which gravitate towards explicit buildings or urban spots. The collectively memorized urban nodes and landscapes, experienced through strolling or commuting on the everyday level, create the sense of belonging to the collective stronger than do the distant pictures of intentional nationality distributed and perceived via visual media. Therefore, the choice of case studies presented in the book depended in the first place on the position within the urban context, and only secondarily as aesthetic artifacts created by recognized names from the architectural profession. The overview of the urban and architectural development of Belgrade, Zagreb and Ljubljana – followed from the beginning of rapid urbanization until the collapse of national ideologies based on middle-class values – tends to show how the ideas of modernization, necessarily correlated to the formation of nations in the modern sense, occurred in the urban environments that most drastically processed the conversion of peasants to citizens. The idea of the modern nation is inseparable from the notion of citizenship, thereby the image of a capital city has been fundamental for representing a national identity. However, the same urban and architectural realization might represent multiple national identities. Thus, verbal and written interpretations by the urbanists and architects in charge of projects provide the reliable witness statements of the original ideological intentions. Yet, it has been the discipline of art and architectural history that stamps the final label on what architecture belongs to whom, as will be discussed in the Conclusion. The intentions of this book are not to challenge the biases, but to point out the fact that defining a national identity by means of urbanism and architecture has been a personal narrative by the scholar in charge despite his or her attempts to be scientifically accurate and objective.

Notes

1 List of publications about Yugoslavia published in English include: John Lampe, *Yugoslavia as History*, Cambridge: Cambridge University Press, 1996; Leslie Benson, *Yugoslavia: A Concise History*, New York: Palgrave Macmillan, 2003; and Marie-Janine Calic, *A History of Yugoslavia*, West Lafayette: Purdue University Press, 2019, enlarged since the dissolution of the country. Depending on different political circumstances, the interpretations and emphasis on historical events have changed and consequently the tone and subject of interest differ from the older literature such as: Vladimir Ćorović, *Istorija Jugoslavije*, Belgrade: Narodno delo, 1933; Dragoslav Janković and Bogdan Krizman, *Građa o stvaranju jugoslovenske države (1.1.–20.12.1918)*, Vol. 1 and 2, Belgrade: Institut društvenih nauka – Odeljenje za istorijske nauke, 1964; Ferdo Čulinović, *Jugoslavija izmedju dva rata*, Zagreb, 1961; and Vladimir Dedijer (ed.), *Istorija Jugoslavije*, Belgrade: Prosveta, 1972.

Introduction 13

2 The "question" was recognized as a political rivalry of big nations over the territories that had belonged to the weakened Ottoman Empire by Karl Marx, *The Eastern Question, Letters 1853–56*, New York: B. Franklin, 1968. The later phrase resulted from a book title by one of most active proponents of the Yugoslav unification from 1911 – more recently published as R. W. Seton-Watson, *The Southern Slav Question and the Habsburg Monarchy*, New York: H. Fertig, 1969.
3 Hans Kohn, *Prelude to Nation-States: The French and German Experiences*, Princeton: D. van Nostrand Company, 1967.
4 Liah Greenfeld, *Nationalism: Five Roads to Modernity*, Cambridge, MA: Harvard University Press, 1992; Liah Greenfeld, "Types of European Nationalism," in John Hutchinson and Anthony Smith (eds.), *Nationalism*, Oxford: Oxford University Press, 1994: 165–171.
5 Johann Gottlieb Fichte, *Address to the German Nation*, New York & Evanston: Harper Torchbooks, 1968 (originally published 1845).
6 Ernest Gellner, *Nations and Nationalism*, Ithaca NY: Cornell University Press, 1983.
7 Discussed in William Wilson, "Herder, Folklore and Romantic Nationalism," *Journal of Popular Culture*, vol. 6, no. 4 (1973): 819–835.
8 Regnum Sclavorum, possibly written in the twelfth century, known only through the later, early sixteenth-century translation to Latin by Marko Marulić, has been considered the cornerstone of South Slavic historiography.
9 Today a disputable fact, discussed by the most prominent Serbian historian from the first half of the twentieth century, Viennese-trained Vladimir Ćorović in *Istorija Srba* [*History of Serbs*] completed right before his death in 1941 – reprinted as *Ilustrovana istorija Srba*, Vols. 1–6, Belgrade: Narodna knjiga, 2005.
10 On the importance of Serbian Orthodox Church for retaining a strong sense of national identity among many sources see: Nicholas Pappas, "Between Two Empires: Serbian Survival in the Years after Kosovo," in Alex Dragnich (ed.), *Serbia's Historical Heritage*, New York: Boulder, 1994: 28–29.
11 In the 1907 elections, Slovenes received fifty-two mandates out of 382 in Carnolian diet, which did not correspond to the number of 131 elected Slovenes. See Janko Pleterski, "Položaj Slovencev pred prvo svetovno vojno," in *Jugoslovenski narodi pred Prvi svetski rat*, Belgrade: SANU, 1967: 785–786.
12 Discussed in Josip Bratulić, "Pavao Ritter Vitezović: utemeljitelj hrvatske zemaljske tiskare u Zagrebu" [Pavao Ritter Vitezović: The Founder of Croatian State Printing House in Zagreb], *Senjski zbornik*, vol. 22 (1995): 179–186.
13 David MacKenzie, *Ilija Garašanin: Balkan Bismarck*, Boulder, CO: East European Monographs, 1985.
14 For Garašanin's ideology of Great Serbia, see Ivo Banac, *National Question in Yugoslavia: Origins, Politics, History*, Ithaca NY: Cornell University Press, 1984: 82–84.
15 R. W. Seton-Watson (1879–1951) recognized the cultural potentials of Zagreb versus the backwardness of Belgrade and accordingly supported the idea of Zagreb as the capital city as the only solution to the "Southern Slav question." In Seton-Watson, *The Southern Slav Question*: 342.
16 About the constitution of Yugoslavia, see John Lampe, *Yugoslavia as History: Twice There Was a Country*, Cambridge: Cambridge University Press, 1996.

17 For the original document of the proclamation of State of Slovenes, Croats and Serbs, see Snežana Trifunovska, *Yugoslavia Through Documents: From its Creation to its Dissolution*, Dorobrecht: Martinus Nijhoff Publishers, 1994: 147.
18 For the document of the proclamation of Kingdom of Serbs, Croats and Slovenes, see Trifunovska, *Yugoslavia Through Documents*: 157.

Part I
The birth of national architectures

1 De-Ottomanized Belgrade

Nationalizing the urban fabric

At the time of the signing of the Hatti-I-Serif of 1830 – the agreement that acknowledged the autonomy of Serbia – Belgrade was a border city of the Ottoman Empire with a military post, dating back to Ancient Rome, placed in the fortification. Through this agreement with the sultan, the leader of the Second Serbian Uprising, Miloš Obrenović, gained the title of the prince of Serbia, a status that enabled him to claim a certain level of independence from Istanbul, and the power to create government institutions on the national and local levels, to address cultural and church affairs, and to establish an educational system in the native language.[1] The Ottoman army, however, still controlled the city and borders with the Habsburgs, at the Sava and Danube rivers. Shortly before Serbian autonomy, Belgrade lived through a quick period of takeover by the Habsburgs, 1789–1791, the last in a sequence of similar eighteenth-century events characterized by sudden urban transformations from an "Oriental" into a "Baroque" city and the reverse.[2] After receiving autonomy, the Serbian center started being reshaped again in accordance with the Austrian urban and architectural doctrines as the most familiar means for diminishing the "Orient." The turnaround from the East to the West was carried out primarily by those connected to the Serbian diaspora, which had been formed after the Great Migrations of Serbs in 1690 and 1737–1739, to the Habsburg territories, while Serbs born in the native land still mingled between the new courses of modernization and long-preserved rural customs – the central theme of Serbian identity construction up to the present day. In a similar fashion, the national ideals in Serbian society still oscillate between a desire towards achieving a Western-looking environment and an inherited tendency to resist any kind of foreign intrusion.

The survey of 1838 recorded a total of 13,000 citizens, among which 8,500 were Serbs, 2,700 Muslims, 1,500 Jews and the rest declared as "foreigners."[3] These numbers already revealed the tendency to push out the Muslims, who had constituted four-fifths of the city's population prior to the First Serbian Uprising of 1804. The entire nineteenth century would be remembered for drastic migrations. Serbs from Vojvodina, as well as from the Ottoman territories still not incorporated into the autonomous principality, saw a great potential for establishing new businesses in Belgrade. On the other hand, the Muslim population, which had been settled within the city moat for over 300 years, was totally removed from the city after the agreement regarding the evacuation was signed between the sultan and Miloš's successor Mihailo Obrenović. The last portion of the Ottoman army left the fortification five years later, in 1867.[4]

The first urban transformation critical for future constitution of Belgrade as the Serbian capital was envisioned by Prince Miloš himself. Besides the constructions of a few large-scale administrative buildings around the reconstructed Archangel Michael's Cathedral – placed on the slope toward the Sava, a traditionally Serbian part of the city within the moat – Miloš established the main directives for future development outside of the civic gates. Despite a poor education, he personally traced the street pattern of a new commercial and administrative center and wanted that center to be established "far enough from the reach of the Ottoman cannons still present at the fortification."[5] Miloš envisioned a road to connect his new military and governmental center outside of the moat, established in the 1830s, with his summer residence in Topčider, from the same period, expanding the city ten kilometers toward the south. This road, later developed into Kneza Miloša [Prince Miloš's] Boulevard, has been and remains the most prominent civic artery, accommodating governmental edifices and foreign embassies. The new residential districts around Miloš's road were planned in accordance with modern urban doctrines from the Central European academies. In 1834, Miloš invited an engineer from the Habsburg Empire, Franz Janke,[6] to help with a cadastral survey, parceling out the land outside of the moat between the road he cut and the old Constantinople Road (today's Bulevar Kralja Aleksandra [King Aleksandar's Boulevard]), and also with the regulation of urban blocks within the moat, around the Archangel Michael's Cathedral. Janke's plan proposed a division into rectangular blocks delineated by straight parallel streets forming a precise grid regardless of the city's hilly topography. Resulting from the proclamation that the expanded city outside of the moat could not be settled by Muslims, a non-Muslim population, primarily Serbs, moved into the regulated areas. At first, the occupancy of the newly parceled lots was chaotic and highly influenced by Prince Miloš's personal decisions. After he was forced to leave the country in 1839, a special committee was formed to establish a more legitimate way to distribute land. The committee paid special attention to the needs of a newly rising class of administration employees, migrating mainly from the Habsburg territories. Trying to be fair while granting the land, the committee created an "urban lottery"; the parcels were given out in an order decided by a lottery drum.[7]

Besides his pioneering involvement in tracing the modern urban fabric, Franz Janke was involved in proposing sites for the construction of public buildings to house Serbian institutions, among which was Đumrukana – the Palace of Customs – which served a broader range of public purposes than simply tolls and taxes. The new public edifices were of a modest scale, yet their shape, construction and ornamentation were Biedermeier-styled like in Central European petit bourgeois environments. On the other hand, the growing class of native-Serbian craftsmen, merchants and small businessmen resisted the influence of the Western building practices for another few decades. Their shops retained indigenous forms of vernacular Balkan traditions until the mid-twentieth century. The single-story buildings with low-sloped, clay-tiled roofs, deep eaves, tall chimneys, small windows on street façades, and wide porches prolonged into deep shadowed gardens at the back, created new neighborhoods, such as Savamala, in a fashion closer to the Orient than to the West.

Looking back through records by Serbian commentators written parallel to Western travelers' reports, the nineteenth-century urban transformations were considered the expression of gained freedom and national pride, a conquest over the backward heritage and bad customs associated with Ottoman rule. Serbian chroniclers educated in the West glorified the pro-European transformations in a similar fashion to the foreign travelers, who researched and documented the Balkans usually as part of political missions financed by the national governments of the countries they arrived from. The Serbian press highlighted the way foreigners applauded the changes throughout the liberated nation, particularly the urban development. Belgrade's sudden rebirth was granted to a Serbian, in other words Christian, takeover, pushing away the "Oriental dirtiness." In 1829, a German researcher, Otto Dubislav Pirch, noticed positive changes in the Serbian section of the city within the moat in comparison to the Muslim quarters.[8] A French traveler, Bois-le-Comte, wrote about Belgrade as "a Christian city which is becoming cleaner and more beautiful every day by kicking out the Turkish settlement."[9] An anonymous traveler from England published an article in the *Times*, which was translated in the daily newspaper *Srbske novine*:

> Since the last time I was here, Belgrade changed to the extent I could not recognize it. Then two thirds of the city looked Oriental, and now the European looking multistory houses raised everywhere, with shops and hotels which could be compared to those on Frankfurter Zeile.[10]

The agreement about the total removal of the Muslim population from the quarters within the moat,[11] and the evacuation of Ottoman army from the fortification, were the precondition for the transformation of urban fabric in the inner city. The removal of the moat and civic gates enabled the synthesis of the old enwalled quarters and the new urban districts traced by Franz Janke. The Regulatory Plan for Belgrade within the Moat by Emilijan Josimović[12] from 1867 was the key event in Belgrade urbanism[13] related to the final evacuation of Muslim inhabitants and army who had been settled in the inner city since 1500. Conceptualized in the years between the removal of Muslim citizens and the final withdrawal of the Ottoman army, the plan proposed the transformation of the previous urban fabric of crooked alleys very often ending in dead-ends into an orthogonal urban scheme created from rectangular blocks and straight streets. Josimović ranked the streets according to their width and urban function, but also defined the position and the shape of the main squares, parks and monumental public buildings essential for the creation of a new image of Belgrade as the nineteenth-century capital of Europe.[14] The new urban course also assumed the replacement of previous Ottoman public and religious structures with the Western-styled buildings. The most radical change in the city's identity resulted from the destruction of dozens of mosques with minarets that had defined the skyline of Ottoman Belgrade for over 400 years.[15] Instead, Josimović envisioned the locations for new cultural institutions, governmental and administrative edifices, and the spot for a new large cathedral, devoted to the first Serbian archbishop St. Sava, who had gained the autonomy of the Serbian Orthodox Church from the Byzantine patriarch, to epitomize the final victory of Christianity. The cathedral was planned at a location of symbolic importance, the Vračar Plateau. St. Sava was a real historical figure, Rastko Nemanjić, the second son of Duke Nemanja, who became a monk named Sava at Mount Athos, and after his death was canonized by the Orthodox church as a saint. Allegedly, the site for the cathedral corresponded to the place where Ottoman official, Sinan Paşa, threatened by the symbolic impact of St. Sava's cult, burned his relics in 1594.

Josimović's urban visions considered both the technical aspects of urban functioning as well as the city's monumental character. Incorporating the ideas of nineteenth-century European urban planning, Josimović paid attention to civic parks for their aesthetic values, and significance of public gatherings and health. The plan for the circular area along the demolished moat was to make it into a green esplanade, a series of parks flanked by wide communication corridors divided into three categories, for pedestrians, carriages and horse-riders. The centuries-old military fortification, the Belgrade Fortress, was to be converted into the main civic park, an idea that began to be realized soon after the evacuation of the Ottoman army. The main civic, commercial and administrative axis, beginning at the fortress and ending with St. Sava Cathedral on Vračar Plateau, determined the future expansion of the inner city. Halfway between the fortification and the cathedral was envisioned a site for the future king's palace, built when the Kingdom of Serbia was recognized after the Berlin Congress of 1878. Josimović also planned the prime communication routes that would make Belgrade an important stop on the way from Europe to the Middle East. Aware of the rising needs for a railway system, he envisioned a railway tunnel under the elevated downtown area to avoid heavy traffic while connecting the two main city ports, one on the Sava and another on the Danube. This idea, like the solution that had been materialized in Budapest in 1853, has remained one of the partly realized urban visions that Belgrade planners are still trying to achieve.

In general, Josimović's interventions have remained celebrated as the birth of Serbian urbanism, synonymous to the idea of city's "Europeanization" and the fight against backwardness. Along with the romanticized descriptions of Serbian rebellions that achieved the national freedom by fighting against the Turks, Belgrade's urban transformations by a planner of Serbian origins were celebrated as an architectural symbol of national victory by future generations of Serbian historians. Indeed, Josimović was a Serb, who grew up within the Serbian ethnic community of the Habsburg Empire and later moved to Belgrade as one of the first educated engineers and planners to be settle there. Yet, with all due respect to the patriotic feelings, his ambition to introduce a rising nation to the values of modernity, rationalism and progress originated from his Austrian-Hungarian background, mostly his training at the Technical Faculty in Vienna, his direct insight into the project for Ringstrasse, as well as into the radical urban transformations of Budapest. Despite the patriotic interpretations of Josimović's role in establishing the national dimension of Serbian urbanism, the transformations of Belgrade coincided with the Tanzimat reforms, conducted in the Ottoman-ruled cities of the Balkans at the same time. It was the Ottoman Porte itself that encouraged the autonomy of local governments, agreed on the removal of the Muslim population from the cities dominated by non-Muslim ethnic groups, and promoted modern city planning as an attempt at reconstructing the empire. In that sense, Josimović's Regulatory Plan of Belgrade, could be compared to similar urban interventions throughout the Ottoman world and considered as another case study of probing the implementation of the Tanzimat reforms.

After gaining the status of capital of the independent Kingdom of Serbia in 1882, further transformations by Belgrade planners succeeded in giving a general impression of being "Europeanized" to at least a limited zone of the city's core (see Figure 1.1).[16] Contemporary commentators, however, complained about the lack of structured planning politics and the insufficient support of both the local and state governments in the improvement of the image of Belgrade as the Serbian capital.[17] The embellishment of the nation's most exposed city often relied on private initiatives of the rising upper-middle class, which gained its economic power mainly from trade with the border countries. The beautification of Belgrade became an important national goal, especially after the initial phase of regulating the urban fabric during the time of autonomy. The Building Law of 1896 established the ideal height for new constructions on prominent streets and near representative public buildings. A height of three stories and richer decoration on the façades were expected for buildings on the main boulevards and a height of at least two stories on narrow side streets. Nevertheless, most Belgrade citizens – primarily newcomers either employed in administration or owners of small shops and craft businesses – was not able to achieve those standards.

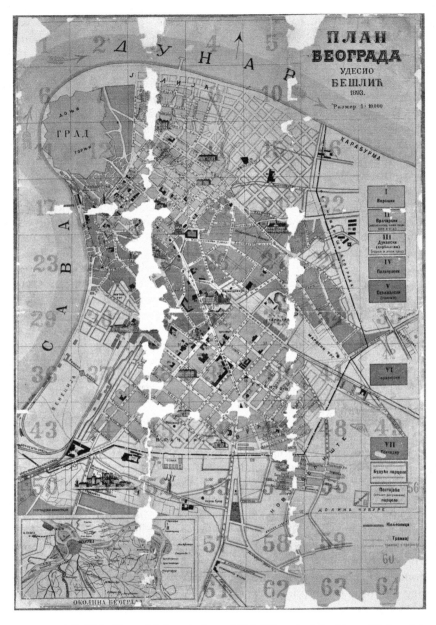

Figure 1.1 Bešlić's Plan of Belgrade from 1893 (Historical Archive of Belgrade)

Due to huge income discrepancies among inhabitants who owned land in the same urban blocks, the appearance of buildings remained unsynchronized. Street façades of homogeneous heights and standardized decorative elements were not common in the Belgrade cityscape until the next expansion of Belgrade after WWI.

Resurfacing streets and pavements also became key to creating an image of a European instead of an Oriental-looking city. The traditional "Turkish cobblestone" started to disappear in the 1870s, but it was only at the turn of the century that the issue of modern surfaces on streets became a hot topic in public debates.[18] The local government could not provide the necessary funds for finishing the streets and sidewalks in a modern-looking way, so in many cases property owners were asked to build sidewalks in front of their entrances at their own expense. Civic infrastructure projects – the sewage system, running water, street lights and public transportation – were upheld during the last two decades of the nineteenth century, but they often collided with the work on street resurfacing.[19] A modern water supply infrastructure, instead of the previously used Ottoman system,[20] was put into service in 1892 using the plan by German engineers. After decades of debates, the city's sewage system was finally completed twenty years after its construction began in 1885.[21] Belgrade has been proud of its first electric power plant, opened in 1893.[22] With its three furnaces and large capacity, the plant was compared to its counterparts in much wealthier European cities; more importantly, it provided the possibility for electric tram public transportation and electric street lighting.[23]

Despite the decent urban growth – from 60,000 in 1895 to over 90,000 citizens in 1910 – Belgrade's economy was still rooted in trade and small businesses. Larger factories emerged only at the turn of the century, and even then, the industrial production was limited[24] because the new enterprises grew mostly from the existing small craftsmanship shops. Most newcomers were employed in the growing state administration. The nineteenth-century social milieu was also determined by the development of the higher educational institutions. The largest number of graduates from the newly constituted Belgrade University came from the Faculty of Law, while engineers and doctors continued earning their looked-for degrees from abroad.[25] Along with elevating the overall educational level, the transformation of the population from rural into urban assumed the acceptance of new norms and ways of public behavior. Together with educational and cultural institutions and professional societies the leading sites of social interactions were "kafanas," meaning the coffee houses, yet if compared to their European counterparts, they were closer to bistros, taverns and pubs.

With the rapid urban growth, the city began to be affected by the problem of social housing – an issue that the municipal government set out to confront in a systematic fashion in 1909.[26] It would be proudly noted in Serbian architectural historiography that the earliest workers' housing colony was realized by a woman architect, Jelisaveta Načić,[27] who belonged

24 *The birth of national architectures*

to the first generation of students who graduated from the Department of Architecture at Belgrade Technical Faculty.[28] However, only a very limited number of the poor enjoyed social support from the Belgrade municipality. Most newcomers lived in rental units with shared closets attached to individual cesspits. As the last phase of the sewage system was put in service only in 1914, right before the outbreak of World War I, there were only a small number of multistory rental buildings with bathrooms available in the limited area of the civic core. The housing shortage along with high rents in comparison to the average income aggravated the living conditions at the time, but more distressingly it has remained one of the toughest problems for Belgrade citizens until the present day.

Between gaining autonomy in 1830 and the outbreak of World War I, the search for a modern Serbian identity could be followed through two distinct phases of drastic urban transformations in Belgrade.[29] The first took place while Serbs were still fighting for independence from the Ottomans and their national leaders insisted on a sudden switch from the Oriental urban fabric to Western-looking urban schemes and modern building types.[30] At that time, any intervention associated with Western European architectural and urban principles, resulting from the Age of Enlightenment, was considered synonymous with a Serbian identity, although some radical conversions of the Belgrade cityscape, oscillating between the Ottoman and the European-looking silhouettes, had already occurred during the eighteenth century, when the Austrian army took control. Therefore, the later, exclusively Serbian attempts at imitating the Western styles and urban schemes could be simply considered as one more page in the long history of Belgrade's urban discontinuity. However, the mid-nineteenth century in Serbia would be remembered for strong optimism about leaving behind its Ottoman heritage, with a leading goal of introducing European urban patterns not only in Belgrade, but all over the principality.

In the second phase, after the Berlin Congress of 1878 and recognition of the Serbian nation-state, the urge for fighting against the Ottoman legacy evaporated, yet the victory over the enemy did not result in the anticipated level of national unity. The new freedom fueled growing tensions between municipal and state leaders, as well as, between the center and the periphery – Belgrade and the rest of the country. Modernization and the overall appearance of Belgrade continued to be a national priority, as were the aspirations for catching up with the leading Western European cities beyond the Central European boundaries. With the anti-Austrian political climate at the eve of Great War, Belgrade authorities leaned toward a French, rather than Central European-looking capital, to be accomplished through the new Master Plan of 1912 and several infrastructural projects. Assigned to Brussels-based, *fin de siècle* architect, Alban Chambon,[31] well-known for glamorous designs in Paris and London, the Master Plan suggested a sequence of regular squares accentuated by immense public buildings, monuments and fountains, tied together into a network of grand boulevards, reminiscent of the Beaux-Arts urban legacies. Despite grand aspirations, Belgrade never came close to realizing the monumental public spaces and palaces imagined by Chambon due to the Balkan Wars, followed immediately by World War I.

The backwardness of Belgrade's appearance as a national capital and her still Oriental character have remained the main theme of lament among architects, politicians and citizens until the present day. Struggling primarily with a weak economy, Belgrade has never achieved the level of necessary infrastructural improvements such as the subway system; however, the main cause of Belgrade's unsynchronized development has lied in the slow modernization pace. The urban population in Serbia at the turn of the century was only 13.9 percent of the total, which was lower than in most countries of the Balkans previously controlled by the Ottomans.[32] The cultural elite started to appear as a significant public voice at that time, but its influence was interrupted by participation in frequent wars. The communist revolution of 1945 interrupted the interwar intellectual growth of the Serbian elite that would start recovering with a new wave of modernization along with the increase of overall level of education since the 1970s.[33] Urban development of the Serbian capital has been continually reflecting the confusion over the varying concepts of nationhood: on one side, a belief that the foundations of nation rely on modernization, while the opposing voices see the nation as synonymous with its ethnic roots – this clash that has been the cause of constant conflict between Belgrade's urbanity versus its ruralness.

Architectural statehood

The first decades of Serbian autonomy introduced remarkable transformations in administrative procedures and legislation codes for building in urban areas. The projects were supervised by the already mentioned Franz Janke, employed by the Ministry of Internal Affairs upon his arrival in Serbia in 1835. Seven years later, in 1842, the ministry established the Building Department upon the German model of Baudirektion.[34] In the earliest stages, the engineers employed at the department were recruited from abroad. Besides Janke, another foreigner, Czech Jan Nevole, recognized for his collaboration on the project for Masaryk Railway Station in Prague, supervised numerous public projects throughout the country during the next two decades. Since its constitution, the department felt the urge to separate infrastructural projects from representational public enterprises, thereby the title of "state architect" was granted to those working specifically on architecture and urbanism. Although the Baudirektion extended into the Ministry of Buildings in 1863, a separate architectural department was established within its shield only after a serious restructuring in 1881. Many Serbian-born architects had been sent by the government to earn architectural degrees from the universities in Vienna, Karlsruhe, Munich, Zürich, Berlin and Budapest,[35] and upon their return to Serbia took leading positions in the Ministry of Buildings. As the most productive chronicler of nineteenth-century architecture in Serbia, Bogdan Nestorović, noticed, "in 1859, only three out of nine employees at the Baudirektion were of Serbian origins, while ten years later all of them were Serbs."[36]

After the proclamation of the Kingdom of Serbia in 1882, the types, scale and forms of public works conceived and executed to serve the state programs started to expand despite the country's weak economy and frequent wars. The designs for large-scale structures and their construction were regulated by the Law for the Construction of Public Buildings, which had been put into effect in 1865.[37] This law recognized the types and hierarchy of structures to be constructed and owned by the state, including the state administration, central and regional government, courts, military facilities, customs, hospitals and schools. The quest for Historicist stylization in public projects, although not codified by the law, corresponded to rising consciousness about the power of architectural images in constituting the national identity. In contrast to the ongoing complaints against Austrian-looking forms in church architecture, the Ringstrasse prototypes inspired most public designs, at least until the dynastical turnover of 1903. While the Viennese forerunners unmistakably paired their programs with the explicitly encoded neo-styles (neo-Classicism for the Parliament, neo-Gothic for the City Hall, neo-Baroque for the theater and opera), Belgrade architects favored the universal or the "International Style" of neo-Renaissance as Jörg Stabenow defined it.[38] The neo-Gothic and the neo-Baroque styles were neglected, due to their overt analogies to the Western medievalism and the Counter-Reformation.

The development of public buildings during the nineteenth century[39] gravitated towards two locations defined in the 1830s: around Archangel Michael's Cathedral within the moat, and around Prince Miloš's army barracks outside of the moat. Unsurprisingly, the first residences for the prince's family and the bishop's residence grew next to the cathedral, while the governmental institutions grew around the military seat. Miloš's Court and the Palace of Soviet (the Council), both completed by 1840, comprised the first governmental institution adjacent to the Great Barrack from 1836. After the relocation of old cemetery (today's Tašmajdan Park), the analogous institutions of the Royal Court and the National Assembly were built a half-mile further on northeast to house the same programs.

Multistory, academically composed edifices had rarely been seen across Belgrade's cityscape before Serbia gained independence. The earliest three-story palazzo built within the moat from 1857 to 1863 was the residence for the family of Mihailo Miša Anastasijević, the second richest man in Serbia and a business partner of Prince Miloš.[40] When the Obrenovićs' totalitarian politics began to be questioned and the public discontent fulfilled by the constitution of first parliamentarian institutions, the Council and the Assembly,[41] Anastasijević took part in political life, fighting against the Obrenovićs in favor of the Karađorđevićs. His oldest daughter Sara married a potential heir of the throne from the Karađorđević dynasty, a reason why the palazzo was initially envisioned as the future court. Yet, Anastasijević's influence on the political scene was short-lived. After the next political turnover in 1859, when Mihailo Obrenovićs resumed power, Anastasijević was forced to leave the country and grant the completed palazzo to the Serbian people, namely the state.

The original program of Kapetan Miša's Endowment (Figure 1.2),[42] as it is known today, was adopted to accommodate the needs of newly formed educational and cultural institutions, including the Great School (the future University of Belgrade), the Ministry of Education, the National Museum and the National Library.[43] Thus, the palazzo unintentionally developed into a national symbol because of the new programs defining Serbia as a *Kulturnation*, yet these were not the only means by which it acquired this significant status. Anastijević chose Jan Nevole, educated at the Technical Faculty and at the Academy of Fine Arts in Vienna during the supremacy of Rundbogen style, to employ the forms commonly connected with medievalism. Nevole respected the Rundbogen compositional schemes in the design, yet heavily interfered with the Byzantine stylization and hence achieved a compilation that could be considered the first attempt at alluding to Serbian medievalism in Belgrade public architecture.

The first intentional project to serve the rise of Serbia as a *Kulturnation* was the National Theater (Figure 1.3). At the initiative of Prince Mihailo Obrenović, the European-educated heir to the throne, Belgrade was supposed to grow into a European-looking city with a vibrant cultural scene. The institution of the Serbian National Theater had existed in Novi Sad, the largest

Figure 1.2 Kapetan Miša's Endowment – the Old University and its future extension behind (Photo Archive Miloš Jurišić)

28 *The birth of national architectures*

Figure 1.3 National Theatre at the place of demolished Istanbul Gate (Photo Archive Miloš Jurišić)

Serb-populated city in the Habsburg Empire, since the 1848 Revolution. The relocation of the Serbian National Theater Company from Novi Sad to Belgrade was a result of Prince Mihailo's decision to proclaim Belgrade the Serbian capital, publicly announced in 1842. Mihailo coordinated the final evacuation of the Muslim population from the area within the moat and the Serbian takeover of the last Ottoman military post situated at Belgrade Fortress, achieving the political success which was to be commemorated by the architectural means. Thus, the National Theater was erected on a piece of land expropriated from the fleeing Muslims at a symbolical site, next to the demolished Stambol Kapija [Istanbul Gate] remembered for cruel executions of Serbian rebellions. Spolia from the Istanbul Gate were inserted into the foundations as a symbolical act of Serbian renaissance, a cultural conquest over the Orient.

The design for the National Theater[44] – granted to Ministry of Buildings employee Aleksandar Bugarski[45] – resembled the neo-Classicist and neo-Renaissance precedents, characterized by a dominating portico with a Doric colonnade and a tympanum above the main entrance, a design that flourished around Europe after Schinkel's pivotal design for Berlin's Schauspielhaus from 1819. The fact that the building – both its exterior and interior – was strongly reminiscent of the Teatro alla Scala in Milan by Giuseppe Piermarini has led to an assumption that Bugarski only adopted a standardized design, previously bought by the government from an unidentified European source, for the location in Belgrade.[46] Moreover, an almost identical composition occurred in an earlier proposal for the theater signed by employee of the Baudirektion, Joseph (Giuseppe) Cassano in 1852,[47] for another location at today's Zeleni Venac. The construction was accomplished in a short period of time soon after Mihailo's assassination in 1868, which inspired his family and the National Council to speedily complete the project and, accordingly, did not leave Bugarski enough time to develop a more original design. The first performance, held on October 30, 1869, presented a piece written by a Serbian writer, translator and future theater director, Đorđe Maletić, who paid tribute to the assassinated leader with a panegyric titled "The Afterlife Glory of Prince Mihailo." The special box embellished with furniture, curtains and royal insignia manufactured in Austria was prepared for the attendance of the late prince's family and later converted into the royal box. The interior was lit by "hundreds of lights" from gas-chandeliers, supplied from a gas plant placed in a nearby abandoned mosque. Together with the Kapetan Miša's Endowment and the Archangel Michael's Cathedral, the scale and form of the theater – despite the unoriginality of its design – overshadowed the inherited skyline of low-rise Balkan houses made from perishable materials, with secluded gardens inserted into the irregular network of winding streets, still encircled by the moat.

Disappointed by Russian support to Bulgaria at the Berlin Congress, Mihailo's successor, Milan Obrenović, turned towards Austro-Hungary, and finally, in 1881, signed the Secret Convention about providing loyalty to the Habsburgs in return for their support for his being crowned as king of Serbia. Although officially crowned only in 1882, Milan initiated the construction of Royal Court as soon as the agreement with the Habsburgs was reached. The location was determined by the position of Stari konak [Old Palace], the residence of Serbian princes since the first Karađorđević *coup d'état*, when Prince Aleksandar relocated to a two-story, Western-looking palace outside of the moat, originally built for a wealthy merchant and politician, Stojan Simić.[48] The edifice, placed on an irrigated pit between the Constantinople Road and Prince Miloš's barracks, was sold to Prince Aleksandar soon after its completion in 1844. It was the site picked by Simić that would determine not only the future position of the Royal Court but also the alignment of one of the most emblematic urban processions traced outside of the moat: the axis linking the Belgrade Fortress at the northwest with the future St. Sava's Cathedral at the southeast. Originating from Josimović's vision, the path lead from the fortress through the newly cut Knez Mihailova [Prince Mihailo's] Street within the moat, via Terazije Square and King Milan's Street outside of the moat, passing by Stari konak and continuing further to Vračar Plateau. The programmatic character of the area within which the Royal Court would be developed was defined after Mihailo Obrenović decided to move the Ministry of Internal and Foreign Affairs into a new palace, designed and executed by Joseph Cassano from the prince's own funds, next to Stari konak. The decision resulted in

30 *The birth of national architectures*

the construction of several ministries on both sides of Kralja Milana Street, which would, together with Kneza Miloša Boulevard, grow into the main corridor to hold governmental programs.

When the building of the Royal Court became a national priority, there was a whole list of architects including Dragutin Milutinović and Aleksandar Bugarski, who took part in proposing the initial drawings. The construction started according to the Biedermeier-looking plans by Bugarski, but then King Milan, dissatisfied with the outcome, invited recently graduated Jovan Ilkić[49] to step in and improve the project. As one of the most talented students of Theophil von Hansen, Ilkić was, after graduation, invited to work on the realization of Hansen's project for the Austrian Parliament; and then, at the age of twenty-five, he moved back to Belgrade to participate in completing the most demanding national endeavor of the time. Bugarski's massing of the Royal Court as a Renaissance palazzo with cortile was finished when Ilkić took over the project. Therefore, Ilkić primarily addressed the compositional issues and the ornamentation[50] to be attuned to the academic, neo-Renaissance precedents of the Ringstrasse era. What differentiated the silhouette of Serbian Royal Court from its Viennese forerunners was the royal insignia placed on three tall domes dominating over Kralja Milana Street: the royal crowns and the two-headed eagles, historical replicas of the heraldic symbols of the Nemanjićs dynasty, were found in Studenica Monastery.[51]

In 1882, when another Viennese-trained architect, Svetozar Ivačković, arrived in Belgrade to work for the Ministry of Buildings, the first plans for the Royal Court were under review, thereby the new stylistic approach to the façades was still uncertain. After graduating from the Viennese Academy in 1874, Ivačković[52] first returned to his native Pančevo, a city ten miles to the northeast of Belgrade, to work on the construction of a new church, the Transfiguration of Our Lord, a project in which he demonstrated a profound academic knowledge of the neo-Byzantine stylization, elaborated on by Hansen and his followers. However, his experience with the neo-Byzantine did not fully prepare him for the proposed style of the Ministry of Justice to be built in the block next to the Royal Court, a realization he undertook as an employee of the Ministry of Buildings.[53] Upon accepting the position of state architect, Ivačković was sent to Rome to study high-Renaissance palazzos and build on his Viennese background of the Historicist styles by looking at the original historical precedents.[54] Yet, this additional training did not take Ivačković's design away from templates he had become acquainted with during his stay at the Academy, namely Hansen's project for the Philharmonic Hall in Brno and Friedrich Schachner's Palace Erlanger in Vienna. In the end, his project for the Ministry of Justice developed into an explicit example of Ringstrasse-styled Renaissance, the first consistent design of this kind in Belgrade architectural history.

Ivačković's switch from the neo-Byzantine to the neo-Renaissance might have resulted from his personal belief that governmental programs needed to employ a more universal language than provided by the neo-Byzantine. On the other hand, a decision about the neo-Renaissance as an adequate style might have been inspired by King Milan's ideas transcoded into some unrecorded stipulation in the Ministry of Buildings. During his long-term employment at the Ministry, Svetozar Ivačković accomplished numerous designs for various public programs including small-scale parochial churches and chapels in towns and villages throughout Serbia, all of which were neo-Byzantine.[55] His church projects set standards for the future development of modern ecclesial architecture, according to which the layouts be cross-in-square or trichoncal concepts and the stylization of either Byzantine or Morava Style precedents from Serbian medieval architecture – by the end of the nineteenth century, these were profoundly researched by architectural scholars Mihailo Valtrović and Dragutin Milutinović. Therefore, the argument about a particularly Serbian passion for the Byzantine and Serbian medieval references in late nineteenth- and early twentieth-century production, suggested in later twentieth-century historiography, was limited primarily to churches.[56]

The neo-Renaissance orchestrations on governmental programs culminated in 1886, when Konstantin A. Jovanović[57] received a commission for the National Bank, near Archangel Michael's Cathedral. Through Jovanović's design, Belgrade architecture reached another level of accuracy and articulation rooted in the Central European legacy. From his early years of studies at the ETH in Zürich, Jovanović became inspired by Gottfried Semper's teaching and practice, and later continued a professional correspondence.[58] He lived and practiced in Vienna when Semper worked on grandiose neo-Renaissance projects for the Museums of National History and Art History on Ringstrasse, adjacent to the Imperial Court. Jovanović's path from Vienna to Belgrade ran through Sofia, as he was first invited by the Bulgarian government to design the Parliament of the Bulgarian principality, when the country became internationally recognized at the Berlin Congress. He received the first commission in Belgrade through his father, Anastas Jovanović, the first professional photographer in Serbia and a close friend of the Obrenovićs. After several small-scale apartment buildings and larger mixed-use palaces, designed for Belgrade leading tradesman and politicians, he received the commission for the National Bank. The governor of the National Bank at that moment, wealthy tradesman and amateur photographer Marko Stojanović, was Anastas Jovanović's close friend. Unsurprisingly, Stojanović served on the building committee that chose the architect in charge of the design.

The National Bank was conceptualized as a massive, sixteenth-century Renaissance palazzo with a robust first zone, in sharp contrast to the dense, previously enwalled urban fabric, still dominated by modest vernacular houses. The lighter upper stories were enhanced by elaborate neo-Renaissance details: pediments and columns framing the windows, pilasters and tympanums around the main entrances, all topped by a heavily molded

32 The birth of national architectures

roof cornice. The main portal, placed at a sharp angle protruding into an intersection of narrow streets, was the most striking element in the composition and led into a well-proportioned courtyard with monumental staircases, smoothly lit by a glass lantern. In the later addition from 1922–1923, executed when the bank was enlarged to meet the new needs of Royal Yugoslavia, Jovanović was invited to submit a plan for the extension. And although the addition did not disturb the integrity of initial palazzo concept with the inner courtyard, the extension managed to turn an originally modest monument to the early Serbian statehood into a powerful logo of the enlarged South Slavic kingdom.

When the Serbian government initiated the construction of a new edifice for its seat to replace the older, small-scale palace close to Miloš's barracks, the commission for the new National Assembly (Figure 1.4) was granted to Konstantin Jovanović based on his previous design for the National Bank. The Minister of Buildings at the time was a Zürich ETH graduate, Petar Velimirović – Jovanović's friend from college and a skillful politician who stayed in power long enough to follow many further transformations of the initial design. The site was chosen at spot of the demolished Batal Mosque[59] on Constantinople Road. The historical importance of the spot laid in the fact that the sultan's Hatti-I-Serif, announcing Serbia's autonomy, was publicly announced there in 1830. The location was still considered too remote from the city core; however, the potential of creating a broader urban ensemble linked to the previously completed Royal Court was recognized in

Figure 1.4 National Parliament designed in 1891 with the Main Post Office and the St. Mark's Church from the 1930s in the background (Photo Archive Miloš Jurišić)

architectural criticism. The main advocate of a comprehensive plan to regulate the urban area around the Assembly in relation to the Royal Court was Dimitrije T. Leko, who himself proposed several solutions. He positioned large-scale edifices to frame a large forum for public gatherings in front of the Assembly's main façade and although this grand vision was not materialized, Leko's attempts to contextualize the urban framework around the Assembly inspired less ambitious decisions to compositionally tie it with the Royal Court complex in the future.[60]

After submitting the initial sketches in 1891, Jovanović worked on developing plans during the next year, evolving the original concept into a more pronounced synthesis of two major edifices on Ringstrasse: the Austrian Parliament by Theophil von Hansen and the history museums by Gottfried Semper. The crowning element on the Serbian Assembly, in contrast to the Austrian Parliament, was an immense dome over the monumental neo-Classical portico, looking as if it had been transferred from Semper's history museums. Jovanović had developed a long-lasting interest in domical structures since his study tour to Rome, after which he published a book about the building of St. Peter's,[61] paying special attention to Michelangelo's design. The transformation of celestial symbolism of the dome into what has been defined as the "sanctified legislative power of the republic"[62] had occurred in American examples of capitol buildings that Jovanović might have been acquainted with through Gottfried Semper. The domical analogy also occurred in the design for the Hungarian Parliament in the nearby capital of Budapest, yet the Serbian project differed both from these American and European counterparts because of its specifically Semperian stylization.

Jovanović's interest in domical structures, elaborated in his booklet about St. Peter's, were profoundly explored in two proposals for St. Sava's Cathedral on Vračar Plateau to create a crowning vista of the processional route through Kralja Milana Street and establish a visual relation to the Royal Court both urbanistically and stylistically. As part of the commemoration of the 300th anniversary of the burning of St. Sava's relics, ideas about erecting his mausoleum – which dated back to Emilijan Josimović's Regulatory Plan of 1867 – started being developed in more detail. All affairs were run by a special committee, appointed in 1894, with Jovanović serving as a member. He anticipated a monumental, trichoncal cross-in-square plan with five domes alluding to the Holy Apostles in Constantinople – the mausoleum of Eastern Roman emperors and a source of inspiration for St. Peter's in Rome. The construction was postponed until the end of the Great War due to the turbulent politics and unstable economy. It was in 1926 that the committee finally assured the finances and announced the competition for a grandiose 3,000-square meter cathedral, in which 6,000 people could be gathered under the same roof.[63] By that time, the knowledge about Serbian medieval heritage and the Byzantine architectural realm had become the grounding source for the discussion about a Serbian national style to be explored mainly in church architecture. Jovanović's international neo-Renaissance could not meet the criteria stipulated by a new intellectual climate. The architecture of St. Sava's Cathedral ended being a compilation of Serbian references found in Duke Nemanja's Studenica Monastery and King Milutin's Gračanica Monastery, but also the early Byzantine precedents: Hagia Sophia as the first imperial cathedral of early Christendom and the Holy Apostles as the first imperial mausoleum, as Jovanović had originally anticipated.

The execution of the National Assembly also took over thirty years, in the end signed not under Jovanović's but Jovan Ilkić's name. The first obstacle in implementing Jovanović's design was that the new Serbian constitution of 1901 reformed the parliamentary system from unicameral to bicameral, requiring the layout to contain two meeting chambers instead of one. Since Jovanović was hard to negotiate with and was not willing to adjust a project to a realistic budget, the government announced a competition for a new solution, in which Ilkić won first prize with a project that closely resembled Jovanović's design. The dynastical shift from Obrenović to Karađorđević in 1903 did not help either, because of Jovanovć's ties to the dethroned dynasty. The construction of the Assembly finally started in 1907 according to the project signed by Ilkić – who proceeded due to his experience in collaboration with Hansen during the construction of the Austrian Parliament – but could not be competed quickly due to the weak economy and the Balkan Wars. It resumed only after World War I, when the Assembly needed to accommodate representatives of the enlarged state. Forty-five years after the project had been initiated, the consecration of what was then the Yugoslav National Assembly took place on October 18, 1936, while the interior decoration, painting and the sculptural program lasted for another year. Thus, the representatives of Royal Yugoslavia gathered in the new edifice for less than four years, until the outbreak of WWII when the Nazis took over the Assembly as their seat. After the end of WWII, on November 29, 1945, the still legitimate pre-WWII Royal Yugoslav Assembly appointees initiated the abolition of the kingdom and the proclamation of the republic. So the Ringstrasse-styled edifice, designed by a student of Semper and another of Hansen, turned into an architectural symbol of Marshal Tito's personal cult, validating his approach toward communism for another forty-seven years.[64]

There is a prevailing argument in historiography on Serbian architecture regarding the preoccupation of Serbian architects with the creation of national architecture rooted in the Serbian medieval past.[65] This assumption is only partly true. Despite fervent debates over the notion of a national style among Serbian architects at the turn of the century,[66] alongside the strong mission of the Department of Architecture at Belgrade Technical Faculty to favor the Serbo-Byzantine code in studio requirements,[67] an overall picture of Belgrade public buildings was rather different. The creation of a universal academic language – at first reminiscent of the Viennese Ringstrasse precedents – for governmental edifices became an imperative since the constitution of Serbian Kingdom, a tendency that would only strengthen when Belgrade became the seat of Royal Yugoslavia. Neo-Classical and neo-Renaissance compositions dominated in expanding governmental programs during the interwar period; however, the sources of influence shifted from the Viennese precedents to an academic manner imported from tsarist Russia. At the time when Aleksandar Karađorđević took the throne, Belgrade welcomed a generation of Russian architects who fled the October Revolution. Their presence opened a new era in monumentalizing the state-run construction campaigns. In the following years, a new kind of academicism, imported from Moscow and St. Petersburg, made a great impact on achieving a grandiose image of Belgrade as an imperial capital.

Notes

1 Charles Jelavich, *The Establishment of the Balkan National States 1804–1920*, Seattle: University of Washington Press, 1986: 56.
2 In only twenty-two years of Austrian rule from 1717 to 1739, Belgrade was transformed into a Baroque city with new fortification walls built to meet the needs of new weapons, new infrastructure, public and administrative buildings, Catholic churches and monasteries, and residential areas. Right after the Austrian defeat, most of the structures were torn down, creating space for the rebuilding of the Ottoman city. The pre-nineteenth-century urban development of Belgrade is discussed in Oliver Minić, "Jezgro Beograda" [The Core of Belgrade], *Godišnjak grada Beograda*, vol. 7 (1960): 441–470.
3 Rajko Veselinović, *Beograd u 19. veku* [*Belgrade in the Nineteenth Century*], Belgrade: Muzej grada Beograda, 1967: 69.
4 About the complex negotiations on the migration of the Muslim population from Belgrade after the agreement between the Sultan and the Serbian Principality in 1862, see Šaban Hodžić: "Migracije muslimanskog stanovništva iz Srbije u sjeveroistočnu Bosnu između 1788–1862 godine" [Migrations of Muslim Population from Serbia to Eastern Bosnia, 1788–1862], *Članci i građa za kulturnu istoriju istočne Bosne*, vol. 2 (1958); Vidosava Nikolić, "Turska dobra i stanovništvo u Beogradu u vreme bombardovanja 1862. godine" [Turkish Property and Population During the Bombing of Belgrade in 1862], *Godišnjak grada Beograda*, vol. 9–10 (1962/1963): 286–287; and Safet Bandžović, "Iseljavanje muslimanskog stanovništva iz kneževine Srbije u Bosanski vilajet (1862–1867)," *Znakovi vremena*, vol. 12 (2009): 67–79.
5 Quoted in Branko Maksimović, "Urbanistički razvitak Beograda od 1815–1941" [Urbanistic development of Belgrade], in Vasa Čubrilović (ed.), *Oslobođenje gradova u Srbiji od Turaka 1862–1867*, Belgrade: Srpska akademija nauka i umetnosti, 1970: 633.
6 For archival documents about Franz Janke's arrival to Belgrade: DAS (State Archive of Serbia), KK-VI-577, 1813–1834.
7 DAS [State Archive of Serbia], P. No. 4314, 19 November 1841. Quoted in Branko Maksimović, *Urbanizam u Srbiji – osnivanje i rekonstrukcija varoši u 19. veku* [*Urbanism in Serbia: The Foundation and Reconstruction of Cities in the Nineteenth Century*], Belgrade: Građevinska knjiga, 1962: 87.
8 Otto Dubislav von Pirch, *Putovanje u Srbiji u godini 1829* [*Traveling through Serbia in 1829*], Belgrade: Akademija nauka, 1899: 30. Translated from *Reise in Serbien im spatherbst 1829*.

36 *The birth of national architectures*

9 Sojan Novaković, *Srbija u godini 1834;pisma grofa Boa-le-Konta de Rinji ministru inostranih dela u Parizu o tadašnjem stanju u Srbiji* [*Serbia in Year 1834: Letters of Bois-le-Comte to de Rigny, the Foreign Minister in Paris about the situation in Serbia*], Belgrade: Državna štamparija Kraljevine Srbije, 1894. Quoted in Tihomir Đorđević, *Iz Srbije Kneza Miloša: stanovništvo i naselja* [*From Knez Mološ's Srbija: Population and Settlements*], Belgrade: Geca Kon, 1924: 288.

10 Anonymous, *Srbske novine* [the first daily newspaper in Serbia], November 13, 1843: 367.

11 The displacement of the Muslim population from Serbian cities was a result of an agreement between the Sultan and autonomous Serbian government, according to which the Serbian party was obliged to pay compensation for taking over the property of Muslim citizens. The majority of these were Muslims of Slavic origins, who moved to the less developed regions of eastern Bosnia.

12 Emilijan Josimović (1823–1897) completed his degree in philosophy and technical sciences at the University of Vienna, after which he moved to Belgrade. Most of his life he dedicated to teaching, at first at the Belgrade Lyceum and later at the newly formed Belgrade University, as the first professor of architecture.

13 Josimović wrote about his plan in Emilijan Josimović, *Objasnenje predloga za regulisanje onoga dela varoši Beograda sto leži u šancu*, Belgrade, 1867.

14 Dragana Ćorović, *Beograd kao evropski grad u 19. veku: transformacija* [*Belgrade as a European City in the Nineteenth Century: The Transformation of Urban Landscape*], PhD thesis, Belgrade: Arhitektonski fakultet, 2015. Comparison to similar European developments is discussed in Andrew Lees and Lynn H. Lees, "Pursuits of Urban Improvement," in *Cities and the Making of Modern Europe, 1750–1914*, Cambridge: Cambridge University Press: 99–128.

15 According to the records of Evliya Çelebi, at the time of great prosperity under the Ottoman rule in the seventeenth century there were thirty-five mosques in the city. The first radical destruction of mosques occurred during the Austrian rule of 1717–1739 and later during the First Serbian Uprising in 1804. In 1826, Joakim Vujić reordered thirty mosques of which most were damaged. Serbian records in 1836 mention sixteen mosques that would remain in the old civic core under the evacuation of the Ottoman army in 1867. See Abdulah Talundžić, "Džamije u Beogradu" [Mosques in Belgrade], *Most: časopis za zobrazovanje, nauku i kulturu*, vol. 24, no. 174 (2004): 76–79.

16 About the urban transformations of Belgrade in the nineteenth and early twentieth century, see Branko Maksimović, "Urbanistički razvitak Beograda od 1815–1941" [Urbanistic Development of Belgrade 1815–1941], in Vasa Čubrilović (ed.), *Oslobođenje gradova u Srbiji od Turaka 1862–1867*, Belgrade: Srpska akademija nauka i umetnosti, 1970: 633; D. Vuksanović-Anić, "Urbanistički razvitak Beograda u periodu izmedju dva svetska rata" [Urbanistic Development of Belgrade between the World Wars], *Zbornik nauka*, vol. 9 (1968); Nikola Nestorović, *Građevine i arhitekti u Beogradu prošlog stoleća* [*Buildings and Architects in Belgrade from the Last Century*], Belgrade: Institut za građevinu i urbanizam, 1972.

17 Dubravka Stojanović, *Kaldrma i asfalt: urbanizajica i evropeizacija Beograda* [*Cobblestone and Asphalt: Urbanization and Europeanization of Belgrade*], Belgrade: UDI, 2008: 90.

18 Ibid., 90–91.

19 Ibid., 117–169.

20 Milka Jovanović, "Snabdevanje Beograda vodom do izgradnje modernog vodovoda 1892" [Water Supply in Belgrade before the Construction of Modern Water Infrastructure in 1892], Godišnjak grada Beograda, vol. 5 (1958): 241–248.
21 Konstantin Vasiljević, Kanalizacija Beograda 1905–1975, Belgrade: Prosveta, 1975.
22 Nikola Vučo, "Beogradska elekrtična centrala," Godišnjak grada Beograda, vol. 24 (1977): 165–180; Dobrivoje Erić, "Prva javna termoelektrična centrala u Beogradu" [The First Electric Power Plant in Belgrade], Nasledje/Heritage, vol. 12 (2011) : 129–144.
23 Anonymous, Tramvaji i osvetljenje [Trams and Street Lightning], Belgrade: DTO, 1932.
24 Dragan Petrović, Ljubodrag Dimić and Ivan Popović, Istorija industrije Beograda: razvoj i razmeštaj industrije Beograda u 19. i 20. veku [History of Belgrade Industry: Development and Distribution through Belgrade in the Nineteenth and Twentieth Centuries], Belgrade: Srpsko grafičko društvo, 2006.
25 Ljubinka Trgovčević, Planirana elita: o studentima iz Srbije na evropskim univerzitetima u 19. veku [The Planned Élite: About the Students from Serbia at European Universities in the Nineteenth Century], Belgrade: Istorijski institut, 2003.
26 Zlata Vuksanović Macura, "Socijalno stanovi Beograda u prvoj polovini 20. Veka" [Social Housing of Belgrade in the First Half of the Twentieth Century], Nasledje/Heritage, vol. 12 (2011): 65–89.
27 Jelisaveta Načić (1878–1955) was not only the first women to earn a degree in architecture, but also the first to accomplish numerous projects in Belgrade. She applied for a job at the Ministry of Buildings but was not granted the position because of the requirement that all employees complete military training. Yet she found a job at the Municipal Building Office, through which she was appointed on numerous large-scale projects.
28 Jelena Bogdanović, "Jelisaveta Načić: The First Serbian Female Architect," Serbian Studies, vol. 18, no 2; Milan Minić, "Prva Beograđanka arhitekt – Jelisaveta Načić" [The First Belgrade Female Architect – Jelisaveta Načić], Godišnjak grada Beograda, vol. 3 (1956): 451–458.
29 Also discussed in Marta Vukotić Lazar and Nataša Danilović Hristić, "The Growth and Development of Belgrade in the Period from 1815 to 1910," Zbornik radova Filozofskog fakulteta, vol. 65, no. 3 (2015): 51–80.
30 The same process was taking place in most cities in the Balkans after the end of the Ottoman rule. Discussed in Tanja D. Conley and Emily G. Makaš, "Shaping Central and Southeastern European Cities at the Age of Nationalism," in Emily G. Makaš and Tanja D. Conley (eds.), Capital Cities in the Aftermath of Empires: Planning in Central and Southeastern Europe, London: Routledge, 2009: 1–28; Alexandra Yerolympos, "A New City for a New State: City Planning and the Formation of National Identity in the Balkans," Planning Perspectives, vol. 8 (1993): 233–257; Maximilian Hartmuth, "Negotiating Tradition and Ambition: A Comparative Perspective on the 'De-Ottomanization' of the Balkan Cityscapes," Ethnologia Balkanica, vol. 10 (2006): 15–33.
31 Jean-Paul Midant, La fantastique architecture d'Alban Chambon, Brussels: AAM, 2010.
32 Yerolympos, "A New City for a New State": 244.

38 *The birth of national architectures*

33 Đokica Jovanović, *Prilagođavanje – Srbija i moderna: od strepnje do sumnje* [*The Adjustment – Serbia and the Modern: From Fear to Suspicion*], Belgrade: Filozofski fakultet, 2012.
34 Bogdan Nestorović, *Arhitektura Srbije u 19. veku* [*Architecture in Serbia in the Nineteenth Century*], Belgrade: Art Press, 2006: 91.
35 For the development of the Ministry of Buildings, see Bogdan Nestorivić, *Arhitektura Srbije u XiX veku*: 164–172. Aleksandar Kadijević, "Pojam 'državnog' arhitekte" [The Concept of "State Architect"], *Arhitektura*, vol. 102 (2006): 12.
36 Ibid., 168.
37 Mirjana Roter-Blagojević, "Pojava prvih zakonskih propisa i standarda u oblasti građevinarstva u Srbiji tokom 19. i početkom 20. veka" [The Emergence of First Legislative Laws and Standards in the Field of Construction in Serbia During the Nineteenth and Early Twentieth Century], *Izgradnja*, vol. 5 (1998): 245–258. Mirjana Roter-Blagojević, "Arhitektura građevina javnih namena izgrađenih u Beogradu od 1868. do 1900. godine – I/II" [Architecture of Public Buildings Built in Belgrade from 1868 to 1900 – 1/2], *Arhitektura i urbanizam*, vol. 12–13 (2003) and vol. 14–15 (2004): 109–121 and 73–90.
38 Jörg Stabenow, "Ljubljana," in Makaš and Conley (eds.), *Capital Cities in the Aftermath of Empires*: 229.
39 The pivotal work on the nineteenth-century architecture was done by Bogdan Nestorović, son of architect Nikola Nestorović. See "Razvoj arhitkturee Beograda od Kneza Miloša do Prvog svetskog rata, 1815–1914" [Development of Belgrade Architecture from Prince Miloš to WWI], *Godišnjak grada Beograda*, vol. 1 (1954): 159–174; "Nosioci arhitektonske misli u Srbiji XIX veka" [Carriers of the Architectural Taught in Serbia of the Nineteenth Century], *Saopštenja IAUS*, vol. 2 (1969): 49–55; "Pregled spomenika arhitekture u Srbiji XIX veka" [An Overview of Architectural Monuments of Serbia of the Nineteenth Century], *Saopštenja RZZZSK*, vol. 10 (1974): 141–169; "Graditelji Beograda od 1815. do 1915. godine" [Belgrade Builders from 1815–1915], in *Istorija Beograda – 2*, Belgrade: Prosveta, 1974: 335–347.
40 Anastasijević accumulated wealth after gaining rights to import salt product from Wallachia and Moldavia.
41 Discussed in Gale Stokes, *Politics as Development: The Emergence of Political Parties in Nineteenth Century Serbia*, Durham, NC: Duke University Press, 1990.
42 Bogdan Nestorović, "Kapetan Mišino zdanje," *Godišnjak grada Beograda*, vol. 9–10 (1962–1963): 81–98.
43 The first exhibition of recorded drawings, sketches and paintings, resulting from Mihailo Valtrović and Dragutin Milutinović's research on Serbian medieval churches took place in Kapetan Miša Endowment.
44 Bogdan Nestorović, "Narodno pozorište u Beogradu" [The National Theater in Belgrade], *Godišnjak grada Beograda*, vol. 3 (1956): 303–324.
45 Aleksandar Bugarski (1835–1891) was born in Prešov, raised in Novi Sad and graduated from Budapest Technical College. In 1869, he accepted an offer from the Serbian Ministry of Buildings to work as state architect. Later in his career, he became a member of the Serbian Academy of Arts and Sciences.
46 Zoran Manević, "Novija srpska arhitektura" [Newer Serbian Architecture], *Čovjek i prostor*, vol. 1 (1972): 7–8; Zoran Manević, "Klasici srpske arhitekture – Aleksandar Bugarski" [Classics of Serbian Architecture – Aleksandar Bugarski], *Arhitektura*, vol. 59 (2002) – part 4.

47 This project was initiated during the rule of Prince Aleksandar Karađorđević, when the Obrenovićs were dethroned for the first time.
48 Ljiljana Miletić-Abramović, *Arhitektura rezidencija i vila Beograda 1830–2000* [*Architecture of Belgrade Residences and Villas, 1830–2000*], Belgrade: Karić fondacija, 2002: 37.
49 One of Hansen's students, Jovan Ilkić (1857–1917) is remembered for the prolific career he achieved, mainly at the Ministry of Buildings where he was employed.
50 The stylization discussed in Aleksandar Kadijević, *Estetika arhitekture akademizma XIX – XX vek* [*The Aesthetics of Academism in Architecture – Nineteenth and Twentieth Century*], Belgrade: Građevinska knjiga, 2005: 301–304.
51 The heraldic symbols from the Royal Court, removed during communist rule, have been reconstructed in drawings. See Marko Popović, *Heraldički simboli na javnim zdanjima Beograda* [*Heraldic Symbols on Public Buildings in Belgrade*], Belgrade: BMG, 1997: 50–53.
52 Svetozar Ivačković (1844–1924) set new directions for the large-scale civic cathedrals, but also for the standardized, widely spread, small village churches. His legacy is evident in modern church architecture of Serbia. See Željko Škalamera, "Obnova 'srpskog stila' u arhitekturi" [The Revival of "Serbian Style" in Architecture], *Zbornik za likovne umetnosti Matice srpske*, vol. 5 (1969): 200.
53 The collaborator in this project was Ivačković's colleague from the Academy of Fine Arts in Vienna, Jovan Subotić, whose role has been neglected and forgotten. See Aleksandar Kadijević, "Palata Ministarstva pravde – ostvarenje arhitekata Svetozara Ivačkovića i Jovana Subotića" [Palace of the Ministry of Justice – the Realization of Svetozar Ivačković and Jovan Subotić], *Godišnjak grada Beograda*, vol. 53 (2006): 199–209.
54 Milica Ceranić, "O arhitekturi Palate Ministarstva pravde u Beogradu i njenim neimarskim uzorima" [About the Palace of the Ministry of Justice in Belgrade and its Analogies], *Nasledje/Heritage*, vol. 10 (2009): 83–90.
55 The most remarkable among Ivačković's small-scale designs in Hansen's manner are the Hariš Chapel at Zemun Cemetery and the New Cemetery Chapel in Belgrade. His projects for standardized village churches were realized in Guncati (1893), Rasnica (1894) and Žlni (1894) – published in *Srpski tehnički list*, no. 5/ 1893 and no. 1–2/1894.
56 Interest in the "Serbian style" grew after the pivotal text Škalamera, "Obnova 'srpskog stila' u arhitekturi." Further elaboration can be found in Aleksandar Kadijević, *Jedan vek traženja nacionalnog stila u srpskoj arhitekturi: sredina 19.–sredina 20. veka* [*One Century of the Search for a National Style in Serbian Architecture: Mid-Nineteenth–Mid-Twentieth Century*], Belgrade: Građevinska knjiga, 1997.
57 For more about Konstantin A. Jovanović or Constantin Jovanovits (1849–1923) see Danijela Vanušić, *Konstantin A. Jovanović: arhitekta velikog formata* [*Konstantin A. Jovanović: A Grand-Scale Architect*], Belgrade: Museum of the City of Belgrade, 2013; Gordana Gordić and Vera Pavlović-Lončarski, *Arhitekt Konstantin Jovanović* [*Architect Konstantin Jovanović*], exhibition catalog, Belgrade: Zavod za zaštitu spomenika kulture grada Beograda, 2001.
58 Tanja Damljanović, "A Semper Student in Belgrade," *Centropa*, vol. 2 (2002): 145–151.

40 The birth of national architectures

59 The mosque was destroyed after the Turkish withdrawal despite its architectural and cultural importance and appeals for its preservation. The initiatives for preservation proposed for the mosque to be converted into a library or archive.
60 Discussed in Branko Maksimović, "Estetička shvatanja kompozicije gradskih centara Beograda početkom 20. veka" [Aesthetic Consideration of the Composition of Public Centers in Belgrade in the Early Twentieth Century], *Godišnjak grada Beograda*, vol. 14 (1967): 83–85.
61 Constantin Jovanovits, *Forschungen über den Bau der Peterskirche zu Rom*, Vienna: Wilhelm Braumüler, 1877.
62 Kendall Wallis, "Bearing Bandmann's Meaning," introduction to Günter Bandmann, *Early Medieval Architecture as Bearer of Meaning*, New York: Columbia University Press, 2005: 5.
63 The competition was first announced in Belgrade daily newspaper *Politika* on November 3, 1926 and reprinted in Zagreb bulletin *Tehnički list*, no. 9 (1927): 30.
64 Further discussed in Tanja Damljanović Conley, "The Backdrop of Serbian Statehoods: Morphing Faces of the National Assembly in Belgrade," *Nationalities Papers*, vol. 41, no. 1 (2013): 64–89.
65 The ideological framework of the Serbian style is further discussed in Bratislav Pantelić, "Nationalism and Architecture: The Creation of the National Style and Its Political Implications," *JSAH*, vol. 56, 1997.
66 A collection of texts by Serbian architects debating on the notion of national style around the turn of the century is published in Zoran Manević.
67 Focusing on specifically Serbian medieval heritage in contemporary design was fostered through the curriculum of the Department of Architecture at Belgrade Technical College after its foundation in 1897.

2 Croationed Zagreb

Tracing a modern Croatian capital

Defining Zagreb as a modern Croatian capital dated back to 1776, when the Croatian Kingdom Council – established as part of Empress Maria Theresa's reformation politics giving more power to separate ethnic entities – was moved to Zagreb from the city of Varaždin. The council was an executive body consisting of five noblemen with different aristocratic titles coming from the native region yet appointed directly by the empress and ruled by the ban, whose title was related to the Croatian medieval state, now incorporated into the hierarchy of the Habsburg administration. Although in control over the local jurisdiction and internal affairs, the council was subordinated to the Hungarian government from 1779, yet even as a Hungarian political subject, the seat of the Croatian ban remained in Zagreb.

When the Hungarian Count Ignác Gyulay started running the office of the ban in 1808, he bought a residence at Gradec – one of two enwalled, medieval urban cores of Zagreb, and turned it into his seat, still known today as Banski Dvori [Ban's Palace]. Situated at the square where the parish church of St. Mark had been standing since the fourteenth century, the new governmental program changed the inherited urban context; the secular political authority was inserted into the existing residential fabric previously oriented only toward the ecclesial center. From the time of completion in the early 1800s, Banski Dvori housed the institution of the ban until the proclamation of the Vidovdan Constitution, an event that became a source of discontent as a sign of disrespect of Yugoslav authorities for the inherited political institutions of Croats. With the collapse of Royal Yugoslavia at the outbreak of World War II, Banski Dvori was the seat of the Ustaša regime, and later after the end of the war, the seat of the Croatian socialist government of Tito's Yugoslavia. Although modest in size and decoration, this late-Baroque town palace played a crucial role in the constitution of contemporary Croatian identity during the civil war of the 1990s, when the central power of Socialist Yugoslavia, the Yugoslav People's Army, bombed the palace as a gathering place of Croatian politicians striving towards the independence. This event only helped in the international recognition of the

42 *The birth of national architectures*

Republic of Croatia in 1992, after which Banski Dvori became the seat of Croatian government and of the prime minister.

The protagonists of the Illyrian Movement engaged in the national awakening under the Habsburgs were the leading developers of modern architectural programs coincident with the spread of the Enlightenment. With good education, well-paid jobs, and decent social status, the Illyrians managed to collect sufficient funds for purchasing a just-completed palace of the Croatian aristocratic family of Drašković for their seat, with some members of the Drašković family being supporters of the movement themselves.[1] Named Narodni Dom [People's House], the building was a meeting place of numerous cultural and political events, and also an initial venue of rising national institutions such as the museum, publishing house, reading room and economic society. In contrast to the existing late-Baroque, mainly residential edifices in Upper Town, the neo-Classical features of Narodni Dom, by the Zagreb-based builder of German origins, Bartol Felbinger,[2] advocated a new type of culturally enlightened society to challenge the Holy Empire's hierarchical order reinforced during the Counter-Reformation. Soon after opening, during the revolutionary year of 1848, the People's House hosted the pivotal events of Croatian modern history – meetings of the National Assembly with representatives from all social and economic backgrounds, including the plebs, which led toward the proclamation of a decree for Croatian national liberation. The following gatherings of the Assembly, which took place in the Old Theater on Upper Town, resulted in a broader political affirmation of the Illyrian Party program, requesting the abolition of villeinage, freedom of speech and equal legislative and electoral rights. The main advocate and supporter of the national program, Josip Jelačić, was the first Croatian ban freely elected by the Assembly, the decision confirmed by the emperor to challenge the Hungarian supremacy over the Croats in the following decade.

The growing Croatian bourgeoisie society was anti-aristocratic, modern-oriented and urbanized independently from the clerical hierarchy. As such, it differed from the Serbian national rebellions, which focused on religious emancipation of the deprived Orthodox-Christian peasantry suppressed by the Ottoman authorities to boost economic prosperity and social mobility. When the rising power of the Croatian middle-class gave a new impulse to urban development outside of the enwalled medieval settlements of Gradec and Kapitol during the 1840s, the area down the hill known as Lower City was fast-expanded. The rising wealth of Croatian merchants and small-service shop owners was first shown in the development of Ilica Street, still present-day Zagreb's most vibrant commercial and retail zone. The main civic gate, Mesnička, along with Dverce on the city's southern rampart and the northern gate at Priest Tower, was pulled down to open up space for growth toward the countryside. The eighteen-century marketplace called Harmica was developed as the end-point of Ilica Street into a planned public place named after Ban Jelačić. The square was regulated in 1866 to hold the sculpture of the ban on horse as its focal point, after an initiative of citizens and municipal authorities to raise money for presenting the ban as hero in the earlier battle against the Hungarians.[3]

By an Imperial Decree from September 7, 1850, Zagreb became administratively united into a single city from two older enwalled settlements, Gradec and Kapitol, and a third, unwalled Lower City, where the trade center had been formed since the 1700s. The urban development of united Zagreb was intensified in the 1880s and 1890s due to the rapid economic and industrial growth, especially after the devastating earthquake of 1880.[4] The willingness of Zagreb authorities to accept and follow the modern urbanistic doctrines was first rectified in the Building Code for the Capital City of Zagreb from 1857, which declared that "the level of built conditions has to be raised to serve the interests of health, comfort, decency and taste and the regularity of streets and public places to be achieved."[5] More detailed, legislatively effective proposals for the development of the Lower City, the Regulatory Plans of 1865 and 1888, defined the character of future urban interventions in more detail.[6] The shape and size of the city were determined, on one side by the two medieval settlements on the hill, from which urban expansion had begun at the beginning of the century; and on the other, by the railway built in the 1870s. As early as in 1862, a train service started operating from Zagreb to the junction in Slovenia where the tracks joined the railroad Vienna-Trieste. After accepting the agreement with Hungary, Zagreb became an important stop on the railroad named the Great Hungary, connecting the capital of Budapest with ports in the Adriatic Sea.

A political deal between Croatia and Hungary known as Nagodba was signed to guarantee the political rights of the Croats within the Hungarian borders a year after the proclamation of the dual Austrian-Hungarian Monarchy. Following Nagodba, the Croatian Assembly with the ban as its head, controlled some spheres of politics, culture and the economy, such as local government and courts, educational institutions and agriculture. The organization of global modern systems such as the postal service, railways, banks, credit unions and industries depended on the central government in Budapest. However, a strong elite of Croatian merchants, industrial capitalists and bank owners started to emerge despite its overall dependence on the centralized monetary system. The early development of industry was initiated in the 1870s, with the number of workers totaling 3,650 by the end of the century.[7] The initial industrialization turned the local shop-owners into the bourgeoisie, with the oldest enterprises being a flour mill, a tobacco factory, two tanneries and a local gas works. At the turn of the century, Zagreb became the largest industrial center in the region with seventy manufacturing works, each of which employed around 100 workers, hence attracting a big population influx into the city.

The urban development and a national program: the Green Horseshoe

The hilly terrain on the north and the emergence of traffic corridors on the opposite side determined the spread of the Lower Town along the east–west direction. This newly regulated urban area was planned as a grid, gravitating towards the central north–south axis between Ban Jelačić Square on the north end and the railway station on the south. The modern extension of Lower Town was defined by the concept of Green Horseshoe, a U-shaped ensemble of two deep parks laid parallel to each other, later connected with the third green prospect on its south side (Figure 2.1). The credit for the whole urban design went to Croatian civil engineer and urban planner Milan Lenuci[8] (after whom it was named Lenuci's Horseshoe in the 1960s), although each segment was considered and executed separately as a piecemeal urban process. The Horseshoe was already drawn into the Regulatory Plan for the Lower City of 1888; however, the urban necklace developed in a sequence of green squares during the timespan of more than thirty years – from the 1890s until the 1920s – growing into the showcase for prominent public national institutions: the Yugoslav Academy of Sciences and Arts of 1880, the National Theater of 1895, the Art Pavilion of 1898 and the National and University Library of 1913. From the standpoint of an urban program aiming to intensify modernization processes leading to political emancipation and strengthening of the Croatian middle class, the Green Horseshoe was a Croatian equivalent

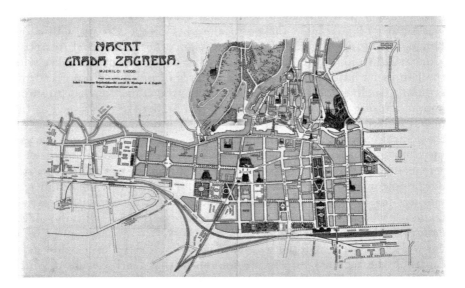

Figure 2.1 Plan of Zagreb 1911 – the Green Horseshoe starts with the National Theatre – the West Esplanade, ends with the Yugoslav Academy – the East Esplanade (National and University Library, Zagreb)

to Viennese Ringstrasse,[9] yet from the perspective of its formal setup, Lenuci's urban vision resulted in a more successful urban achievement than its celebrated Viennese predecessor.

The Zrinjski Square, originally known as the New Square or the Cattle Market, halfway between the Jelačić Square and the railway station, was the first to be developed in the Horseshoe's East Esplanade.[10] The square was already included in the Regulatory Plan of 1865 along with a proposal for the future use of buildings placed along its four sides with a market hall in the center and a new church, seminary and music center along the regulatory lines. Later attempts at transforming the Cattle Market into a landscaped public space and parceling the land into building lots attracted new landowners, eager to confirm their growing wealth through the construction of representational, multistory, neo-Renaissance-styled palaces with business on the street level. In 1870, Zagreb municipality calculated the budget for leveling, installing sewage drainage and planting trees in honor of the 300th anniversary of the death of Croatian nobleman and army leader Nikola Zrinjski during the siege of Szigeth against the Ottoman army. A fully developed horticultural plan for the square's central space was signed by the head of the Viennese civic garden office, Rudolph Siebeck,[11] and executed together with the installation of gas street lightning in the mid-1870s. Initially, the municipality intended to save surrounding parcels of land for the development of public and administrative institutions, yet the development ended up relying on the private initiative of wealthy nobleman and the rising upper middle-class. Therefore, besides the Court House completed in 1879 and the Yugoslav Academy of Sciences and Arts completed in 1880 and opened in 1884, the monumental, multistory buildings flanking the square were residential palaces built for Baron Dragan Vranyczany-Dobrinović, Baron Buratti and Ljudevit Vranyczany – reminiscent of the high-Renaissance Roman palazzos of noblemen and clergy. The oldest surviving house at the square, Halm House, built in 1859 by prominent mid-century Croatian architect Janko Nikola Grahor, housed the earliest pharmacy-shop of the Lower City.[12]

Aware of the importance of the new site in formulating an architectural program of Croatian identity, the Croatian government along with the municipality accepted an initiative for building of a new seat for the Yugoslav Academy of Sciences and Arts (Figure 2.2) at the head of Zrinjski Square in 1877. One of the founders, Bishop Josip Juraj Strossmayer, donated a large grant for relocating the Academy from the People's House to a new palace, and through his personal connections invited a professor at the Academy of Fine Arts in Vienna and author of numerous projects on Ringstrasse, Friedrich von Schmidt, to develop the plans. These two became acquainted when Strossmayer served as bishop of Đakovo-Bosnia-Srem and Schmidt inherited the project for Đakovo Cathedral from Karl Rösner.[13] Friedrich von Schmidt had been recognized as an expert in modern appropriation of the Gothic vocabulary both in projects for cathedrals and public buildings, including the Viennese City Hall, designed approximately at the same time as the Yugoslav Academy. Therefore, his decision to engage the neo-Renaissance

Figure 2.2 Yugoslav Academy of Sciences and Arts at Zrinjevac Square – the East Esplanade of Horseshoe (National and University Library, Zagreb)

instead of Gothic stylization at the Academy was symbolically relevant to the nature of a new national program, similar to Ivačković's decision to wrap the Ministry of Justice in Belgrade in the neo-Renaissance instead of the neo-Byzantine code. As the neo-Renaissance was deemed appropriate for academic institutions – such as the university and the Museum of Art History – the Yugoslav Academy in Zagreb translated the social connotations of Ringstrasse into the Croatian setting. Moreover, instead of alluding to late-Renaissance palazzos of Roman cinquecento, which had affirmed the strengthening of the Catholic clergy within the boundaries of the Holy Roman Empire including the Croatian lands, Schmidt suggested a lineage with the early Florentine rulers of quattrocento, when most power was in secular hands. As the palazzo of knowledge, the Academy was strictly composed; its simple, modestly scaled square plan with an elegant inner courtyard was covered with a flat-coffered glass lantern illuminating the monumental staircase and galleries on all four sides. The precise forms of architectural elements – piers, columns, and semicircular archivolts – were accentuated only by the different shade of stone on arches and cornices in contrast to vertical supports. From the outside, the sturdy composition felt impenetrable in the lower zones as opposed to the lightness of the last, disproportionally higher third floor, accentuated with dynamic pattern of solid and open surfaces, rows of pilasters and wide-arched windows, as could have been expected on the piano nobile. A classical portico in front of the main entrance, topped by a balustraded terrace accessible from the second floor, was the only segment openly communicating with Zrinjski Square. The design stylistically evoked neo-Renaissance palaces of the Ringstrasse era, Theophil von Hansen's realizations characterized by sturdy massing and contrasting façade textures, rather than Schmidt's meticulously crafted neo-Gothic stylization.

How was the political program of integrated Yugoslavism, originally pursued by the Academy and its leaders, altered along the Croatian identity line in the next century? Rooted in the Illyrian Movement, yet approved and recognized by the Austrian throne in 1866, the institution promoted the research of language, history and culture of South Slavs with all respect to the Habsburg authorities. Its leading figures, founders and patrons, Juraj Strossmayer and Franjo Rački, were Roman Catholic priests with a long interest in the unification of all Slavs and overcoming the long-lasting gap between Western and Eastern Christianity, the main cause of South Slavs' split into different ethnicities. The Academy had close ties to the university, which grew from a Jesuit school opened in Zagreb in the 1600s, with an aim to integrate forces of Enlightenment into the Catholic hierarchy and encourage the underdeveloped Slavic population to join the European modernization processes. Yet, Strossmayer hoped to unify the South Slavs under the leading role of Croats, an idea which was finally spoiled after the constitution of Royal Yugoslavia. The Serbian counterpart to the Yugoslav Academy had existed since 1842; since 1886 it was run under the name of the Royal Serbian Academy and after the dissolution of the kingdom into the Serbian Academy. On the other hand, the Yugoslav Academy of Sciences and Arts in Zagreb held the Yugoslav name and promoted a Yugoslav idea for 125 years in continuity after its foundation, with its name altered to Croatian only after the proclamation of independence.[14]

The first seed of Green Horseshoe on its west side was the Old Fairground, where a Romanesque-styled, three-story hospital[15] was built after the plans of a Viennese architect Ludwig von Zettl from 1856 to 1859. After the municipality decided to move the rectorate of Zagreb University into the hospital in 1882, the first elaborate plans for today's Theater Square were conceived. This time, it was Milan Lenuci who submitted several proposals defining an academically conceptualized green park, flanked by wide streets and palaces for national institutions to replace the Fairground. The first building to appear on the south regulation of the Theater Square was the Croatian Sokol from 1884, followed by the Teachers' Society built five years later, on its east side. The monumental Croatian National Theater (Figure 2.3) arose in the center during the early 1890s and was encircled by pavement and formally landscaped flowerbeds with no trees – the first design of this kind in

48 The birth of national architectures

Figure 2.3 Croatian National Theatre at the West Esplanade (National and University Library, Zagreb)

the sequence. In the future development of the West Esplanade, none of the public squares would be fully emerged into greenery as was the case with Zrinjski Square and the rest of the East Esplanade but composed from geometrically shaped pieces of grass and flowers inserted into paved surfaces.

The construction and opening of the National Theater in Lower City coincided with the strengthening of Hungarian national appetites along new movements in conceptualizing a Croatian national ideology at the turn of the century. Previously settled in the Old Theater House in Upper Town, the institution was born out of its German predecessor in 1861.[16] Named the Theater of the Yugoslavs, it run programs in the native language, established a school of drama and the first South Slavic opera all under the supervision of the elected council of trustees appointed by the Croatian Assembly. The building had severely damaged in the earthquake of 1880, but a consensus about the location for a new building could not be easily reached, so the Hungarian Count Károly Khuen-Héderváry – the Croatian ban at the time – made the decision on his own in 1893. Upon his invitation, the respected Vienna-based firm Fellner & Helmer, well known for theater designs over the monarchy, submitted a project to be developed in a very short period, only sixteen months – an effort made in honor of Emperor Franz Joseph's visit to Zagreb. The first performance, a piece by a Croatian composer Ivan Zajc, was attended by the emperor on October 14, 1895. Since the Hungarian instead of Croatian flag was flaunted at the opening, the event was considered as a signal of the political strategy of Magyarization, against which Croatian riots protested at Ban Jelačić Square at the time of the performance.

The imposing size and forms created by Fellner & Helmer also respected the Ringstrasse concept of pairing the style with the program, as was seen on the Yugoslav Academy, in this case the neo-Baroque suitable for the theatrical function. The firm took part in designing theaters in many regional centers of the monarchy such as Prague, Pressburg, Cluj and Szeged, but was also hired outside the Austro-Hungarian borders: in Odessa, the major port of Russian Empire, and Sofia, the capital city of recently recognized Bulgaria. Since its opening, the theater provoked debates over the pompous architectural features symbolizing the Habsburgs – considered the suppressors of equal rights by the poor, hence the criticism referred to class issues as a limitation for Croatian national emancipation. Intellectuals of leftist political affiliation, such as a Croatian writer and critic Miroslav Krleža, attacked the theater as an example of provincial Austro-Hungarian Historicism, the occurrence of which could not supplement a lack of a meaningful national architecture.[17] Although the leftist-oriented thinkers continued attacking bourgeois iconography after the victory of communism, a new interest in the Historicism, and analogously in architecture of the National Theater, grew parallel to the struggle for Croatian emancipation from Yugoslavia at the peak of the communist regime in the 1960s.[18] With the emergence of Postmodernism in Yugoslav architectural historiography in the early 1980s, reinterpretations of cultural significance of the nineteenth-century achievements, along with the place of National Theater as a national monument prevailed as the means of challenging the assertively modernistic dogmas tied to the communist era. The symbolical power of the building as a carrier of the new national program has been amplified since the proclamation of Croatian independence.[19]

The construction of Zagreb's main railway station at the bottom of the East Esplanade also inspired controversy over the issue of hidden Magaryzation. After long negotiations between the municipality and the representatives of Royal Hungarian Railroads, the decision about location was finally reached in 1890 with an outcome that granted the construction of the monumental edifice to an employee of the Hungarian Railroads, Ferenc Pfaff, the leading architect of numerous projects for railway stations in the Hungarian portion of the monarchy. The almost 200-meter-long structure was built on undeveloped land, then considered remote from the city core, for an important reason; to demarcate and anchor the south wing of the Horseshoe, and consequently define a new spatial barrier, a threshold between the inner versus the outer city. The strongly articulated main façade oriented toward the city became a symbolic civic gate, as well as the focal point of the Horseshoe's eastern axis starting at Zrinjski Square. Both by its size and architectural rhetoric, the main façade of the railway station was a theatrical backdrop for the future arrangement of Franz Joseph Square, setting the tone for new buildings as the largest urban and architectural ensemble in the Lower City.

The chief civic gardener, Franjo Jaržabek, oversaw the landscaping and maintenance attuned to the French Baroque schemes, which had become popular in representational green ensembles throughout the monarchy. The square was finalized with the completion of the Art Pavilion of 1898 set on the East Esplanade's axis between the Yugoslav Academy and the railway station.

A flamboyant juxtaposition of the neo-Baroque and the Secessionist façades for the Art Pavilion, executed as a combination of traditional masonry and modern materials, iron and glass, has remained a monumental vista to be absorbed from the entrance podium of the railway station upon the arrival to Zagreb. The design presented the next step in the development of an imperial architectural script by Fellner & Helmer around the turn of the century[20] and was Ban Károly Khuen-Héderváry's present to the Croatian people, built as a replica of the previously constructed building for the Croatian Pavilion at the Millennium Exhibition of 1896 in Budapest. As part of the celebration of 1,000 years of Hungarian statehood, the Croatian art was exhibited in Budapest in a smaller pavilion by the Hungarian architectural firm Korb & Giergl. Khuen-Héderváry was involved in choosing architectural firms[21] for executing the pavilions in both cities and defining a location for the permanent display of Croatian art at Franz Joseph Square in Zagreb.[22] The public reaction to the project was twofold: one faction of Croatian politicians – mostly nobleman, set against the unification of Croats with other South Slavic ethnicities and the Illyrian Movement – supported the Hungarian leadership and responded positively. On the other hand, the Illyrians, anticipating the strengthening of the Hungarian authority as a threat to the pan-Slavic political program, remained hesitant. Overall, the Hungarian authorities were given credit for the economic growth and cultural revival despite the attempts at assimilation conducted through the compulsory use of the Hungarian language in state administration. The rebuilding of the Art Pavilion confirmed the Hungarian-Croatian political coexistence, yet even more pronouncedly the strength and resilience of the Habsburg realm in adjusting to the processes of nationalization and modernization within the existing imperial boundaries.

The future architectural verbalization of the Green Horseshoe as an urbanistic Gesamkunstwerk was an idea central to all of Milan Lenuci's activities as the head of the Municipal Building Department.[23] The composition of Franz Joseph Square, based on his regulation plan from 1897, presented a starting point for numerous sketches and developed plans for the West Esplanade, dated 1901, 1903 and 1906. However, the final decisions about the character of public spaces and edifices in the West Esplanade overlooked Lenuci's initial vision, whose long-lasting idea was to develop this portion of the Horseshoe into public area reserved primarily for pleasure and sports as an extension of the Croatian Sokol. Instead, the municipality granted the southern area of the West Esplanade for the development of the university complex with a library.

The University Library, the most significant architectural statement of the West Esplanade due to its post-Historicist features,[24] was the first building to be proposed and executed within the new university complex. The bureau of Karlsruhe-trained Rudolph Lubynski[25] received the commission through an architectural competition of 1909, a choice that was made based on Lubynski's previous experience with a large-scale project for Heidelberg University Library that he had participated in from 1902 to 1905. Although the entry failed to meet all the stipulations put forth in the competition, the success of Lubynski's design lay in a neo-Classical monumental aesthetic adjusted to the up-to-date Secessionist stylization, which matched the overall tone expected for the Green Horseshoe.[26] The formal, box-shaped layout with two inner courtyards was wrapped into rows of Classicist pilasters on all four sides, lending a sober tone to the composition which was interrupted only with a portico and pediment over the main entrance and an enormous dome covered with copper. The library's contour and symmetrical arrangement, respecting the inherited processional character of the Horseshoe determined by the nineteenth-century urbanistic aesthetics, was a reason why the upcoming generation of rebellious Modernist voices, gathered around recently arrived Viktor Kovačić, reacted negatively upon the project's completion. Despite its meticulously crafted Secessionist details, Lubynski's project was considered by a rising generation of architects and critics as an illustrative example of mediocrity failing to reach an intrinsic expression of a national spirit, the foremost goal for Croatian art and architecture in the early 1900s. Among them was a young art historian, Kosta Strajnić, who argued that key examples of national architecture had to be designed only by unique national genius, recognized in the rising figure of Viktor Kovačić, instead of an "average follower of the already seen prototypes."[27]

Although not finally conceived before the revised regulatory plan from 1913 was put into effect, Marulić Square in front of the library also respected the nineteenth-century urban doctrines. Its urban arrangement envisioned a composition of two symmetrical, identical-looking edifices framing the processional path towards the library. The first to be completed, the Chemical Institute by Vjekoslav Bastl, was built in the following year as a stylistic homage to Lubynski's design. On the other hand, the construction of its mirroring counterpart, the Institute of Physics by Egon Steinmann,[28] lasted for more than twenty years.[29] Although fully subordinated to the predetermined urban setting from 1913, Steinmann realization's spoke for the next golden era of Croatian architecture – the interwar Modernism.[30]

The last portion of the Horseshoe, the South Esplanade, connecting the east and the west wings, was conceptualized during the 1920s around the Botanical Garden, an "open classroom" for the Faculty of Natural Sciences, as the starting point. The Botanical Garden had been aligned with the Old Fairground, the later Theater Square, at the time of its establishment in 1889, when the planners had anticipated the potentials of this location in spatial relation to the Lower Town. With the completion of

52 *The birth of national architectures*

Marulić Square, the Botanical Garden became the endpoint of the West Esplanade beginning with the Theater Square, but also the west edge of the South Esplanade determined by the railway station and the train tracks. The position of the railroad and ground transportation corridors was the subject of long-lasting debates between the Hungarian railroad company and local planners and architects,[31] with the final decision reached in 1913. When the railway tracks permanently cutting off the continuous spread of the city toward the south, the Municipal Building Department made final decisions about the future development of the South Esplanade. Its central content was to become a luxurious hotel with an elevated terrace conjoined with an elegantly articulated garden, opening toward the entrance zone of the railway station. Following this urban vision, the Hotel Esplanade was built in 1925 after the winning entry in the international competition[32] by a well-established Zagreb architect Dionis Sunko,[33] who envisioned a design as a welcoming showroom of luxury and splendor to visitors arriving by train. The travelers were to be rapt by the hotel's massive yet elegant features: stoic massing, gigantic colonnades and immense pediments projecting out from all four façades, a glamorous respite on the Orient Express voyage "nostalgically evoking the pre-War I Belle Époque sensibility."[34] The façade opening toward the station was robust and heavy yet elaborately perforated by vertical strips of doors and windows rising over the elevated terrace. Besides its connection to the plateau in front of the railway station, the hotel defined the shape of Ante Starčević Square dedicated to the controversial politician, considered the father of Croatian nation because of his deliberate fight against Habsburg authorities in favor of the South Slavic unification under the Croatian name. Because of his uncompromising personality, Starčević neglected personal wealth, frequently dwelling in inappropriate housing conditions. Yet, for this reason he was admired by members of his political party and the Croatian people, who raised money through donations to erect a large neo-Renaissance palace, known as Starčevićev Dom [Starčevićev's House], today serving as the City Library, in honor of the leader who lived here for the last few years of his life. The design and execution were granted to the most prolific architectural firm of the late nineteenth century, Hönigsberg & Deutsch,[35] who thereby determined the street façade of the north side of the future Starčević's Square. Although large in scale and elegant in its stylization, the architectural tribute to Starčević would be overshadowed by the sturdy volume and exaggerated forms of the later-built Hotel Esplanade.

The Green Horseshoe, as a single urban concept and a piecemeal development process, with its contents – public spaces and edifices of national importance – ended being one of the most synchronized urban resemblances in service of a modern national ideology in Europe. Since its formation, certain segments built by the local authorities from domestic funds, such as Zrinjski Square, continuing into Strossmayer Square with the Yugoslav

Academy of Sciences and Arts from the 1860s and Marulić Square with the University Library from the 1910s, have been undisputedly verifying a Croatian identity, while the others with sources in the centralized source of power, the Hungarian government, like Theater Square with the National Theater and Franz Joseph Square with the Art Pavilion and the railway station remained questioned and re-evaluated as Croatian national symbols until Croatia became an independent state.

National architecture / modern architecture

The first generation of Croatian architects – Josip Vancaš, Martin Pilar, Janko Holjac and Josip Grahor, essential in constituting the Croatian architectural profession – was educated under Friedrich von Schmidt at the Academy of Fine Arts in Vienna.[36] Yet, with the opening of Zagreb's School of Arts and Crafts in 1882, the first generation of native pupils from underprivileged, mainly peasant families received an education that would allow them to trace a path toward the conceptualization of national architecture. The initiative for establishing the school with such a specific program came from an urgent need for skilled craftsman in the reconstruction of Zagreb Cathedral. Originally built as the bishop's seat within the enwalled settlement of Kaptol between the ninth and twelfth centuries, the cathedral was severely damaged during the earthquake of 1880, and turned into an overwhelming project taking most of the resources from the entire community for the next two decades. Like its many Central European counterparts, the original cathedral went through numerous stages of construction and reconstruction since its foundation until the late-Baroque transformations in the eighteenth century. With the rise of national consciousness and the unification of Zagreb from two separate medieval fortifications, Kaptol and Gradec, the idea of replacing the cathedral's unbalanced silhouette grew into an important national agenda fostered by Strossmayer.

It was Herman Bollé, invited to Zagreb by Strossmayer after they had met during Bollé's study trip though Italy, to become the leading architect of the reconstruction.[37] As a collaborator in Schmidt's studio at Viennese Academy of Fine Arts, Bollé was acquainted with projects for neo-Gothic transformations of medieval clerical seats in Central Europe. After his recognized work on St. Stephan's in Vienna, Schmidt contributed to the reconstruction of Matthias Church at Buda Castle hill with his Hungarian student, Frigyes Schulek, and to St. Vitus' in Prague with a Czech student, Josef Hlávka. In Croatia, his original project for Đakovo Cathedral was assisted by Bollé, who was already acquainted to projects of a similar nature through his father, who had supervised the reconstruction of Cologne Cathedral. After completing the work in Đakovo, Bollé continued collaborating with Schmidt on the project for the Yugoslav Academy, completed right before the earthquake. Although signed by Schmidt, the project was developed and executed by Bollé, a job that kept him in Zagreb longer than originally

54 *The birth of national architectures*

anticipated. He oversaw all stages of the development of the Academy, along with educating and recruiting younger collaborators to become ready for the reconstruction of the cathedral.

An idea of correcting the cathedral's silhouette was Strossmayer's preoccupation since the completion of the bishop's seat in Đakovo and, according to his romantically written commentary from 1874, in that way changing Zagreb's cityscape to make its image breathtaking to visitors arriving from the west and north:

> When somebody approaches Zagreb, the messiness of Zagreb Cathedral hurts his view even from the far distance… It is a pity for Zagreb, whose natural disposition asks for high bell towers, to still have reminiscence of Baroque construction hiding the original Gothic building.[38]

Although originally Strossmayer's, the idea of re-Gothicizing the cathedral was pushed forward by Izidor Kršnjavi, an influential Croatian art historian, who at first appealed to receive the government's funding for the reconstruction based on Schmidt's expertise. Yet, while Schmidt suggested a one-tower scheme, based on the accurate historical remains, neither Strossmayer nor Kršnjavi were pleased. Under their influence, Bollé proposed a plan with two lace-looking spires,[39] a scheme widespread through Central Europe after the discovery of the original, late-medieval plans for Cologne Cathedral, the reconstruction of which grew into an stirring architectural event, supporting rising national ideologies across the region.[40] With two tall, elaborately crafted spires, Zagreb Cathedral was finally completed in 1898, and ever since then it has acted as the foremost symbol of the Croatian national capital, just as Strossmayer had anticipated. After reaching independence in 1992, the state government together with the Zagreb municipality recognized a new reconstruction of the cathedral as a national priority, a project that has been in progress up to the present day.

When the early twentieth-century generation of architects started challenging the age of Historicism, Herman Bollé and Izidor Kršnjavi became the subject of sharp criticism. The leading proponents of modern architectural ideas pejoratively defined the late nineteenth-century attempts at formulating a national program under the shield of Austria-Hungary as "Bolléistics stylization."[41] Describing Bollé's architecture as catastrophic, many in the architectural profession emphasized the fact that Bollé was a foreigner and never able to speak the Croatian language fluently. Touchingly, Bollé insisted on labeling himself a Croatian nationalist and only after decades of being neglected have Bollé's Historicist aesthetics, his leadership in all stages of reconstruction of the cathedral and his organizational contribution to establishing the Arts and Crafts School have been re-evaluated attuned to the dissolution of communist Yugoslavia and the rise of Postmodernism in the 1980s. Instead of being understood as a forcefully imported builder in the service of the old Austrian regime, he has become considered "our

Croatian" Bollé, whose architectural genius was unjustly neglected by his native followers.

The name of Viktor Kovačić,[42] on the other hand, has been uninterruptedly celebrated as a synonym of a modern as well as an intrinsically national architecture since his appearance on the Croatian scene in 1899. Kovačić was born to a peasant Croatian family, but was raised in Graz by his uncle, who supported him to complete his education at the Building and Crafts High School. After his graduation he moved to Zagreb and being recognized as a unique talent was soon employed at Herman Bollé's atelier as a construction manager. After a while, Kovačić developed a hostile relationship with Bollé, arguing against his strong presence on the Zagreb intellectual scene, which allegedly inspired him to go back to Austria and enroll at Wagner's Academy of Fine Arts in Vienna. If turn of the century Vienna was recognized for a struggle between the generation of Ringstrasse-style fathers and their Secessionist sons, to use Carl Schorske's explanation, Zagreb of the same period was remembered for Kovačić's attempts to find his place as the founder of a new national architecture by contrasting his work to Bollé's nineteenth-century Historicism. Like his contemporary fellows from the underestimated European national groups, Kovačić attacked Historicism not only for its false stylistic approach, but also for being imported by "foreign builders, who had no intrinsic feeling for the national authenticity."[43] Upon his return to Zagreb, after leaving the Viennese Academy, his tone demonstrated even more pronounced hostility toward the older generation, along with a high level of self-esteem, which might be understood as a common behavior among the Wagnerschule disciples.

The still-unemployed Kovačić, while looking for a job to help him settle in Zagreb, claimed:

> I came back to establish new foundations to Croatian architecture. I am a ray of sun illuminating the path towards new tendencies. [...] Those tall spires of Zagreb Cathedral [built by Bollé] are monsters which should be demolished by cannons.[44]

Biographers have emphasized Kovačić's friendship with Adolf Loos,[45] from whom he imported not only a specific approach of architectural creativity, but also an eccentric behavior.[46] A prominent art historian and the first curator of the Modern Gallery in Zagreb, Ljubo Babić, observed:

> Those who liked him were rare. It was hard to get along with him. He was oversensitive, stubborn and arrogant, becoming sleazy while facing the authorities and turning into a rude character before those who were weaker than him.[47]

Like Loos, Kovačić searched for ingeniously modern expressions, holding a full awareness about architectural knowledge accumulated through

56 The birth of national architectures

historical continuum: "Laws of evolution lead us to appreciate our fathers' heritage. Modernity itself has not started from tabula rasa."[48] As part of the Wagnerschule, he was a strong opponent of "false Historicism," although he never advocated a radical break with the past. In none of his projects did Kovačić experiment with radical avant-garde ideas; on the contrary, he stayed attuned to universal architectural concepts and historical precedents, re-evaluated regarding contemporary needs. His attitudes about the new architectural age were formulated and popularized through an essay "Modern Architecture," titled the same as Otto Wagner's influential book, in which he argued:

> New technologies, new materials and a new way of life tell us that the forms of building must change. By doing this we should not dispose the old styles instantaneously. Moreover, some of the stylistic elements should find their place in the composition if they were applied organically.[49]

Some sources understood Kovačić's proclamation as a summary of Otto Wagner's book developed from his inauguration speech for the membership at the Viennese Academy;[50] however, the tone of Kovačić's words rather resembled Adolf Loos's statement written in response to the Secessionist attack against history: "for me the tradition is everything, a free unfolding of the imagination is secondary."[51] Kovačić' also adopted and reinterpreted Loos's criticism on the Secession, which neglected the Biedermeier ideas of "plainness and reserve."[52] On the occasion of Kovačić's early death, a devoted follower, architect Edo Schön interpreted his anti-Secessionist attitudes:

> The Secessionist credo – the liberation from "dressing" for the sake of exposing the naked construction, is as bad as the "polytechnic" stylization. We must free ourselves from both prejudices: the unconditional denial of tradition, as well as the Secessionist nakedness. Kovačić succeeded in liberating himself and founding his own personality.[53]

Kovačić's large-scale designs – the unrealized, winning competition entry for Palace Russia in Belgrade from 1905 and the Stock Exchange in Zagreb from 1919 – were strikingly reminiscent of the highly appreciated Looshaus on Michaelerplatz in Vienna. The early project for Belgrade, today better known as Hotel Moscow, was submitted in the international competition, with Otto Wagner serving as the chair, but never advanced toward realization. The drawings found in Kovačić's endowment[54] show an intriguing similarity with the famous Looshaus, designed four years later. Along with the similar trapezoid layouts, accentuated by the centrally positioned vestibules, the articulations of ground floors in form of a monumental entrance zone with overwhelming Classical colonnades look intriguingly analogous in both projects. The same could be said about Kovačić's Stock Exchange in Zagreb, designed in 1919 upon the scheme of the Russia Palace, the realization of which would remain recognized as the peak achievement of Croatian national, as well as modern architecture.[55]

Yet, Kovačić's first realized large-scale public commission in Zagreb was the Church of St. Blaise (Figure 2.4), dedicated to the patron of the city. The idea of building a seat for the new Zagreb diocese dated back to the 1880s, and the building campaign intensified when Izidor Kršnjavi became a member of the building committee in 1892. Kršnjavi had a strong personal vision for Zagreb's development in general, within which the urbanization of the city's west side, including a new religious landmark, was of special interest. It was Josip Vancaš, a Croatian architect with strong professional connections and public influence, who together with Kršnjavi had envisioned a domical cruciform composition for St. Blaise's. The monumental, centrally planned church with a dome was imagined as the crown of an elaborate urban ensemble, the School Forum, flanked by educational and cultural institutions of national importance. However, since this ambitious plan never received enough funds, it was in 1908 when the building committee announced an open competition for the church within a less ambitious urban layout. Kovačić won the first prize, proposing a new concept for a centrally planned structure with a dome, as had been suggested by Kršnjavi. After the decision had been reached, the architect was granted a study trip

Figure 2.4 Kovačić's St. Blaise (Nationalism and Architecture, p. 101)

58 The birth of national architectures

to Ravenna to become better prepared for developing of the domical structure.[56] Despite his previous criticism against "the generation of fathers" of which Kršnjavi and Bollé were the leading figures, Kovačić enthusiastically accepted their offer. Upon his return to Zagreb, he transformed the original proposal, developed the plans and supervised the construction, which took place between 1912 and 1915.

The St. Blaise's domical, cross-in-square concept with a bell tower was delicately incorporated into the existing urban setting. Both because of its layout, as well as the external features – a sturdy silhouette, the rusticated ground floor versus smooth texture and subtle details in the upper zones – the project offered a new interpretation of early medieval churches spread along the Adriatic coast and its vicinity, which coincided with the territory of the first Croatian medieval state. A similar amalgam of early Romanesque features, infused into the cross-in-square domical concepts, existed throughout the entire region of today's Western Balkans, which had fluctuated between the Carolingian and Byzantine spheres of dominance during the Middle Ages. Therefore, St. Blaise's presented a radical departure from its neo-Gothic precedents, the earlier heralds of a national revival during the 1880s, understood by Kovačić's generation as synonymous with the long-lasting German dominance, since Schmidt and Bollé, who had introduced this foreign style, were both Germans. "The Gothic in Croatia could only represent German tribal origins [...], while the St. Blaise is a combination of our old churches, which we find in good condition in Bosnia and Serbia,"[57] claimed Croatian writer Vladimir Lunaček in an article published right after the completion, while the historian and museologist, Gjuro Szabo, paid more respect to St. Blaise's close ties to the early Byzantine heritage in Ravenna.[58] In more recent interpretations of St. Blaise's, the scholars have pointed out the neglected sources from which Kovačić drew his inspiration: the old Croatian churches of Dalmatia, which were, according to them, far away from the Byzantine sphere of influence:

> Forms of St. Blaise comprise political aspirations for the inclusion of Dalmatia into Croatian territory with the center in Zagreb [...]. Yet, Kovačić's patriotism was of "good taste", his leading idea was to create forms to symbolize the elevation of the concept of nation.[59]

When the enthusiasm for the unity of all South Slavs was at its peak in the first decades of the twentieth century, and even during Royal Yugoslavia, St. Blaise's references were understood within a broader framework of the medieval heritage of the Balkans, while with the rise of the Croatian fight for national independence from 1970 to 1990, the interpretations acknowledged the references to a particularly Croatian heritage. While more recent Croatian scholarship has made an effort to extricate a national character of St. Blaise, a Viennese architect of Slovene-Italian origins born in Belgrade, Boris Podrecca, has overlooked any explicitly ethnic message of

Kovačić's work. It seems that Podrecca's tracing of Kovačić's architecture in "an ingenious spirit, at once individual and collective, manifested though an ambiguity between the modern and the inherited"[60] exceeds the limits of a singular, narrowly defined geography.

Kovačić's role as the father of Croatian architecture addressed the national and the modern attributes inseparably. In 1908, eight years after publishing "Modern Architecture," Kovačić took part in the most debated national competition for the historical urban area of Kapitol, the fortified medieval bishop's seat, with the reconstructed cathedral being its focal point. Kovačić's proposal was anti-Bolléian, an argument based on the different views of the medieval gate flanked by Bakač Tower and its incorporation into a public square in front of the cathedral. According to Kovačić, the square was supposed to hold a mausoleum to Zrinski-Frankopan families, remembered for their martyrdom in the name of Croatian people. Nikola Šubić Zrinski, the national hero remembered for his heroic fight for Christianity at the time of the Ottoman penetration into Europe in the Battle of Szigeth of 1566, had been acknowledged in the layout of Zrinski Square within the Horseshoe. Yet, in the early 1900s, the myth about heroic deaths of Petar Zrinski and Fran Krsto Frankopan, two rebels against the Habsburgs killed in Wiener Neustadt in 1671, was actualized because of growing anti-Habsburg sentiments. In 1907, the Brothers of Croatian Dragon excommunicated the Zrinski-Frankopan remains and temporarily reburied them with more dignity, while waiting for a right spot to be found for their mausoleum in Zagreb. This event coincided with the separation of national parliament from the Catholic Church authorities, and the construction of the Croatian Assembly in the Upper Town. Inspired by those events and the new political climate, Kovačić proposed for the Kapitol to become the central national memorial, an architectural symbol of the integration of Croats into a modern nationhood.[61] Like the Kosovo Battle had been in Serbian national memory, the broader myth of Zrinski's sacrifice, dating back into the lost Battle of Szigeth, grew into the essence of national integrative ideology.[62] Within this context, Kovačić's idea of the mausoleum at Kapitol was to become "a distinctive historical sight for Croatian people, an urban carrier of vital national narrative, right at the defensive rampart in battles against the Turks."[63] The mausoleum might be inspired by Ivan Meštrović's Kosovo Battle shrine[64] assuming that Kovačić attempted to integrate other South Slavs into the Croatian historical myth.[65]

Kovačić succeeded in replacing Bollé as the father of Croatian national architecture primarily as the inaugurator of a modern architectural discourse. The reason for emphasizing Kovačić's pivotal status lay in his role as an educator of the first generation of domestic architects, who followed the Modernist doctrines. His pupils: Alfred Albini, Juraj Denzler, Stanko Kliska, Egon Steinmann and Ernest Weissman, who had studied under Kovačić's supervision during his short appointment at the Technical Faculty in 1919–1924, became leading protagonists of the Modern Movement, parallel

60 The birth of national architectures

to their colleagues in Austria, Germany and Czechoslovakia. Despite the explicit statement that modern architecture "does not start from tabula rasa," Kovačić built up his professional image as the unprecedented hero who had started conceptualizing Croatian architecture from ground zero. Until the present day, most surveys on Croatian architecture consider his work as the starting point.[66] Coming from diverse ethnic and national backgrounds, Kovačić's direct followers leaned toward supranational attributes such as the concept of the International Style. Certainly, Kovačić's role as the father of national architecture along his fundamentally international mindset, influenced the next, radically Modernist, generation of his Croatian disciples.

Notes

1 There were about sixty members of the Illyrian Movement in Zagreb at the time, which was a large percentage, considering the total number of 8,000 citizens. See Celia Hawkeworth, *Zagreb: A Cultural and Literary History*, Oxford: Signal Books, 2007, 49.
2 Lelja Dobronić, *Bartol Felbinger i zagrebački graditelji njegova doba* [*Bertol Felbinger and Zagreb Builders of his Time*], Zagreb: Zadužna štampa, 1971.
3 The role of Ban Jelačić in the Revolution of 1848 has been understood in various ways. While contemporary Croatian historiography reaffirms him as the leader of Croatian national revolution against Hungarian domination, other sources see him as a loyal warrior on the side of Austrian throne against the Hungarian revolutionaries. See Jonathan Sperber, *The European Revolutions 1848–1851*, Cambridge: Cambridge University Press, 1994: 224.
4 For the review of urban development in the nineteenth century, see Marko Vidaković, "Prolegomena principima urbanizma" [Prolegomena to the Urbanistic Principles], *Arhitektura*, vol. 3–4 (1933–1934): 144–166; Andre Mohorovičić, "Analiza historijsko-urbanističkog razvoja grada Zagreba" [The Analysis of Historical and Urban Development of the City of Zagreb], *Rad JAZU*, vol. 287 (1952); Darja Radović-Mahečić, *Urbanizam i arhitektura 19. stoljeća u kontinentalnoj Hrvatskoj* [*Nineteenth-century Town Planning and Architecture in Continental Croatia*], Zagreb: Školska knjiga, 2007.
5 *Bauordung für die Landeshauptstadt Agram* (4 January 1857), no. 439.
6 Darko Kahle, "Građevinski propisi grada Zagreb u razdoblju 1850–1919" [Building Codes for the City of Zagreb between 1850 and 1918], *Prostor*, vol. 12, (2004): 203–215.
7 Ivan Kampuš, *Tisućljetni Zagreb: od davnih naselja do suvremenog velegrada* [*One Thousand Years of Zagreb: From Old Settlements to Contemporary City*], Zagreb: Školska knjiga, 1994: 199.
8 Snješka Knežević, "Lenuci i 'Lenucijeva potkova'" [Lenuci and Lenuci's Horseshoe], *Radovi Instituta za povjest umjetnosti*, vol. 18 (1994): 169–185.
9 Discussed in Olga Maruševski, "Arhitektonsko-urbanističke veze Zagreba i Beča na prijelomu stoljeća" [Architectural and Urbanistic Links between Zagreb and Vienna at the Turn of the Century], in *Fin de siècle Zagreb-Vienna*, Zagreb: Školska knjiga, 1997: 197–229.

10 Discussed in Snješka Knežević, "Mjesto Zrinskog trga u genezi zagrebačke 'Zelene potkove'" [The Role of Zrinski Square in the Genesis of the Green Horseshoe], *Radovi IPU*, vol. 11 (1987): 61–93.
11 Rudolph Siebeck studied garden design in Altenburg and Munich. He became head of Viennese Gardens Office in 1857.
12 Stella Fatović-Ferenčić and Jasenka Ferber-Bogdan, "Tracing the Painting of Nikola Šubić Zrinski: Chronology of Royal Pharmacy at Zrinski," *Medicus*, vol. 12, no. 1 (2003): 143.
13 Schmidt inherited the project, which had started in 1866. See Dragan Damjanović, *Đakovačka katedrala* [*Đakovo Cathedral*], Zagreb: Matica hrvatska, 2009: 185–215.
14 The Nazi regime during WWII was the first to disregard its Yugoslav mission and consequently any possibility for the existence of a Yugoslav identity.
15 The plans were altered from the administrative function to the hospital.
16 The first theater in Zagreb was built in the 1840s by a merchant passionate about theatrical performances. After winning the premium lottery, he spent the money on the construction of the first stage in his hometown. Until 1861, most pieces on this stage were performed in the German language.
17 Miroslav Krleža, "Slučaj arhitekte Iblera" [The Case of the Architect Ibler], *Književna republika*, vol. 2, no. 4 (1924).
18 The first movement to announce aspirations toward national independence in Socialist Yugoslavia was the Croatian Spring or Mass Movement (MASPOK), which started in the 1960s and was suppressed in 1971.
19 The crowning event in obtaining a new layer of national affiliation with the building was Pope Benedict XVI's arrival to Zagreb in 2011, when he visited the theater. The ceremonial importance of the pope's visit can be compared only to Emperor Franz Joseph's appearance at its opening in 1895.
20 Stylistic analogies have been found between Paul Wallot's Reichstag in Berlin and Friedrich von Tiersch's Justizpalais [Justice Palace] in Munich. See Dragan Damjanović, "Croatian Pavilions at the 1896 Millennium Exhibition in Budapest," in Miklós Székely (ed.), *Ephemeral Architecture* in *Central and Eastern Europe in the 19th and 21st Centuries*, Paris: L'Harmattan, 2015: 62.
21 Acquainted with Fellner & Helmer during their engagement on the National Theater, Héderváry chose them again for the design of Art Pavilion in Zagreb.
22 Olga Maruševski, *Gradnja Umjetničkoga paviljona: okrunjeni trg* [*The Building of the Art Pavilion: The Crowned Square*], exhibition catalog, Zagreb: Umjetnički paviljon, 1998.
23 Milan Lenuci was the head of the City Development Department until 1912. Therefore, he signed the majority of acts, agreements and plans that resulted from political negotiations between the city authorities and the national government, with Ban Khuen-Héderváry at its head.
24 Nenad Fabijanić, "Između secesije, neoklasicizma i moderne: prilog interpretaciji zgrade Sveučilišne knjižnice Rudolfa Lubynskoga u Zagrebu" [Combining Secession, Neo-Classicism and Modernism: Rudolph Lubynski's University Library in Zagreb], *Prostor*, vol. 18 (2010): 2–25.
25 Rudolph Lubynski (1873–1935) studied at the polytechnic in Karlsruhe 1896–1899, and later worked at the firm of his professor Josef Durm during the construction of Heidelberg Library. See Mladenka Dabac, "Rudolf Lubynski

i njegovo doba" [Rudolf Lubynski and His Time], *Arhitektura*, no. 189–195 (1984/1985): 160–166.
26 Together with the leadership of the University Library, Lubynski had spent a few months on a study trip, exploring recently finished buildings with the same programmatic parameters all around Europe, before the final design for the Zagreb counterpart was developed.
27 Kosta Strajnić, "Viktor Kovačić – povodom otvorenja zagrebačke Burze" [Viktor Kovačić – for Occasion of the Stock Exchange Opening], *Pregled*, no. 31 (1927): 8–9.
28 Steinmann had completed an architectural internship in Paris; therefore, he stepped away from the secessionist mode in favor of the "purified" neo-Classicism of by August Perret.
29 Steinmann's project was submitted in 1927, yet the Institute opened only in 1936 due to unstable financing slowing the construction.
30 Arijana Štulhofer and Iva Muraj, "Sportski i sveučilišni sadržaji na Mažuranićevu i Marulićevu trgu u Zagrebu" [Sports and University Facilities on Mažuranić and Marulić Squares in Zagreb], *Prostor*, vol. 14, no.1/31 (2006): 43–53.
31 Snješka Knežević, *Željeznička pruga, kolodvor i strojarska radionica kao problem prostornog razvoja Zagreba od polovice 19. stoljeća do 1918* [The Railway Tracks and the Station as a Problem of Zagreb Spatial Development from the Second Half of the 19th Century until 1918], Zagreb: Gradski zavod za planiranje razvoja i zaštitu čovjekova okoliša Zagreba, 1992.
32 The competition entries are in the City Museum of Zagreb: MGZ (A 586-111/112).
33 Dionis Sunko (1879–1935) graduated from Karlsruhe Polytechnic and later enjoyed the support of an older colleague, Josip Vancaš, who published a monograph about Sunko. See Josip von Vancaš, *Dionis Sunko*, Geneva: Meisters der Baukunst, 1930.
34 Architectural historian Aleksander Laslo noticed that the myth of the Esplanade as the backdrop for "Orient Express" mysteries fades away after checking the train schedule of the time. The passengers were arriving at the Zagreb railway station in the middle of the night and stayed there for less than an hour. See Aleksander Laslo, "Scenografija za Poirota: okvir slike vremena" [Scenography for Poirot: The Framework for an Image of the Time], in *Art Deco: Art in Croatia between the Two World Wars*, exhibition catalog, Zagreb: Muzej za umjetnost i obrt, 2011: 93–118.
35 The owners Leo Hönigsberg and Julio Deutsch were both educated at Viennese polytechnics under the supervision of Hainrich Ferstela and Karla König, consequently they were stylistically close to the neo-Renaissance manner of their teachers in Vienna in the late 1800s.
36 Among those, Josip Vancaš (Josip von Vancaš, 1859–1932) was well known across the Croatian boundaries. He was born in Hungary but finished high school in Zagreb. After graduating from the Academy of Fine Arts under Friedrich von Schimdt, he worked at Fellner & Helmer studio. His works could be found in most of the key cities of Austria-Hungary predominantly inhabited by South Slavs; as well as Croatia, he built extensively in Sarajevo and Ljubljana.
37 Hermman Bollé (1845–1926) was born and raised in Cologne, but soon after graduation from the Viennese academy he moved to Croatia and remained

there until the rest of his life. See Dragan Damjanović, *Arhitekt Herman Bollé*, Zagreb: Leykam Int, 2013.
38 Josip Juraj Strossmayer, "Nekoliko rieči o stolnoj crkvi zagrebačkoj" [A Few Words about the Cathedral Church of Zagreb], *Katolički list* (October 3, 1874): 1.
39 Hermann Bollé, *Program o obnovi prvostolne crkve zagrebačke*, Zagreb, 1884, reprinted in Lelja Dobronić, *Zagrebački kaptol i Gornji grad nekad i danas*, Vol. 3, Zagreb: Školska knjiga, 1988: 93–96.
40 The idea of reconstruction was tied to the German rivalry with France, in which the position of Cologne Cathedral held special importance. The fact that the king of Prussia participated in the inauguration of Cologne Cathedral, while the highly ranked representatives of the Catholic Church ignored the event due to a political disagreement with the secular leadership shows the importance of the project for German national pride.
41 Edo Schön, *Arhitekt Viktor Kovačić: mapa-monografija*, Zagreb: Grafičko nakladni zavod, 1927: 9; and Miroslav Krleža, "Slučaj arhitekte Iblera," *Književna republika*, vol. 2, no. 4 (1927): 172.
42 Viktor Kovačić (1874–1924) studied at the Academy of Fine Arts under Otto Wagner. Similar to Slovenian Jože Plečnik and Czech Jan Kotěra, Kovačić has been considered the father of Croatian architecture.
43 Schön, *Arhitekt Viktor Kovačić*: 9.
44 Kovačić allegedly said this during his visit to a government-employed architect. Recorded in daily newspaper *Narodne novine*, no. 66 (1900): 260.
45 Recent research proves that the friendship between him and Loos was deeper than previously believed. Sketches with the reconstruction of Agapa Therme in Rome, signed both by Kovačić and Loos have been found in an unclassified folder in the City Museum of Zagreb.
46 Noticed by Ljubo Babić, "Arhitekt Viktor Kovačić," *Obzor*, vol. 69, no. 37 (Zagreb 1928): 2–3; and later by Olga Maruševski, "Kovačić u kontekstu svoga vremena" [Kovačić in the Context of His Time], in Miroslav Begović (ed.), *Arhitekt Viktor Kovačić, život i djelo* [*Architect Viktor Kovačić: Life and Work*], Zagreb, HAZU: 2003.
47 Babić, "Arhitekt Viktor Kovačić": 3.
48 Viktor Kovačić, "Modern Architecture," *Život*, no. 1 (1901): 46.
49 Ibid., 46.
50 Aleksander Laslo, "Život i djelo Viktora Kovačića" [Life and Work of Viktora Kovačić], in Begović (ed.), *Arhitekt Viktor Kovačić, život i djelo*: 100.
51 The quote is translated from Adolf Loos, "Ein Wiener Architekt," *Dekorative Kunst*, no. 1 (1898): 227, in Christopher Long, *The Looshaus*, New Haven: Yale University Press, 2011: 26.
52 Long, *The Looshaus*: 27.
53 Edo Shön, *Arhitekt Viktor Kovačić: mapa-monografija* [*Architect Viktor Kovačić: Portfolio-Monograph*], Zagreb, 1927: 7.
54 These are kept in the archive of the Croatian Institute for Cultural Heritage: RZZ – 91 ID 563.
55 The Stock Exchange will be discussed in the next chapter.
56 Kovačić sent reports from his trip to Ravenna to Izidor Kršnjavi.
57 Vladimir Lunaček, "Izložba hrvatskog društva umjetnosti" [The Exhibition of the Croatian Art Society], *Savremenik* (1913): 7.

64 The birth of national architectures

58 Gjuro Szabo, "U spomen Viktora Kovačića," *Savremenik*, no. 2 (1928).
59 Maruševski, "Kovačić u kontekstu svoga vremena": 37–39.
60 Boris Podrecca, "Viktor Kovačić i njegovi suvremenici u europskoj arhitekturi," in Begović (ed.), *Arhitekt Viktor Kovačić, život i djelo*: 22.
61 Discussed in Krešimir Galović, *Viktor Kovačić – otac hrvatske modern arhitekture* [*Viktor Kovačić – the Father of Croatian Modern Architecture*], Zagreb: Jutanji list, 2015: 39–43 and 165–170.
62 Mirjana Gross, "Nacionalno-integracijske ideologije u Hrvata od kraja Ilirizma do stvaranja Jugoslavije" [National Integration Ideologies among the Croats from the End of Illyrian Movement until the Constitution of Yugoslavia], in *Društveni razvoj u Hrvatskoj od 16.–20. veka*, Zagreb: Liber, 1981.
63 Maruševski, "Kovačić u kontekstu svoga vremena": 36–37.
64 Discussed in the next chapter.
65 Galović, *Viktor Kovačić – otac hrvatske modern arhitekture*: 166.
66 Žarko Domljan "Arhitektura XX stoljeća u Hrvatskoj" [Architecture of the Twentieth Century in Croatia], in *Art in Yugoslavia – Architecture of the 20th Century*, Zagreb: Spektar, 1986: 35; Tomislav Premerl, *Hrvatska moderna arhitektura između dva rata*, Zagreb: Nakladni zavod Matice hrvatske, 1990.

3 Architectural affirmation of the Yugoslav idea

The search for a Yugoslav art

When the Croatian Party of the Rights, led by Ante Starčević, promoting a program for South Slavic unification under the Croatian name, reached a dead-end, a faction named the Progressive Youth, comprised mainly of young intellectuals of different ethnic origins based in Zagreb, accepted Belgrade as the unifying center.[1] They did so believing that Serbian political power would have served as the main cohesive factor for the existence of an independent Slavic state able to oppose the Habsburgs' aspirations to dominate the Balkans. According to their beliefs, the liberation of South Slavs from the Habsburgs relied on their unification with the already independent Kingdom of Serbia. Most of the Youth members studied in Prague, when Tomaš Masaryk's campaign for the pan-Slavic brotherhood was at its peak. Inspired by political actions toward the constitution of Czechoslovakia, they established a political platform for creating the southern counterpart. From the start of the Youth's political engagement, however, there was no clear consensus if the future state of South Slavs should be a fusion of different ethnic groups into a single nation or a looser federation, encouraging the growth of multiple national identities.

The Youth members keenly advocated for Belgrade to be a center of the Yugoslav political program and promoted Serbian history, myths and folk epics as the keystone of the common Yugoslav heritage. The Serbian capital welcomed intellectuals from Croatia, Dalmatia, Bosnia and Herzegovina who inclined towards the unification, especially after the dynastic shift of 1903, when the overall political course of the Karađorđevićs turned anti-Austrian. The enthusiasm about "integral Yugoslavism" reached its peak after Austria-Hungary annexed Bosnia and Herzegovina in 1908 and lasted for at least a decade, until Royal Yugoslavia was internationally recognized with Belgrade declared as the capital city.

Official Belgrade supported the growing enthusiasm by organizing the First Exhibition of Yugoslav Art to bring together works by Serbian, Croatian and Slovenian artists under the same roof. Organized by the student association Pobratimsvo [Brotherhood], with the advisory committee consisting of professors from Belgrade University, the show put together at the Belgrade University, Kapetan Miša's Endowment, presented 500 art pieces inconsistent both in quality as well as in themes. The grand opening, attended by the future king of Yugoslavia Petar I Karađorđević, took place three days prior to his coronation as part of the centennial celebration of the First Serbian Uprising of 1804. Accordingly, the Serbian section – the largest due to the practical matters of transportation and lowest expenses – included titles such as the "Coronation of Tsar Dušan" and "Wedding of Tsar Dušan," alluding to Serbian ambitions at re-achieving territorial success of the most prosperous medieval ruler, while the others such as "Great Serbia" and the "Dawn of Serbia" carried either allegorical patriotic messages or celebrated the Karađorđevićs, whose founding father Karađorđe led the uprising. On the other hand, the Croatian selection, presented by fifteen painters cultivated under the leadership of Izidor Kršnjavi, was politically disengaged. Majority of works on display came from the Strossmayer's Gallery, yet not a single art piece depicted the Illyrian Movement, even though the most celebrated name from the Strossmayer's collection, Vlaho Bukovac, had completed a few large-scale patriotic compositions celebrating the Illyrian ideology. Even a rare politically colored painting by a Croatian artist was Marko Murat's "The Arrival of Tsar Dušan to Dubrovnik," bluntly suggesting the Serbian rights over the city was not presented in the Croatian but in the Serbian section. The hesitation in Croatian committee was related to the ambiguous position of the Croatian government which tried to maintain unspoiled political relations with the Austro-Hungarian authorities but also please the rising sympathies toward the Yugoslav idea by covering the transportation costs of the art pieces. Another reason for political neutrality could be caused by uneasiness about mixing the Illyrian ideals with the Karađorđević coronation.

The following Exhibitions of Yugoslav Art – held in Zagreb in 1908 and again in Belgrade in 1912, instead of Ljubljana – became less programmatically consistent. Already during the first event, the artists started clustering into groups around various political programs, offering different answers to the question of Yugoslav integration. The Lada Society, organized as the largest network of well-established middle-generation artists with headquarters all over the region soon gained full control over the organization of Yugoslav art gatherings, which irritated younger, more energetic activists opposing to the Lada's weak position regarding Yugoslav integration. This animosity gave birth to two new art organizations, one from Belgrade called the Yugoslav Art Colony and another from Dalmatia, the society of young artists named Medulić. The leading protagonists of the Medulić, Tomislav Krizman and Emanuel Vidović, had taken part in the Croatian section at the First Exhibition of Yugoslav Art, after which they decided to start a more aggressive political campaign toward the synthesis of Yugoslav art. They were joined in Belgrade by a young Ivan Meštrović,[2] at that time still a student of the Fine Arts Academy in Vienna, who would soon become the key figure of the Medulić's program and activities. Meštrović would grow into the leading protagonist of the politically colored art projects, supporting and promoting the Yugoslav ideology eagerly, fighting for the national beliefs both through sculptural themes and public speeches especially before an international audience. For two decades, since the time of his debut show at the Viennese Secession in Meštrović 1910 until the participation in the Exhibition of Yugoslav Artists at the Petit Palais in Paris in 1919, Meštrović's voice was a leading weapon in fighting for the Yugoslav nationhood and statehood.

Ivan Meštrović: from the Vidovdan Temple to the Tomb of the Unknown Soldier

The 1904 art show in Belgrade was Meštrović's first presentation to the Serbian audience,[3] an opportunity he used to approach influential Serbian politician and future prime minister Nikola Pašić, suggesting to him the construction of a Yugoslav national shrine, "the structure to be built systematically, year after year across several generations, in a manner of collective undertaking,"[4] to commemorate the Battle at Kosovo Plain of 1389. It was Serbs who lost the territory of Kosovo, the heart of their medieval kingdom and consequently the keystone of national history; however, the Kosovo myth grew into a cohesive narrative applicable to all people of the Balkans, challenging the long-lasting foreign dominations. The passion for Serbian revenge grew within all the peoples from the region after the Austrian annexation of Bosnia and Herzegovina, inspiring a broader optimism about the end of both imperial supremacies. The Serbian dream of recapturing Kosovo from the Ottomans was finally fulfilled in the Balkan Wars of 1912–1913, when Meštrović resided in Belgrade, working on his gigantic sculpture The Victor – an homage to Serbian success. Meštrović's plans for the Yugoslav shrine were completed at the same time. Parallel to working on The Victor he executed the wooden model for the Vidovdan [St. Vitus Day][5] Temple (Figure 3.1), to be built one day on the real site of the Kosovo Battle[6] as a "container" of the elaborate sculptural program, known as the Vidovdan Fragments, depicting Serbian national heroes and myths. The temple was intended to commemorate the fallen at Kosovo Plain, who were remembered in oral national poetry through generations of gusle players. Meštrović himself grew up in a remote Dalmatian village, near the town then called Little Kosovo,[7] listening to the vibrantly interpreted stories about the heroes of the Kosovo Battle, the loss of national freedom and the long-lasting suffering under the Turks.

Meštrović started carving the Fragments during his stay in Paris in 1908 and 1909 and put his work on display for the first time at the Thirty-Fifth Secession Exhibition in 1910, which resulted in the sculptor's much

Figure 3.1 St. Vitus Day Temple – cover page of Strajnić's monograph on Mestrovic from 1919

desired international recognition and significant acquaintances. The powerful pieces, depicting Serbian mythological heroes and historical figures such as the knight Miloš Obilić, who killed Sultan Murad, and his fellow warrior Srđa Zlopogleđa, both remembered through national oral poetry, occupied the central spots at the Secession Pavilion. The sense of being primitive and modern at the same time, associated with the South Slavic identity, inspired the re-evaluation of the West. It was expected that the same binary condition would have removed the stigma of being inferior, ignorant and savage from South Slavs; moreover, that it would have turned them into the rescuers of Europe. The role of discovering and presenting the underestimated heritage of the Balkans to the European academia was fostered by art historian Josef Strzygowski, who not only shaped public opinion about the roots of an authentic Slavic art and architecture throughout Europe, but also applied his findings to the promotion of Meštrović's work.[8]

The same year, a more elaborate version of the Fragments was displayed at the Medulić exhibition in Zagreb – with the provocative title "To the Timid Times, Despite" – organized as a reaction against the weak political message spread by the Third Exhibition of Yugoslav Art of 1908. This time, a more powerful prophetic message about the national mission of Yugoslavism was finally sent from Zagreb through Meštrović's "incomplete sculptures – an image of the national temple in ruins, bespeaking the condition of a nation that has been unaltered since the Battle of Kosovo."[9] On

Affirmation of the Yugoslav idea 69

this occasion Meštrović's Viennese fellow, Slovenian architect Jože Plečnik[10] delivered a perspective drawing of the Vidovdan Temple, after which Meštrović executed the wooden model two years later.[11]

The positive reception at the Secession inspired the Austro-Hungarian authorities to invite Meštrović to take part the in dual monarchy's presentation at the International Exposition in Rome of 1911. Yet, the invitation required the artist to avoid politically involved pieces, namely those referring to the Kosovo Battle, which Meštrović refused to do.[12] Instead of placing the sculptures in either the Austrian or Hungarian pavilion, Meštrović decided to exhibit under the name of the Kingdom of Serbia and emphasize its importance for the future national status of South Slavs.[13] This profound political statement was reinforced by the fact that the International Exposition in Rome celebrated the fiftieth anniversary of Italian unification. After Meštrović acknowledged his unconditional participation under the Serbian flag, the Fragments became the central theme around which the Serbian Pavilion was conceptualized,[14] primarily to serve as the backdrop for Meštrović's sculptural narrative. Honored by the invitation to participate in the Exposition among only a few other European states – Great Britain, Austro-Hungary, Germany, France, Russia, Spain and Belgium, plus the USA and Japan outside Europe – the Serbian government paid remarkable attention to the country's presentation, synonymous with the promotion of Meštrović's work.[15] In his memoires, the sculptor intensely described the way the art work by him and other Croatian artists was illegally transported from Croatia to Belgrade to be sent all together to Rome.[16]

The Serbian government appointed architect Petar Bajalović[17] to develop the pavilion inspired by Meštrović's and Plečnik's vision. Accordingly, Bajalović employed universal historical references fluctuating between the Archaic and the Ancient Mediterranean art rather than focusing solely on the Serbian past. Set on the hilltop of the Guilia Gardens right across from the Hungarian Pavilion, the structure ended being an uncanny mixture of Mesopotamian, Egyptian and Archaic Greek architectural associations, which contemporary criticism found disgusting. Serbian writer and critic Marko Car from Dalmatia, close to the region where Meštrović was born, claimed:

> Meštrović's bizarre art obviously dazed Bajalović with its stinky breath. This creepy building, with its Assyrian dome and Egyptian pylons, attacks a viewer as a question mark to which nobody could respond with satisfaction,[18]

On the other hand, an art critic of Serbian origins from Herzegovina, Dimitrije Mitrinović, the official spokesman of the show, appointed to inform the Yugoslav public about the value of Meštrović's sculptures and

70 *The birth of national architectures*

advertising their political message to the international public, tried to establish a positive picture:[19]

> Concerning Meštrović's Archaic stylization, which irritates the ignoramuses and the Orthodox nationalists, the answer is very simple. His stylization is immanent to the national poetry, albeit not expressed explicitly; there is as much Mycenaean, Egyptian and Assyrian in Meštrović's style as it is in Serbian national poetry. I believe there is a basic similarity between the two, obvious even without a thorough analysis. Fatalism and ornamental elements of our folk songs and, even more, of our vernacularism are so like those of the "Eastern" peoples.[20]

The representations of a barbaric character of South Slavs' past and future were also generously applauded by the Viennese *fin de siècle* critics, who keenly observed the Archaic and Oriental art as a sublime expression of the relegated powers, suppressed by a two-millennium-long supremacy of Western traditions. So were the fragmentary forms understood as carriers of the intrinsic forces of national rebirth and reminders of the nation's broken history, announcing its potential for transformation into a leading force not only of the Balkans but of all Europe.[21]

The presentation of Meštrović's work under the Serbian flag provoked as much controversy in Belgrade intellectual circles as it did among the Croatian fellows. While Croats were bitter about Meštrović's neglect of the Croatian national name at the Rome exhibit, Serbian critics, on the other side, complained about the de-Serbianization of the pivotal historical event. Despite the negative or ambiguous attitudes coming from the domestic critics and some of the international commentators,[22] an intriguing political message was sent to the entire world by the Serbian government. Meštrović's Fragments were received with ovations, resulting in his earning the Grand Prix for sculpture despite a tough competition with recognized artists from the other participating countries.[23]

Meštrović's vision for the national shrine displeased many, beyond the most obvious discontents coming from the Serbian Orthodox or the Croatian Catholic separatists, since the criticism was not simply based on the Croat–Serb antagonisms. A stronger opposition was rooted in the aesthetic discourse, either the avant-garde Modernist or the Academic fellows, both arguing against Meštrović's neglect of universal values. The anti-Classical forms were the main target of criticism coming from the École des Beaux-Arts architect Milutin Borisavljević,[24] who attacked the Temple as a "lexicon of common phrases" and the "resurrection of Egyptian architecture" that had nothing in common either with the notion of national architecture or the architectural principles in general.[25] From the other side of the ideological spectrum, the explicitly avant-garde and ultra-leftist thinkers, such as Miroslav Krleža, linked Meštrović's proposal with "false and faithless Egyptian Osirism, coupled with the dogmas of the national style and pompous agitation!"[26] Meštrović himself was stretched between the strong attachment to Catholicism and the belief in a new cult of Yugoslavs – a "religion of ultimate devotion"[27] for which he had proposed the principal sanctuary. Yet, whenever the Serbian part initiated serious talks about the execution of the structure at the site of the Kosovo Battle, the request was that the temple should be affiliated with Orthodox Christianity in the first place, with an extra chapel for Catholic prayers.[28]

From the first Exposition in Rome until the beginning of World War I, the five-meter-long and two-meter-wide wooden model, together with sculptures (eighty-three pieces among which forty-three belonged to the Kosovo Cycle) executed in stone and bronze or plaster casts, was exhibited in London in 1913 and in Venice at the World Fair of 1914, right at the outbreak of the war. Recognized as a political enemy and deserter by the Austro-Hungarian authorities, Meštrović and his family were forced to flee from Croatia. During the exile, Meštrović took the leading role in the Yugoslav Committee, a political organization formed mainly of intellectuals from Croatia with the mission of achieving national unification.[29] After being formally established in Paris on April 30, 1915, the Committee moved its seat to London[30] due to the support of influential public figures, including historian Robert Seton-Watson, journalist Wickham Steed and archeologist Arthur Evans. Led by a belief that the art and the culture of a nation are the most powerful means of its political propaganda, Seton-Watson and Steed initiated a colossal exhibition of Meštrović's work at the Victoria and Albert Museum – in the Central Court and the West Hall, from June through August of 1915.[31] Not only was the Yugoslav sculptor the first to have a one-man show at the V&A, but his overly provocative Vidovdan Temple – whose model and sculptural fragments were transported from Split and Belgrade in spite of the escalating war – was its focal theme, placed right in the middle of the Central Court. "This gigantic project has become the epitome of centuries-long torment, agony and humiliation that finally turned into a fountain of national hope and honor,"[32] claimed the sculptor in numerous interviews. The extremely effective press campaign brought enormous publicity to Meštrović's work. As important was the sculptor's presence in England during the show, because his speeches and vibrant live interpretations of the exposed pieces spread a strong political message. The popularity of the show was such that it became the most visited event since the museum opened.[33] The strong advocates of South Slavs unification went so far in their writings[34] as to set the Vidovdan Temple against national monuments like the Arc de Triomphe and Valhalla.

Throughout the entire war, the exhibit traveled throughout Great Britain: it was put on display at the City Art Gallery in Leeds, from December 1915 to May 1916,[35] the Royal Glasgow Institute in 1916, the National Galleries of Scotland in Edinburg in 1917 and again in London at the Grafton Gallery at the end of the year. The last event, preceded by the troublesome negotiations about the status of the South Slavs union at Corfu, was slightly changed,

72 The birth of national architectures

both its contents and the title of the show, now called the Serbo-Croatian Exhibition[36] instead of the previously used Southern Slav Show. Troubles over the name of a future nation, however, did not interrupt the "Meštrović fever" in England, finally resulting in a monograph about the sculptor being published there in 1919.[37]

In the same year, a great show of Yugoslav art with the Vidovdan Temple as the central theme was staged at the Exhibition of Yugoslav Artists in Petit Palais in Paris, at the time of Peace Conference prior to the Treaty of Versailles when the Yugoslav delegation was seeking the recognition of new state. The arguments for recognition in the Conference were fortified by pro-Yugoslav scholars – from historians and literary experts to anthropologists and geographers – eager to legitimize this new nation in the international community. Yet, a more persuasive assertion that the South Slavs had always been a single nation once again came from Ivan Meštrović and his artistic compatriots. This time the artists represented in the show were from all over the country; Serbs, Croats and Slovenes all showed their works under the Yugoslav name. "The way it is presented [...] this exhibition is less an artistic manifestation than it is a national manifest," observed a prominent French art historian, André Michel, while writing about the political mission of the Yugoslav art on display and continued: "the artists here are the Yugoslav delegates at the Congress."[38] The Yugoslav critics also underlined a devoted aim of "manifesting our [Yugoslav] unity in cultural terms" and the "vigor and dynamism" of Meštrović and his fellows were seen as "the most obvious forerunners of a new, Yugoslav art."[39]

However, the 1919 Paris show was one of the last moments when Meštrović was eager to present the Vidovdan Temple. Soon after the Kingdom of Serbs, Croats and Slovenes was formed, Meštrović gradually distanced himself from Yugoslav political issues. The Yugoslav government bought the sculptures and the wooden model from the artist, while the last attempt to build the Vidovdan Temple at the site of the medieval battle failed to materialize.[40] Meštrović settled in Zagreb to serve as the first director of the newly founded Academy of Fine Arts, and after the communists overtook power, emigrated to the USA. The biblical themes, which had already absorbed Meštrović's artistic imagination, along with those connected with the history of Croats, lead him to become the harbinger of the dissolution of cohesive Yugoslav ideology. However, despite the withdrawal from distressing Yugoslav politics, Meštrović remained closely tied to the Karađorđević dynasty and continued accepting numerous commissions from the royal throne with considerable enthusiasm, completing many large-scale public sculptures both in Zagreb and Belgrade. His work continued to be widely promoted in Europe[41] and also in the United States, where he exhibited for the first time in 1924.[42] The great success of the exhibition at the Metropolitan Museum in New York City, the first one-man show to be presented there, resulted in many commissions in the Unites States, the largest being the "Indians with the Bow," a public monument set at the Chicago Waterfront in 1926. Those

Figure 3.2 Tomb of the Unknown Soldier (Photo Archive Miloš Jurišić)

pre-WWII connections he had established in the new world helped him and his family to settle in the USA.[43]

Instead of the Vidovdan Temple, Meštrović received the commission directly from King Aleksandar Karađorđević[44] for a national monument dedicated to the unknown soldier at Avala Mountain, twenty kilometers south of Belgrade[45] (see Figure 3.2). As if it had been a tribute to his previous vision for a national shrine, the consecration of the cornerstone for the Tomb of the Unknown Soldier took place on Vidovdan of 1934, only a few months before the assassination of King Aleksandar in Marseilles. The inauguration of the memorial was held also on Vidovdan, four years later, at the time of significant constitutional changes providing new borders and more autonomy to the Croatian portion within the kingdom. Surprisingly, during the site preparations for the construction of the Tomb in the spring of 1934, the remains of a Serbian medieval town, Žrnov, together with the older layer of a Roman fortification, were blown up by dynamite under the supervision of King Aleksandar himself.[46] Suddenly, Meštrović's Ancient and Archaic reminiscences were not simply symbolic, but rather a supplement for the destroyed legacy.

The Tomb was conceived as a ziggurat-like structure on which a temple in the form of a late-Roman sarcophagus was laid.[47] Four caryatides, which symbolically presented different geographic areas of Yugoslavia, were placed in front of both entrances, stressing the regional rather than the ethnic diversity of the nation. The characteristics of these figures were created out of specific regional folk costumes, not upon the official separation on the three ethnic, sub-national groups or "tribes." While shaping the Vidovdan Temple, Meštrović tried to resemble both Western and Eastern Christian church traditions, attempting to emphasize a possible unity of the two antagonistic zones of Christianity, the Catholic and the Orthodox. In the Tomb, on the other hand, the architectural analogies were solely remote, varying from Mesopotamian and Ancient Egyptian to Ancient Roman, thereby completely unrelated to any characteristics of the South Slavic architectural heritage. Instead of the nascent sculptural repertoire previously showed in the Vidovdan Temple – the characters from the medieval epic poetry, history and myths representing the single South Slavic spirit, boosted by a unifying national narrative – he shifted toward abstract representations of diverse regional entities with identical bodily attributes, slightly altered only by their folk costumes.

The universalism of forms in the Tomb of the Unknown Soldier was as much criticized as in the Vidovdan Temple. Meštrović's patriotic message relied on the epic narrative, just adjunct to the sculptural opus, rather than on the visual syntax. The harshest attack on this matter dated to the time of an intense pro-Yugoslav campaign in Great Britain during the Great War. On one side, Meštrović became glorified as a unique artistic genius sprung from his race while, on the other, the uniqueness of his work was questioned because of his Viennese education and tight connections to the Central European cultural sphere of influence. Some art critics doubted not only the possibility that the barbaric warriors had simply grown out of Meštrović's Sothern Slavic soul, but also the very nature of representing a particularly Yugoslavian political mission through the universal formal expression. Meštrović's cosmopolitanism was inevitable, pointed out a commentary from the time of the V&A exhibit: "In an era of greater cultural isolation, he might have been more Serbian; as it is, his work is simply European being no more Serbian than English."[48] A similar observation appeared in the Catholic weekly *The Tablet*:

> The legends and the history of Meštrović's race are nothing beside the triumph of expressing in sculpture the human anatomy swayed and tossed and stricken by thought and emotion and disaster.[49]

Sculpturally, the caryatides carved for the Tomb of the Unknown Soldier were more realistic than those in the Vidovdan Temple, yet the architectural character of the Tomb could have been attached to any national identity, as much to Slavic and European as to any other pancontinental, modern nation. In contrast to the unrealized first memorial, referring to both Catholic and Orthodox traditions, the universal Archaic, Oriental and Classical forms of the second project were dissociated from any links with Christianity, even though Meštrović's interest in biblical themes grew over that time. The architecture of the Tomb and its immediate setting were appropriated to project a desired Yugoslav cohesion. In addition to the structure itself, the entire landscape of Avala, including the indigenous botanical spices, was fused into a natural and cultural "symbiosis to create an extensive national diorama."[50] The temple to the secular religion of Yugoslavism, to use Benedict Anderson's words, was set in the context of a preborn state of the nation prior to its subdivisions, where there had been no "need to identify the nationality of the Tomb's occupant. What else could he be"[51] if not the Yugoslav?

The statement that the unknown soldier was simply a Yugoslav, however, did not provide a satisfactory answer for most Yugoslavs. The body placed in the Tomb was a young man from the Serbian Army originally buried by the enemy: the Austro-Hungarian soldiers that could have been any subject of the ex-Habsburg Empire including Serbs, Croats or Slovenians. By being placed into the Tomb, the Serbian soldier's grave was left with no confessional signs, emphasizing the monument's role as a secular shrine. The lack of Christian-Orthodox insignia, however, was found disrespectful – a neutralization of over one million Serbian victims in WWI, which came on the top of the vandal destruction of Serbian medieval heritage blown by a dynamite to clear up the spot for Meštrović's work. On the other hand, the complaints coming from the western parts of the country predominantly addressed spending state funds on such an unnecessary venture, despite the official claims that the budget had come from the king's pocket. The peoples from other "tribal" entities remained indifferent about the Tomb, completed at the outbreak of World War II when the aspiration of Croats toward autonomy reached its peak. The Tomb developed into a visual resource of Yugoslav individuation after the victory of communism with Tito's attempts to bring Meštrović back from the exile. The original, ideologically neutral forms were as suitable for Tito's "brotherhood and unity" narrative standing for plurality of national identities as they had been for the Karđorđevićs's ideology of synthetized Yugoslav nation. Today, a quarter-century after the dissolution of Yugoslavia, the Tomb has become generally observed as one of the many voided communist memorials that have lost almost any potential for collective identification except for nostalgia.

The fate of the Yugoslav Pantheon

Besides Meštrović's explicitly engaged works, the integral Yugoslavism was architecturally promoted primarily in the form of unrealized designs, competition entries and architectural exhibits. The Fourth Yugoslav Exhibition of 1912, held in Belgrade, was the first to include architectural contributions mostly by Belgrade- and a few Zagreb-based architects. Thematically, it was quite an inconsistent collection of drawings and photographs of large public buildings, residential units and urban designs. Stylistically, the late nineteenth-century Historicism was a predominant mode, with only a few names showing more provocative Secessionist buildings. Random displays of architectural works continued in the subsequent Yugoslav shows in 1922

76 *The birth of national architectures*

and 1927, while more ambitious promotions of synthetized Yugoslav architecture turned into significant national events after the proclamation of dictatorship in 1929.

Since the preparations for the last Yugoslav Exhibition in Belgrade in 1927 until the king's decree about the erection of the Tomb of the Unknown Soldier in 1932, many unrealized projects named Pantheons conceived as memorials to the unknown soldier appeared in the press and periodicals. Croatian architectural historian Tomislav Premerl pointed out that Zagreb architects submitted entries in the architectural competition for the Pantheon announced in Belgrade in 1926,[52] the event which either overlapped or was the same as the competition for the St. Sava Cathedral from the same year. The construction of St. Sava on the Vračar Plateau, the spot where his relics had been burned by the Ottomans, had been a prime national goal since the keys of the city were given back to Serbs in 1867. Yet, after the constitution of the tripartite kingdom, the pursuit of a solely Serbian agenda to become the capital's foremost architectural symbol was considered inappropriate by many. When Belgrade daily newspaper *Politika* published the stipulations for the St. Sava, the public reaction was furious,[53] culminating with Kostra Strajnić's appeal to abandon the idea as inappropriate for national cohesion.[54] Born to a Serbian family in Croatia, Strajnić developed pro-Yugoslav attitudes after being trained by Josef Strzygowsky, under whose influence he developed admiration for Meštrović. As Meštrović's passionate promoter and political compatriot, Strajnić published a booklet complaining to state officials against the construction of a national cathedral limited to only Serbian history in the capital of all South Slavs, half of which were not Orthodox Christians:

> While gaining funds for such a cathedral from the state budget, the officials do not dare to claim that the building must become the most grandiose structure of the whole country, a unique national monument which would serve as the Pantheon. However, the officials imagine the cathedral as the representative of only one (Serbian) and not of all three (Serbian, Croatian and Slovenian) tribe-nations. Is it possible that they have not heard of the model for a Vidovdan Temple, the masterpiece of Ivan Meštrović?[55]

Debates over the construction of St. Sava continued fluctuating between similar arguments about the validity of the enterprise for the multi-religious nation and discussions about the aesthetic qualities of projects submitted in the competition. Exhausted by the long-lasting polemics, the Orthodox Church authorities insisted that the agonizing process stop in pursuance of construction as soon as the funds were assured; however, the decision about the beginning of construction was not reached until King Aleksandar issued a decree on the matter in February 1932.[56] As if he had tried to neutralize this move prioritizing the Serbian side, the king took more forceful steps in realization of the non-confessional Tomb of the Unknown Soldier at the same time.[57] As a result, the Tomb was consecrated on St. Vitus Day 1938, while the cornerstone for St. Sava was only laid a year later, at the eve of World War II.

After Meštrović abandoned the themes emphasizing rejuvenating potentials of the Slavic barbaric origins, a new generation of Zagreb-based artists gathered around a similar idea in an ultra-avant-garde movement named Zenitism.[58] The main concept promoted by its members was a deliberate departure from the leftovers of the already dissolved European culture, while the rebirth of Europe was to be achieved through the strength of "Barbarogenius," the superman's spirit rooted in the intrinsic soil of the Balkans. The group's initial manifesto was written and published in Zagreb by the poet and critic of Serbian origins Ljubomir Micić, but soon the group was forced to move to Belgrade in search for a more welcoming intellectual setting. From 1921 to 1926, their journal *Zenit* was publishing provocative art projects attuned to the Europe avant-garde movements of the time such as Expressionism, Futurism, Dadaism and Constructivism.[59] Works by Pablo Picasso, László Moholy-Nagy, Wassily Kandinsky, Filippo Marinetti, Karel Teige, Kazimir Malevich, Walter Gropius and Hannes Meyer were among many others presented in the journal during the five years of its existence. One of the first mass distributed prints of the never realized project for the Monument of Third International by Vladimir Tatlin appeared on the cover of *Zenit* in February 1922.[60]

During Meštrović's politically engaged phase, the barbarous character of the Balkans was a dominating concept, however, the role of Meštrović's Balkan superman was far less provocative than in Micić's vision. While Meštrović aimed to make Europe comfortable in front of the rising national soul of the South Slavs, the Zenitism promoted the superiority of Slavic spirit as the only remaining force that could stop the rapid decline and final disappearance of European values. In an attempt at overcoming the existing antagonist relationship between the Balkans and Europe, the Zenitists introduced a dynamic opposition, the new Balkans – old Europe, holding an "energetic imperative" pivotal for a constructive process by which Europe would be Balkanized, instead of the Balkans Europeanized.[61] Micić believed that vital native primitivism of the Balkans, so evident in the history of the South Slavs, could have reinvigorated a European civilization, whose moral, cultural and political fatigue had become manifested in the expansion of the Great War.[62] According to some opinions, the initial philosophy of Zenitism was initiated by a positive energy after the constitution of Royal Yugoslavia, which set in motion Micić's ambition to define its specific cultural identity,[63] yet even if this was the case, it was the state authorities who abolished any further activities of the group in 1926.

The main architectural protagonist of the Zenit movement was a Croatian architect Josip Seissel,[64] who settled in Belgrade at an early age to finish high school. Here, he joined Micić and his circle, becoming the first and only

Zenitist to experiment with architectural forms using various techniques and different kinds of visual arts, mainly in graphic design. His drawings and collages were published under the pseudonym Jo Klek, usually typed in Cyrillic script, which could be understood either as a wish to overcome the Serbo-Croatian tension over the predominate national alphabet or as an attempt to adjust to the Constructivist typography. In *Zenit* issue 35, published in December 1924, Jo Klek published two ambiguous projects named Zeniteum I and Zeniteum II, and although unrealizable, the monumental schemes called for the building of a Zenitist central temple, the home for all underestimated Barbarogenii. The purified idealistic forms of both proposals responded to the rising concessions about L'Esprit Nouveau[65] and similar programs coming from the Expressionists architects,[66] yet the monumental central plan for the Zeniteum, especially in the first version of the project, was explicitly tied to the concept of the Pantheon and the Cathedral of Holy Wisdom – Hagia Sophia in Constantinople. A possible link between the Zeniteum and sacred spaces of Byzantium[67] were found in Micić's manifesto on architecture prepared for publication in the Dutch Bouwkunde,[68] in which he stated that "only a few surviving examples of vernacular structures and one modest monastic building with white walls and simple domes could be considered architecture in Belgrade."[69] Finding vernacularism to be the only truly authentic expression of the region recalls Le Corbusier's observation about the Balkans in his traveling to the Orient and Balkans, when he also expressed evident enthusiasm about the gusle instrument[70] after he had studied Meštrović's gusle-inspired Vidovdan Fragments in the Serbian Pavilion in Rome. The Zenitists' focus on the Balkan vernacular, however, bore one more dimension; they did not want only to be inspired by, but to epitomize the creativity of the Balkans, whose people had been seduced by foreign influences and plagiarism, including Meštrović himself. Micić understood Meštrović's use of the Kraljević Marko legend as forgery, believing that his art was promoting his ego rather than the Balkan soul:

> Our nation certainly has held one of the ugliest destinies of the world. Even if any authentic creative soul still works in some remote jungles of the Balkans, he should do that unselfishly, with sacrifice, with heroism, as deserved by this land of suffering. The true sons of this country today are Zenitists, the owners of a new a brighter future. Let us believe![71]

While the utopian dream of Zenitism remained unfulfilled, its only architectural protagonist, Josip Seissel,[72] had one of the most successful careers in Royal Yugoslavia and continued being the leading Yugoslav architect until his death in 1987. He became internationally recognized at the World Exposition in Paris of 1937,[73] where he received the Grand Prix for architecture for design of the Yugoslav Pavilion,[74] built in front of the Palais de Chaillot on the plateau above the Trocadéro Gardens (see the cover

Affirmation of the Yugoslav idea 79

photo). The Pavilion attracted public gaze by a brisk composition, clear proportions and abstract forms against the pompous concave surfaces of the just-completed Chaillot Palace, yet both projects fitted into an ongoing trend tied to the rise of totalitarian regimes of the late 1930s.[75] In comparison to the Czechoslovakian Pavilion,[76] which retained the Functionalist enthusiasm of the previous decade, the heaviness of its Yugoslav counterpart displayed a different political climate resulting from the dissolution of the Little Entente and the rise of fascism.

Seissel's original proposal, submitted in the competition of 1936, was explicitly Functionalist. His entry was rewarded with the highest second prize, since the jury[77] concluded that none of the submitted entries would respectfully represent the country. When the government appointed a new special committee to reach a decision about the final design, asking for a "monumental spirit and explicit use of precious building materials from the homeland, like marble, onyx and bronze,"[78] Seissel, made the best effort to alter his previously submitted project and meet the requirements for desired monumentality. While the plans remained almost untouched, the previous ultra-modernist façades characterized by light, industrially produced materials was changed into "naked plain surfaces cladded in stone which calmness was decently interrupted by four free standing neo-Classical columns crafted from the Prilep marble[79] and three perforations between them."[80] Seissel turned the front façade into monumental statement in conflict to his previous belief that "any monumental attempt at the Yugoslav Pavilion set against the Trocadéro Palace would be a failure while horizontality and modest scale as contrast to the immense architectural backdrop should be a priority."[81] He still insisted on the necessity for calmness, retaining a flat simple screen of the main façade "speaking for itself in its surrounding"[82] in the altered project; however, his Modernist rhetoric was heavily compromised by purely representational neo-Classical elements, the non-load-bearing columns poured from reinforced concrete and only clad with the precisely cannulated marble sheets. The columns dominated not only by the power of shape, proportions and unfinished contour with no capitals, but also by their intense, contrasting, dark shadows, projected onto the bright façade surface over the main entrance.

> Four de-capitalized fluted marble columns with no bases, of De Chirician sensibility, deprived from the structural function, and consequently with no essence might be interpreted as an analogy to the ancient traditions of Yugoslavia, but also as a surrealist provocation. The columns behind which an atypically small door was hiding were the only element without which the of Pavilion would have been deducted to elementary form of a shelter.[83]

Although the dramatic effect of this architectural scene might have resulted from the authoritative vision of Milan Stojadinović, serving as the prime minister in the years prior to WWII,[84] it is not clear if Seissel simply obeyed the dictatorial request, or switched to a more ambiguous collage of sturdy forms with intrinsic enthusiasm.

The zone of main entrance was further reinforced by programmatically incorporated art works by Serbian painter Milo Milunović[85] and Croatian sculptor Toma Rosandić.[86] Milunović's mosaic-painting Three Girls was inserted into the flat, solid façade surface like a precisely positioned rectangular window engraved together with "Yugoslavia" behind the four neo-Classical columns. Like mosaics in "medieval Byzantine churches,"[87] it depicted three figures in the folk costumes of Serbia, Croatia and Slovenia set in an imaginary garden of paradise as the personifications of three tribe-national identities in the kingdom. Rosandić's sculptural composition, on the other hand, alluded to the wild and the masculine potentials of the nation struggling for its affirmation while "demonstrating its constructive strengths."[88] Rosandić's work was reminiscent of Meštrović's earlier representation of a titanic dimension of Yugoslav origins, resulting from their friendship and involvement in the previous exhibitions on Yugoslav art. The tone and the position of Rosandić's piece were imposed by the Yugoslav authorities, insisting on the already tested models from the Rome Exposition of 1911. The attempts were successful, as the Paris presentation was, as well accepted, in the eyes of foreign critics, as the two-and-half-decade earlier show in Rome. What was displayed had the power to persuade the contemporary commentators of the strength of the country and the cohesion of its peoples, as a French commentator noticed:

> Yugoslavia is revealing its true face, vital and healthy, and at the same time mystical and full of respect for the traditions of its fathers. Yugoslavian Pavilion, laid solely on its own at the Trocadéro terrace, reminds of a noble and dignified Ancient temple.[89]

Seissel's Pavilion was the last successful attempt at creating the temple of Yugoslavs during the short existence of Royal Yugoslavia. Despite Meštrović's absence, due either to his shifted attitude about the Yugoslav nationhood or simply a lack of motivation, the Croatian side put remarkable effort into preparing the Yugoslavian presentation there. The architectural design was done by a Zagreb-based architect, most of the art works were created by Croatian artists, and Croatian politicians took a leading role in organizing the country's appearance.[90] The monumental tone might have resulted from the "tough hand" of Belgrade political leadership, leaning toward the totalitarian regimes and establishing ties with Hitler and Mussolini. However, the international recognition, the Grand Prix Josip Seissel received for architecture in Paris, proved the superiority of a native genius. The Pavilion was demolished soon after the show ended, thereby it shared a similar destiny with the country itself: they were both short-lived.

Notes

1 For a review of the role of the Progressive Youth see the introduction to "Art and Nationalism" by Antun Gustav Matoš, in Ahmet Ersoy, Maciej Górny and Vangelis Kechriotis (eds.), *Modernism: Representations of National Culture: Discourses of Collective Identity in Central and Southeast Europe 1770–1945: Texts and Commentaries*, Vol. 3/2, Budapest: Central European University Press, 2010: 287–289.
2 Ivan Meštrović (1883–1962) is the most celebrated Croatian and Yugoslav sculptor. The bibliography on him is vast, written both in Serbo-Croatian and English. Chronologically, it covers his early works (including the Vidovdan Temple), the broad opus of the period between the world wars, and the post-WWII work after Meštrović immigrated to the USA. Early monographs mainly focused on the Vidovdan Temple; these include Kosta Strajnić, *Ivan Meštrović*, Belgrade: Ćelap i Popovac, 1919; Milan Ćurčin (ed.), *Ivan Meštrović: A Monograph*, London: Williams and Norgate, 1919.
3 The artist himself emphasized the political importance of his participation in the First Yugoslav Exhibition, in Ivan Meštrović, "Umjetnost i slovenska umjetnost na jugu" [The Art and Slavic Art of the South], *Sloboda*, no. 3–5, (1905): 2–3.
4 Ivan Meštrović, *Uspomene na političke ljude i dogadjaje* [*Memories about Politicians and Political Events*], Zagreb: Matica Hrvatska, 1993: 22.
5 Vidovdan or St. Vitus Day on which the Kosovo Battle took place has been considered a symbolic date in Serbian history. Consequently, many important events in the new history took place on Vidovdan. For example, the Constitution of the Kingdom of Serbs, Croats and Slovenes, called the Vidovdan Constitution, was proclaimed on June 28, 1919.
6 Today, the wooden model is at the Municipal Museum of Kruševac, next to the medieval Church of Lazarica – the site from which Prince Lazar allegedly took the Serbian Knights to the Battle of Kosovo in 1389.
7 Milan Ćurčin, "The Story of an Artist," in Ćurčin (ed.), *Ivan Meštrović – A Monograph*: 16.
8 Josef Strzygowski, "Meštrović in der Sezession," *Die Zeit* (January 19, 1910): 17.
9 Milan Šević, "Kosovske pesme u kamenu: vajarski radovi Ivana Meštrovića," [Kosovo Poems in Stone: Sculptural Works of Ivan Meštrović], *Letopis Matice srpske*, vol. 86, no. 265 (1910): 88.
10 Jože Plečnik (1872–1957), recognized as the father of Slovenian architecture, was one of the most authentic Central European architects coming from Otto Wagner's school. Discussed further in Chapter 6, and the Conclusion.
11 Also noticed in Norka Machiedo Mladinić, "Političko opredjeljenje i umjetnički rad mladog Meštrovića" [Political Inclinations and Artistic Contributions of Young Meštrović], *Časopis za suvremenu povjest*, vol. 41, no. 1 (2009): 143–170. Meštrović's drawings of the architectural vision for the Vidovdan Temple were first presented at this exhibition.
12 Mladinić, "Političko opredjeljenje i umjetnički rad mladog Meštrovića": 143–170.
13 For Meštrović's association with the Pavilion of Serbia at the World Exhibition written in English, see Andrew Baruch Wachtel, *Making a Nation – Breaking a Nation: Literature and Cultural Politics in Yugoslavia*, Stanford: Stanford University Press, 1998: 109–117.

82 The birth of national architectures

14 Finally, there were more Croatian than Serbian artists presented in the Serbian Pavilion. However, they were all signed as Serbian, upon the request of the Austro-Hungarian government.
15 Discussed in Aleksandar Ignjatović, *Jugoslovenstvo u arhitekturi, 1904–1941* [*Yugoslavism in Architecture, 1904–1941*], Belgrade: Građevinska knjiga, 2007: 67–72.
16 Ivan Meštrović, *Uspomene na političke ljude i događaje*, Zagreb: Matica Hrvatska, 1993: 77.
17 Petar Bajalović (1876–1947) studied at Karlsruhe polytechnic. He was professor and founder of the descriptive geometry field of studies at Belgrade Faculty of Architecture.
18 Marko Car, "S jubilarne izložbe u Rimu" [From the Jubilee Exposition in Rome], *Letopis Matice srpske*, vol. 87, no. 7 (1911): 564. Quoted in Ignjatović, *Jugoslovenstvo u arhitekturi*: 68.
19 Dimitrije Mitrinović was born and raised in Bosnia and Herzegovina during Austro-Hungarian control. Turning into a bitter opponent to the Austro-Hungarian authorities, he took part in the foundation of Mlada Bosna [Young Bosnia], an extremist political group fighting for the end of the Habsburg domination over Slavs. He was the only member of the group who survived the Austrian prison. During the first half of the twentieth century, he was strongly connected to the leading avant-garde art groups and movements that propoted the pan-European supranational spirit.
20 Dimitrije Mitrinović "Reprezentacija Hrvata i Srba na Međunarodnoj izložbi u Rimu" [Representation of Croats and Serbs at the International Exposition in Rome], *Savremenik*, vol. 6, no. 9 (1911): 525.
21 Discussed in Aleksandar Ignjatović, "Images of the Nation Foreseen: Ivan Meštrović's Vidovdan Temple and Primordial Yugoslavism," *Slavic Review*, vol. 73, no. 4 (2014): 828–858.
22 The Italian press was full of positive commentaries about young Meštrović and his work. Negative criticism came mostly from the circle gravitating towards Benedetto Croce's aesthetic position. See Duško Kečkemet, *Ivan Meštrović*, Belgrade: Publishing House Jugoslavija, 1964: 77. Besides Italy, positive criticism about the presentation of Meštrović in Rome appeared in France, Belgium and Great Britain.
23 Together with Meštrović, Gustav Klimt received the Grand Prix for painting.
24 Milutin Borisavljević (1889–1969), architect and esthetician, internationally recognized for his theory of proportion. Published in English as Miloutine Borissavliévitch, *The Golden Number and the Scientific Aesthetics of Architecture*, London: Louis Hautecoeur, 1953.
25 Milutin Borisavljević, "Meštrovićev Vidovdanski hram – kritika njegove arhitekture" [Meštrović's Vidovdan Temple – the Criticism of his Architecture], *Srpski tehnički list*, vol. 25, no. 15–16 (Belgrade, 1914): 117–132.
26 Miroslav Krleža, "O Ivanu Meštroviću" [About Ivan Meštrović], *Književnik*, vol. 1, no. 3 (1928): 73–85.
27 Meštrović, *Uspomene na političke ljude i događaje*: 1–2.
28 Ibid., 27.
29 Norka Machiedo-Mladinić, "Prilog proučavanju delovanja Ivana Meštrovića u Jugoslavenskom odboru" [Contributions to Research about the Engagement

Affirmation of the Yugoslav idea 83

of Ivan Meštrović in the Yugoslav Committee], *Časopis za suvremenu povjest*, vol. 39, no. 1, (2007): 135–156.

30 Milada Paulova, *Jugoslavenski odbor* [*Yugoslav Committee*], Zagreb, 1925.
31 James Bone and R. W. Seton-Watson, *Exhibition of the Works of Ivan Meštrović*, catalog with photographs by E.O. Hoppé, London: V&A, 1915.
32 The responses of the foreign press were described in Ivan Meštrović, "Ideja Kosovskog Hrama" [An Idea of the Kosovo Temple], *Jadran* (1915/1916): 1–2.
33 Elizabeth Clegg, "Meštrović, England and the Great War," *The Burlington Magazine*, vol. 144, no. 1197 (2002): 746–747.
34 Seton-Watson stated that the Vidovdan Temple was meant to serve as the Valhalla of the free and united Southern Slavs nation. R. W. Seton-Watson, "Meštrović and the Jugoslav Idea," in Ćurčin (ed.), *Ivan Meštrović – A Monograph*: 58. In the first monograph published in Serbo-Croatian, Kosta Strajnić described the Vidovdan Temple as a more powerful national symbol than the Arc de Triomphe and Valhalla: Kosta Strajnić, *Ivan Meštrović*, Belgrade: Ćelap i Popovac, 1919: 21.
35 Parallel to the exhibit, Dimitrije Mitrinović gave a lecture at Leeds University at the invitation of Vice-Chancellor Michael Sadler.
36 Ironically, the show was named "Serbo-Croatian" despite the fact that it presented only three Croatian artists: Ivan Meštrović, Toma Rosandić and Franjo Rački.
37 Ćurčin (ed.), *Ivan Meštrović – A Monograph*. This monograph includes essays by Sir John Lavery, Ernest H. R. Collings, James Bone, R. W. Seton-Watson, Ivo Vojnović, Bogdan Popović and Milan Ćurčin.
38 André Michel, *Exposition des artistes Yougoslaves au Palais des beaux-arts 12/04/1919-15/05/1919*, catalog, Paris: Petit Palais, 1919, translated to Slevenian "Razstava jugoslovanskih umetnikov v Parizu" [The Exhibition of Yugoslav Artists in Paris], *Ljubljanski zvon*, vol. 39 (1919): 591–598.
39 Boško Tokin, "Izložba jugoslavenskih umetnika u Parizu," *Plamen*, vol. 1, no. 13 (1919): 24–29.
40 The sculptor himself remembers the reasons why the temple was not executed in Meštrović, *Uspomene na političke ljude i dogadjaje*: 26–28. The Serbian government bought the largest number of sculptures for the Vidovdan Temple, today kept at the National Museum in Belgrade. According to Meštrović's memoires, he was never adequately paid for his work.
41 František Táborský, *Ivan Meštrović*, Prague: Orbis, 1933; Milan Ćurčin, *Ivan Meštrović*, Zagreb: Nova Evropa, 1933; Ivan Meštrović and Ernest Collings, *Meštrović*, Zagreb: Nova Evropa & Oxford University Press, 1933.
42 Christian Brinton, *The Meštrović Exhibition*, catalog, New York: Brooklin Museum, 1924.
43 Post-WWII literature: Norman Rice, Harry Hilberry and Estelle Hilberry, *The Sculpture of Ivan Meštrović*, Syracuse: Syracuse University Press, 1948; Milan Ćurčin, "Meštrović u Americi," *Arhitektura*, vol. 7, no. 4 (1953): 29–32; Laurence Schmeckebier, *Ivan Meštrović: Sculptor and Patriot*, Syracuse: Syracuse University Press, 1959; Zeljko Grum, *Ivan Meštrović*, Zagreb: Matica Hrvatska, 1962, Duško Kečkemet, *Ivan Meštrović*, Belgrade: Publishing House Jugoslavia, 1964; Željko Grum, *Ivan Meštrović*, Zagreb: Matica hrvatska i Grafički zavod Hrvatske, 1969; Duško Kečkemet, *Ivan Meštrović: The Only Way to be an Artist is to Work*, Zagreb-Ljubljana: Spektar i Delo, 1970.

84 *The birth of national architectures*

44 The decision to erect the monument designed by Ivan Meštrović at the top of Avala Mountain was initiated by the king in 1933. The funds came from the king's personal account, as Meštrović remembers in his memoires. Discussed in Ignjatović, *Jugoslovenstvo u arhitekturi*: 212.

45 Stevan Živanović, *Spomenik neznanom junaku* [*The Tomb of the Unknown Soldier*], Belgrade: Turistička štampa, 1968; Aleksandar Ignjatović, "Od istorijskog sećanja do zamišljanja nacionalne tradicije: Spomenik neznanom junaku na Avali" [From the Historical Memory to the Imagining of a National Tradition: The Tomb of the Unknown Soldier at Avala], in Olga Manojlović Pintar (ed.), *Istorija i sećanje: studije istorijskog sećanja* [*History and Memory: Studies in Historical Consciousness*], Belgrade: INIS, 2006: 229–252.

46 The Žrnov Fortification was recorded and studied by the most prolific architectural historians of the time: Đurđe Bošković, "Grad Žrnov" [The City of Žrnov], *Starinar*, vol. 15 (1940): 70–91; Aleksandar Deroko, *Srednjovekovni gradovi u Srbiji Crnoj Gori i Makedoniji* [*Medieval Fortifications in Serbia, Montenegro and Macedonia*], Belgrade: Prosveta, 1950: 101–102. The destruction of Žrnov was harshly criticized by professional associations such as the Society for Historical Monuments, the Institute for National Art and the Architecture Club. Until today, the rumors about the destruction of the medieval landmark have remained a hot topic in the press: "Top 5 misterija Beograda: grad Žrnov na Avali" [Top Five Mysteries of Belgrade: The City of Žrnov at Avala], *Telegraf* (March 23, 2012).

47 Meštrović's tomb has often been compared to the mausoleum of the Persian king, allegedly King Cyrus, in Pasargadae, Iran. Živanović, *Spomenik neznanom junaku*: 13–14.

48 Robert Ross, "Monthly Chronicle: Meštrović," *The Burlington Magazine*, vol. 27 (1915): 206. Quote is taken from Clegg, "Meštrović, England and the Great War": 748.

49 Anonymous, "Meštrović in South Kensington," *The Tablet*, vol. 3, no. 921 (July 30, 1915): 6. Quote is taken from Clegg, "Meštrović, England and the Great War": 748.

50 Ignjatović, *Jugoslovenstvo u arhitekturi*: 215–216.

51 Benedict Anderson, *Imagined Communities: Reflections on the Origins and Spread of Nationalism*, London: Verso, 1991: 10.

52 Tomislav Premerl, *Hrvatska moderna arhitektura između dva rata: nova tradicija*, [*Croatian Modern Architecture between the Two Wars: A New Tradition*] Zagreb: Nakladni zavod Hrvatske, 1990: 56.

53 Anonymous, "Stečaj za Hram Svetog Save" [A Competition for St. Sava Cathedral], *Politika* (November 3, 1926): 5; reprinted in Anonymous, "Stečaj društva za podizanje Hrama Svetog Save u Beogradu na Vračaru," *Tehnički List*, vol. 11 (1927): 30.

54 Kosta Strajnić, *Svetosavski hram – javni apel zvaničnim faktorima srpske crkve i jugoslovenske države* [*St. Sava Cathedral – a Public Appeal to the Serbian-Orthodox Church and Yugoslav State Officials*], Belgrade: independent press, 1926.

55 Ibid., 32.

56 Anonymous, "Odluka o izgradnji Svetosavskog Hrama" [The Decision about the Construction of St. Sava Cathedral], *Vreme* (February 13, 1932): 6.

57 A letter about the regulation and preparation of the building site for the tomb was sent from the court on May 22, 1934. This is kept in the Archive of Yugoslavia,

AJ. 365 f.369 – reference taken from Ignjatović, "Od istorijskog sećanja do zamišljanja nacionalne tradicije": 229. It means that the detailed plans for the construction had been made by at least 1933. It would be hard to prove when the idea about the tomb first crossed the king's mind, but it could be speculated that the first talks with Meštrović about this project dated back to 1932.

58 Miloš Perović, "Zenitism and Modern Architecture," in Jelena Bogdanović (ed.), *On the Very Edge: Modernism and Modernity in the Arts and Architecture of Interwar Serbia (1918–1941)*, Louven: Louven University Press: 85–96; Irina Subotić, *Od avangarde do Arkadije* [*From the Avant-garde to Arcadia*], Belgrade: Clio, 2000.
59 Vida Golubović, "Časopis Zenit" [The Journal *Zenit*], *Književnost*, vol. 36, no. 7–8 (1981): 1477–1482.
60 Ljubomir Micić and Ivan Goll (eds.), *Zenit*, vol. 2, no. 11 (1922).
61 Vida Golubović, "Eksperiment Zenita" [The Zenith Experiment], in *Zenit i avangarda 20-tih godina*, Belgrade: Narodni muzej, 1983: 35–48.
62 Steven Mansbach, *Modern Art in Eastern Europe: From the Baltics to the Balkans 1890–1939*, Cambridge: Cambridge University Press, 1999: 231.
63 Miloš Perović, *Srpska arhitektura XX veka – od istorizma do drugog modernizma* [*Serbian Twentieth-Century Architecture: From Historicism to Second Modernism*], Belgrade: Faculty of Architecture, 2003: 60.
64 Josip Seissel (1904–1987), known under the pseudonym Jo Klek, graduated from Zagreb Technical Faculty under Hugo Erlich in 1929, after which he became involved in the work of Radna Grupa Zagreb (RGZ), which will be discussed in the next chapter. He moved back to Zagreb after the legal action against the Zenithism in 1926.
65 In 1922 Micić had published a text about new architecture using ideas and quotations from Le Corbusier's writings on Purism. Ljubomir Micić, "O estetici purizma" [About the Aesthetics of Purism], *Zenit*, vol. 2, no. 15 (1922): 34–35.
66 The most obvious analogy is the Goetheanum by Rudolph Steiner.
67 Discussed in Jelena Bogdanović, "Evocations of Byzantium in Zenitist Avant-Garde Architecture," *Journal of the Society of Architectural Historians*, vol. 75, no. 3: 299–317.
68 Perović, *Srpska arhitektura XX veka*: 70.
69 Ljubomir Micić, "Beograd bez arhitekture" [Belgrade Without Architecture], *Zenit*, vol. 5 (1925).
70 Ljiljana Blagojević, *Modernism in Serbia: The Elusive Margins of Belgrade Architecture, 1919–1941*, Cambridge, MA: MIT Press, 2003: 5–8.
71 Ljubomir Micić, "Nova umetnost' [The New Art], *Zenit*, vol. 4, no. 34 (1924).
72 Josip Seissel (1904–1987) was trained at the Technical Faculty in Zagreb. After graduation, he worked at Zagreb municipality on the regulatory plans. He was closely tied to Josip Pič. His passion for urbanism would remain unchallenged through the rest of his career.
73 *Exposition Intenationale des Arts et Techniques dans la Vie Moderne.*
74 Discussed in Tamara Bjažić-Klarin and Jasna Galjer, "Jugoslavenski paviljon na Svjetskoj izložbi u Parizu 1937 i reprezentacijska paradigma nove državne kulturne politike" [Yugoslav Pavilion at the Paris World Exhibition in 1937 and the Role of Zagreb's Public School of Crafts in Creating the Representational Paradigm of the State's New Cultural Policy], *Radovi instituta za povijest umjetnosti*, vol. 37 (2013): 179–192.

86 The birth of national architectures

75 The most often mentioned is a "totalitarian" image presenting the vivid pair of German and Soviet pavilions, symmetrically positioned on both sides of the Eiffel Tower in the main axis from the Trocadéro Gardens.
76 The Czechoslovakian Pavilion by Jaromir Krejcár has been broadly publicized in recent literature.
77 The competition jury included prominent representatives from all three sub-national centers: Pater Bajalović (creator of the Serbian Pavilion in Rome) from Belgrade, Edo Schön from Zagreb, and Ivan Vurnik from Ljubljana.
78 The documentation is kept in the Archive of Yugoslavia (fond Ministarstvo trgovine i industrije, AJ 66–275). See Aleksandar Ignjatović, "Politika predstavljanja Jugoslovenstva: jugoslovenski paviljon na Svetskoj izložbi u Parizu 1937. godine" [Politics of Representing Yugoslavism: Yugoslav National Pavilion at the Paris World Exhibition of 1937], *Godišnjak za društvenu istoriju*, vol. 11, no. 2–3 (2006): 69.
79 The stone was cut from the Nabregovo quarry near Prilep in today's Macedonia.
80 Ivan Zdravković, "Paviljon Kraljevine Jugoslavije na Međunarodnoj izložbi u Parizu" [The Pavilion of the Kingdom of Yugoslavia at the International Exposition in Paris], *Umetnički pregled*, vol. 1, no. 3 (1937): 27–28.
81 Josip Seissel, "Natječaj za jugoslavenski paviljon na međunarodnoj izložbi 1937 u Parizu" [The Competition for the Yugoslav Pavilion at the International Exposition 1937 in Paris], *Građevinski vjesnik*, vol. 5, no. 17 (1936): 150.
82 Josip Seissel, *Jugoslavenski paviljon na Međunarodnoj izložbi u Parizu*, Zagreb, 1937: an unpaginated booklet.
83 Bjažić-Klarin and Galjer, "Jugoslavenski paviljon na Svjetskoj izložbi u Parizu 1937": 184.
84 Zoran Manević, "Arhitektura i politika, 1937–41" [Architecture and Politics, 1937–41], *Zbornik za likovne umetnosti Matice srpske*, vol. 20 (1984): 293–306; Alaksandar Kadijević, "Ideološke i estetske osnove uspona evropske monumentalne arhitekture u četvrtoj deceniji dvadesetog veka" [Ideological and Aesthetic Basis for the Rise of European Monumental Architecture in the Fourth Decade of the Twentieth Century], *Istorijski časopis*, vol. 45–46, (1998–1999): 255–272.
85 Also Montenegrian, but considered as such within the three-tribe national scheme of Royal Yugoslavia.
86 Born under an Italian name in Dalmatia, Croatian sculptor Toma Rosandić spent most of his life in Belgrade.
87 Seissel, "Natječaj za jugoslavenski paviljon na međunarodnoj izložbi 1937 u Parizu."
88 Quote by Gilles-Defalon, "La pavillon yougoslave", *Beaux-Arts* (July 23, 1937) from Ignjatović, "Politika predstavljanja Jugoslovenstva": 73.
89 Anonymous, *L'Evenment* (June 22, 1937): 7.
90 The Kingdom's General Commissioner at the Paris Expo was Adolf Cuvaj, the general secretary of the Croatian Trade and Commerce Chamber.

Part II
National architectures in the unified nation

4 Imperial Belgrade

Projecting an 'imperial' capital

The geographical position of Belgrade was radically changed by the redefinition of state borders after the Versailles Treaty. The city was no longer the border settlement but the center of a noticeably larger territorial unit and the royal seat of the Karađorđevićs – now the rulers of all Yugoslavs. Prior to the war, Belgrade was not much bigger than Zagreb, with populations of 95,000 and 74,000 respectively. Although the cities grew at a similar pace in the first decade after the war (Belgrade's population reached to 226,000 and Zagreb's 185,000), the transformation of Belgrade, with its new role and geographic position, was far more visible.

Despite massive destruction during the Great War, interwar Belgrade developed into a relatively large city with most of its middle-class population employed in administration. Administrative jobs were offered in the state and city governments, the seats of political parties, growing central banks and trading companies, the specialized high schools and the university. The war reparations played an important role in the reconstruction of destroyed urban areas, the rebirth of industry and the development of infrastructures. The textile industry dominated in overall production, yet the percentage of workers in factories was far below the number of clerks. Belgrade was becoming a sizable urban center in rural and backward territory, disproportionally bigger than any other urban conglomeration in the area. Migrations from the Serbia's countryside were intensive, but flows of immigration also accumulated in other parts of Yugoslavia (mostly Dalmatia and Vojvodina) and in some foreign countries (Russia predominated with about 30,000 incoming refugees fleeing the Red Revolution).

Building activity was tremendous, making the construction industry the most profitable job, especially for peasants who were taking contracts only temporarily and never became permanent residents, or for craftsmen whose know-how had not yet been replaced by new technologies. Apartment renting was a popular way to make easy money, especially among the wealthy, who were able to invest into housing projects. Statistics show that in 1921, newly erected buildings outnumbered the existing housing stock.[1]

90 *National architectures in the unified nation*

Between 1921 and 1939, the total number of buildings in Belgrade doubled, from 7,465 to 15,103,[2] despite the very poor financial situation in the entire country. Even as the administrative center, hosting the four leading banks of the whole country, the city owned less than a quarter of the total capital invested in its built stock. In fact, the building industry attracted foreign capital: the main loans for the construction of urban infrastructures were granted by the Chase Security Corporation of New York City and by a Swiss firm, received as compensation for the rights for using one of the city's electric power stations. War reparations and American donations from the Carnegie Endowment also helped in establishing a new university library, along with other higher education facilities.

Belgrade's urbanization was supposed to be controlled by a master urban plan, for which the municipality announced an international competition in 1921. The number of received entries was unexpectedly high, showing to what extent Belgrade was considered as a rising European capital in the European press. The proposals arrived from Austria, Hungary, Germany, Czechoslovakia and France, with no domestic teams taking a chance. Among the twenty-two, two were named "Great Belgrade." In April 1922, the jury revealed the results, with no winner since none of the proposals could be implemented. The second prize was shared equally by three teams from Austria, France and Hungary, all of which had submitted grand urban schemes that swept away most of the existing urban fabric.[3]

The best-accepted ideas from the awarded proposals were fused in the Master Plan (Figure 4.1), approved by the municipality and put into effect in 1924. Following the central theme proposed in a few competition entries, the plan envisioned a grand prospect starting from the fortress via the ancient forum, continuing further through widened Vasina and Kosovska streets all the way to the old racecourse. This never-realized avenue would have run parallel to Via Militaris – today's Boulevard of King Aleksandar – flanking the back side of the National Assembly and through a sequence of monumental public spaces and buildings that would later be developed as the University District adjacent to Tašmajdan Park at the place of medieval cemetery. The fortification was also to be converted into a public park, Kalemegdan,[4] as was the ancient forum, the largest formally arranged green space of the old town, as part of the Royal Square (since WWII called Studentski Trg – Students' Square). Redefining the existing boulevards and constructing new ones, embellished by public parks, squares, monuments and representational edifices, was to be conducted in regard to the academic models, verified in European metropoles prior to the war. Reaching an image of the monumental metropolis was prioritized, yet the plan also took into consideration the issues of efficiency, social wellbeing and hygiene. It defined the position of new railway stations and transportation corridors and provided comprehensive zoning of mixed-use and residential areas, including those for the poor. The foremost ambition of the plan was to incorporate Zemun and Pančevo – previously Serbian and Croatian

Imperial Belgrade 91

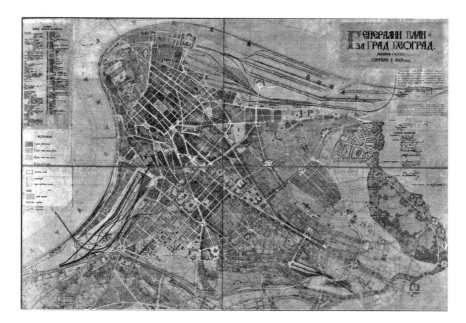

Figure 4.1 Master Plan of Belgrade from 1923 (Urban Planning Institute)

enclaves on the Habsburg territory – into Belgrade metropolitan area, and at least symbolically overcome the previous boundaries that had separated the South Slavs in the previous centuries.[5] The banks of the Sava and the Danube were to be connected by bridges and public transportation.

Despite high expectations, bright planning ideas and strict administrative measures, the urban growth during the interwar period was inconsonant and uncontrolled. The newcomers, mainly poor villagers, usually settled in "avlijske zgrade" [backyard houses] built by rentiers who used to illegally attach rows of small rooms to existing houses in shared backyards. Some other managed to build ad-hoc planned single family units, usually consisted from a kitchen and a bedroom, in illegal residential areas reaching out in different directions, with only a few figuring out sneaky mechanisms of how to attain full-fledged infrastructures.

What rapidly changed an average image of the everyday to everybody was the acceptance of new, modern realities, different paces and habits caused by new technological innovations. The modernization process affected everybody, both the old inhabitants and the newcomers, eager to quickly improve their previous social positions. The new means of fast transportation by buses, cars and planes, along with long-distance communication by telephone and telegraph created the potential for unprecedented mobility and information exchange. Technologies such as film and radio opened a new age of collective performances and large-scale urban gatherings. The expansion of the movie industry across the entire country was intensified after the first public projection of sound film in 1929. By the end of 1938, Belgrade had nineteen movie theaters and a broad public fond of Hollywood productions. The most advanced movie theater hall, run by the MGM Company, was placed at Terazije Square, a short distance from the National Assembly.[6]

Overall, Belgrade was a city of large contrasts with the vernacular-Balkan looking dining shacks next to the high-end hotels and commercial palaces at the most prominent public locations. Changing the inherited customs while becoming used to new metropolitan environments was a painful process, as it was elsewhere during the first decades of the twentieth century. Yet, the modern transformations were far more dramatic in those areas of Europe that frantically ran away from their "Oriental backwardness," so that the unsynchronized development and surprising contrasts have remained typical in Balkan cities until the present day. Contemporary contradictions sound more comprehensible when placed against the past pictures of everyday life. A childhood memory of an active contributor to Belgrade urbanism, architect and planner Miodrag Ferenček, recorded in a recent study about the interwar housing by Zlata Macura, vividly depicts those contrasts:

> My aunt Polda who had grown up in the Habsburg Monarchy came to the Belgrade – the capital of her new "homeland" – for the first time around 1930. She had no wishes to come ever again after walking through Balkanska Street on her way from the Railway Station. Her hesitation resulted from her brief stop at a pub where she saw people eating food poured into digs carved directly into wooden table surfaces, which would be wiped by a filthy wet cloth after one meal was finished and a new customer served [...] Fortunately, my other aunt Olga owned a top-fashion shop just a few blocks away, on the same street. Her husband often traveled to Paris, Vienna and Budapest to pick up merchandise for the shop, so Aunt Polda finally turned fascinated not only by the up-to-date fashion but also by new technical gadgets brought back to Belgrade [...] Belgrade has always been the city of dynamic and contextual contrasts. What can one do except to acknowledge and chronicle them?[7]

What attracted the migration of the well-off from all around the country were new opportunities for developing business, trade and banking, cultural enlightenment and higher education, prestigious jobs in the state government or the army. The greatest advantage of Belgrade, however, lay in the administrative organization of the country. In 1922, the kingdom was divided into thirty-three territorial units all directly subordinated to the capital city. The trend of centralization was radicalized after the proclamation of dictatorship, despite a new division into "banovine" [provinces], in which major cities gained more pronounced role in managing internal affairs.

Although technically the capital of the three-tribal kingdom, Belgrade tended to perform as if it had been only one nation. The ambitions were huge yet understandable. A young European nation, which had never been a colonial power, put as much effort into monumentalizing its capital city as if it had been.

A monumental manner for the extended state

The constitution of the Yugoslav state government, significantly bigger than that of the Kingdom of Serbia, looked to immediate enlargement of the existing and construction of new edifices to house the new political leadership and state administration. For example, the existing State Council, (which would be moved to the already-started National Assembly more than a decade later, in 1936), the National Bank, the Ministry of Buildings, the Ministry of Military Affairs and Military Academy were altered in a quick period of only three years after the proclamation of the controversial Vidovdan Constitution. A radical transformation of Belgrade's urban scenery was articulated through the size of upcoming grand projects, purposively clustered around the historically defined topoi, such as the early nineteenth-century Great Barrack. Still, the question of style played a persuasive role in anticipating an image of the majestic capital. The first wave of extensions paid tribute to the existing compositional and formal schemes, thereby the newly added wings, usually protruding into the neighboring parcels, unreservedly mimicked their neo-Renaissance predecessors, rooted in German and Austrian polytechnic teachings. However, the commitment to the previously canonized Central European codes was short-lived. The generational shift in the profession on one side, and the influx of Russian architects, on the other, opened a new page of development within the public sector. Until the late 1920s, a new version of academic Historicism, still connected to the neo-Renaissance yet with significant stylistic and proportional twists, dominated on most public projects – the style defined by architectural historians as Belgrade post-Academism.[8]

Fueled by enthusiasm about Belgrade's new role, Milan Stojadinović, the minister of finances, and Nikola Pašić, the prime minister, considered the most powerful Serbian politician of all time, initiated the urban transformation of the area around the Great Barrack, along Knez Miloša Boulevard. Their vision resulted in the development of the "state-axis,"[9] a bunch of large-scale edifices for state administration flanking the ceremonial path toward the royal residence in Topčider. The development started from Miloš's demolished residence next to the military headquarters and was envisioned as a complex of governmental institutions named Financial Park, compositionally culminating at the crossing between Knez Miloša and Nemanjina [Duke Nemanja's] streets. It was at this precisely regulated intersection, opening dawn through Nemanjina Street toward the semicircular Wilson Square and the Railway Station, where three new ministries were built during the mid-1920s – the Ministry of Agriculture, the Ministry of Finances and the Ministry of Defense.

The Ministry of Agriculture[10] was the first to be conceptualized through an architectural competition, announced in 1921, when enthusiasm for building in the capital city still blossomed among Croatian and Slovenian architects. The excitement in the architectural profession throughout the country, however, lasted until the jury proclaimed the winning entry. It was a busy compilation of historical forms, alluding mostly to the neo-Byzantine stylization, hung over the academically conceptualized pavilion with a dome above the main entrance that attracted the jury members to award young Dragiša Brašovan[11] the first prize. The choice of winning design provoked negative criticism against unskilled composition and naïve "national"-colored ornamentation; yet even more irritating were the power games in decision-making and irregularities in the work of the jury, whose chair Nikola Nestorović was no less than the father of Brašovan's collaborator in the winning project, Bogdan Nestorović. Brašovan's neo-Byzantine, or Serbo-Byzantine episode would remain a hot theme in further discussions as a paradoxical experiment in respect to the rest of architect's otherwise highly respected career:

> What pushed Brašovan and [Bogdan] Nestorović to consequently develop their project for the Ministry of Agriculture in a spirit of Serbian style, although it is well known that they personally did not incline towards such a manner, remains an unanswered question [...] The authors' willingness to work in this style reveals their pragmatism in attempts to please the jury. The luck of true romantic sensibility instead of picking up from the catalogues of academism is what they missed in this project [...] Brašovan's next competition project for the Ministry of Finances already showed more liberal and imaginative approach to interpreting of old Byzantine heritage, yet it was still far away from immediate Serbian traditions.[12]

What has been the most confusing part in discussion about Brašovan's problematic experiment with medievalism lies in the vague understanding of a Serbian-national style, delivered from the romantic design process, and its correlation to a broader context of Byzantine heritage, subordinated to Central European academic schemes. To please the jury, consisted solely of Serbian architects, Brašovan took a chance to experiment with what he saw as the Serbo-Byzantine, and from that perspective his approach was romantic. It was exactly this departure from the learned academic solutions that attracted the most Serbian criticism after he had been announced as the winner. "Brašovan's vibrant and luxurious Byzantine tone did not achieve a quality of 'official solemnity' necessary for this type of buildings,"[13] claimed the renewed architectural critic, Dimitrije M. Leko,[14] and, in a similar tone, wider Serbian criticism attacked Brašovan's homage to only

Orthodox-Christian heritage in the program to represent the "tri-tribal" instead of a solely Serbian identity.

Architectural societies from Croatia and Slovenia also reacted against the chosen project, yet no attention was paid to the question of style in service of a national program. Their frustration resulted from the luck of transparency and clear procedure in the work of jury and their competence to judge, because of low respect for the Serbian architectural establishment in comparison to Croatian and Slovenian architectural circles, which had grown from the Habsburg educational system. The reaction was even worse when the politicians not the architects discarded the competition results and made new decisions about development of the Financial Park away from the public eye.[15] Finally, out of blue, the Ministry of Agriculture ended in hands of Nikolai Krasnov,[16] employee of the Ministry of Buildings,[17] previously engaged on projects for the Russian court.

Following the crisis of Brašovan's wining proposal, Krasnov, who had just fled from the communist takeover in Russia, received an opportunity to execute a monumental ensemble of two ministries – one for agriculture and another for finances, which would, because of their volume and pompous tone, define the most prominent intersection on the state-axis. Their coherent composition, consisting of identical façades accentuated by domes over semicircular vestibules, was not only configuring the strategic intersection but also framing the vista towards the Railway Station (Figure 4.2). The concept was adopted from some older commissions for Russian tsar that Krasnov had received after an architectural competition entry held in

Figure 4.2 Krasnov's Ministries at the intersection with the State Axis (Photo Archive Miloš Jurišić)

St. Petersburg in 1908.[18] Once the final decision about the project was signed by the government administration, the construction of two structures was completed in a stunningly short period of only three years. King Aleksandar was personally pleased by their impressive look, rich decoration, oversized details and vibrant volumes.[19]

Besides Krasnov, an entire generation of experienced Russian emigrants found Belgrade a welcoming place for settling down after the Red Revolution. Recent studies have shown that over seventy Russian architects practiced throughout the territory of today's Serbia, enjoying a privileged status.[20] They became highly ranked associates at the government-run institutions, the Ministry of Buildings and the Ministry of Defense, and were appointed professors at the Faculty of Architecture. King Aleksandar was personally involved in making the "Russian brothers feel like working for their own country, for their people, for their ruler and king."[21] This Russian presence also served as a tool for promoting multiculturalism, although tsarist Russian emigrants only settled in the larger Yugoslav cities with predominately Serbian, meaning Orthodox-Christian, populations. Despite the fact that many of them were Russian Jews, their background was a tool for emphasizing the pan-Slavic brotherhood linked to the East Roman imperial context.

Governmental edifices continued growing around the Financial Park and state-axis through the 1930s, yet this was not the only fast-developing area of public projects financed from state funds. Recognized as the leading center of higher education in the country, Belgrade University spread its new facilities within the area of the University District, previously vacant land used for horse racing at the Boulevard of King Aleksandar, behind Tašmajdan Park. Although some pre-WWI initiatives had already recognized the potential of this location for dislocation and enlargement of the faculties, the precise function and disposition of buildings were not defined until the approval of regulatory plan from 1921, which coincided with the competition for the Master Plan of the same year.

Similar to the vague procedure in appointing architects for designs of governmental buildings on the state-axis, the architects assigned to the university projects were also chosen thanks to their strong connections with politicians. In this case, it was the rector of Belgrade University and the professor of law, Slobodan Jovanović, skillful in maneuvering through the everyday politics who ensured the influx of money for this significant national development. As a country where more than 50 percent of the population was illiterate, the kingdom received immediate funds for the improvement of education, considered as urgent as the reconstruction of destroyed building stock and infrastructures, after the Treaty of Versailles of 1919, when the Western powers decided to support modernization processes of the new member of the League of Nations. The first large donation of $100,000 arrived from the Carnegie Endowment, eager to invest into the construction of the first University Library in today's Serbia, yet under the condition that progress was quick and that the benefactor would have full insight into the design.

Karlsruhe and Berlin-trained Nikola Nestorović and Dragutin Đorđević,[22] well-established professors from the first generation of the Belgrade architecture faculty, received the commission for the University Library probably based on their pre-WWI reputation and connections with the rector. Their preliminary design was done on short notice due to the request by Carnegie to receive the project by a certain date. Upon the approval from the United States, Jovanović managed to exploit not only the initial sum from Carnegie but also to raise extra funds from the state budget and convince the municipal government to waive the land costs. By the end of the same year, the cornerstone was ceremonially laid by the king and the prompt work on construction was completed in 1926. The fully equipped library was consecrated on the University Day dedicated to the saints Cyril and Methodius – Greek missionaries who translated the Bible from Greek to the Old Slavonic language, and thereby celebrated among all Slavs since the ninth century.[23]

The success with the University Library inspired further development in the University District, and the politicians in charge of fundraising reacted quickly, taking advantage of Belgrade's role as the main capital city. The same day the library was consecrated, the cornerstone for the first student dormitory was laid in the neighboring block, in today's Saints Cyril and Methodius Park. The inauguration speeches at both events announced the construction of the Technical Faculty between these two sites,[24] also to be designed by Nikola Nestorović. Both of Nestorović's monumental compositions for the University District were developed quickly as free-standing, academically conceived tripartite palazzos, with immense entrance zones topped by tympani, facing the boulevard (see Figure 4.3). Placed on the same regulation

Figure 4.3 University Library, Technical Faculty and the Students' Dormitory in the University District (Photo Archive Miloš Jurišić)

line right next to each other, their position assumed further development of an urban ensemble, with the library being the focal point. A coherent urban scheme anticipating the development in the neighboring lot toward the city and on the other side of the Boulevard was verified through the Master Plan in 1924. Yet, it differed from Nestorović's original vision inserted into the regulatory plan of 1921, put into effect in a rush at the request of foreign benefactors. Nestorović managed to maintain his idea, stepping over the newer concept verified through the Master Plan, therefore the completion of the University District as a coherent urban whole was corrupted. This would be particularly noticeable after the next two projects, the State Archive and the Student Dormitory, designed by the government-employed Russian architects were completed, showing the inconsistencies of the urban planning of Belgrade's second most important district to be urbanistically monumentalized.

Architectural critics addressed the weaknesses of Nestorović's design for the Technical Faculty, addressing the issues of authenticity as well as the context:

> The project for Technical Faculty [...] looks like as if was placed accidentally without any relation to the surrounding buildings. Its layout is almost identical to the polytechnic in Berlin-Charlottenburg, yet all of the good features from Charlottenburg were neglected, while only the bad ones were adopted [...] Keeping in mind the high aspirations of our technical studies, we wonder why the picture of central building for Technical Faculty in Belgrade is so sad. Why isn't the picture as it should have been can be explained only by the lack of knowledge, lack of seriousness and lack of love and commitment for the project.[25]

The negative words of accusation on behalf of the oldest generation of professors for plagiarism were emphasized by the fact that Nestorović's collaborators Dragutin Đorđević and Andra Stevanović – at some point rector himself – took over the realization of the Serbian Royal Academy of Sciences and Arts a year before the design for Technical Faculty. After a rough, negative campaign, they managed to turn down an earlier project for the Academy by Konstantin Jovanović due to its monumental scale and ambitious details,[26] yet the submitted project for the Technical Faculty turned to be oddly similar to the outline, composition and neo-Renaissance detailing of Jovanović's terminated design.

Nikolai Krasnov received the project for the State Archive, on the lot perpendicular to the University Library, based on the reputation of the two ministries on the state-axis, while another Russian, Georgy Pavlovich Kovalevsky, designed the Student Dormitory. As a young employee of the municipality building office, Kovalevsky received the chance to build the first modern facility of that kind in the country, considered modern because of the technological innovations and attentiveness to hygienic conditions. The formal code of this lavish palazzo incorporated into landscaped greenery with traditional layout and robust decoration bore imperial Russian reminiscences. King Aleksandar was personally involved in supervising the project, after the scandal regarding Milan Stojadinović, the minister of finances who was a bitter political opponent to his rule. Allegedly, Stojadinović abused money from the German war reparations through some illegal transactions, an affair that ended with the confiscation of his private bank account. Despite a widespread belief that King Aleksandar paid for the project, the construction was mainly supported from the account confiscated from Stojadinović and free labor provided by prisoners. Kovalevsky was also in charge of the urban position of the Student Dormitory at the top of the triangular park across the Technical Faculty (see Figure 4.3), attuned to his broader vision for completing the University District.

The tone of all new edifices in the new university area, like the development on the state-axis, was distinctively "anti-Modernist," stylistically closer to the nineteenth-century developments than to the up-to-date Art Deco trends. Despite the growing tensions between Russians and domestic architects during the 1920s, it was the monumental Academism that dominated all state-funded public programs from governmental to higher-educational. Even those architects who had grown as advocates of the Art Nouveau stylization, such as Nikola Nestorović and Andra Stevanović, shifted towards more traditional academic patterns during the 1920s. Despite the tight competition with Russian émigrés, their late works remained celebrated as the epitome of what Bogdan Nestorović defined as Belgrade post-Academism.[27]

Had the monumental "post-Academism" continued dominating the Belgrade architectural scene after the proclamation of King Aleksandar's dictatorship it could have provided persuasive evidence of his totalitarian politics. Yet, the climate in the architectural profession was changing and 1929 was to be remembered for several architectural events that heralded the shift from Academism to Modernism.

The pivotal indication of Modernist "victory" was the competition for Terazije Terrace, an undefined slope linking the city's epicenter with the bank of the Sava River, won by a young graduate from Czech Technical University, Nikola Dobrović.[28] His radical solution, characterized by plain, "weightless" volumes, an open-grid structural system, cascaded flat roofs and transparent façades, was an unprecedented design, "anticipating such advanced urban visions to never be fully understood neither by his contemporary fellows nor by the future generations."[29] Dobrović's Terazije Terrace has been discussed in a tone of dignified piety and written about by only a few self-confident scholars.[30] Either because of certain "eyes which could not see [and] failed in perceiving its authentic value" or some other mundane, practical matters, the project never advanced toward realization, despite being incorporated in the regulatory plan of 1938.

The penetration of Modernist aesthetics on the government-funded buildings was visible only outside the city limits. The first large-scale ensemble

Figure 4.4 Dubovy's Observatory (Photo Archive Miloš Jurišić)

to be recognized as a Modernist breakthrough was the off-campus science center, the Astronomic Observatory (see Figure 4.4) moved from the district of Vračar to Zvezdara hill. Founded in the 1880s, the observatory was an internationally recognized institution, run by world renowned scientists Milan Nedeljković and Đorđe Stanojević. When the government agreed to spend a part of World War I reparation monies on higher educational facilities, three million gold German marks or $600,000 went on optical and meteorological equipment for the observatory facilities.[31] In 1923, some of most advanced telescopes in Europe arrived from the Zeiss Company, but could not be installed in the existing nineteenth-century pavilions. It was under the leadership of a new director, Vojislav Mišković, that the institution managed to ensure funds from the state budget for the new construction on a five-acre piece of land at Zvezdara. The land was granted by Belgrade municipality, which also provided an architectural design from its technical department. The architect in charge was a Czech native, Jan Dubový, who started working for the municipality in 1924, after leaving a position at Matěj Blecha architectural firm, through which he arrived in Serbia right after his graduation from Czech Technical University. Matěj Blecha was a well-established practice from Prague with branches spread through the region, recognized for its distinct Historicist-flavored designs. Dubový had been exposed to Modernism through his professor Anonín Engel, known for Podolí Water Station in Prague, which synthesized the latest technologies with refined Modernist aesthetics, recognized in Czech historiography as "Purist neo-Classicism."[32] Dubový was also a keen follower of new urban theories addressing uncontrolled growth of the industrial city and its impact on housing for the unprivileged citizens – a theme he explored in articles published in *Tehnički list* from Zagreb and *Savremena opština* from Belgrade.[33] Dubový was one of the four founders of the Grupa arhitekata modernog pravca or GAMP [Group of Architects of Modern Orientation].[34]

With the commission for the observatory, Dubový gained an opportunity to probe the "garden-city" concept on a concrete site. He conceptualized the complex as a cluster of pavilions irregularly sunk into the greenery, following the configuration of the sloped terrain and the cardinal directions. The size and shape of pavilions depended on their functions, either the experimental stations, with telescopes and measuring devices, or residential units with research and study areas. The pavilions were connected only by a web of pavements mingling towards the largest building of the complex for the research, the administration and the library. With its sober, classically articulated portico, topped by the technologically equipped dome allowing for star observations, it was the focal gathering point for the researchers, most of whom lived there. The organic urban layout intermingled with the natural surroundings along with the bold aesthetics: plain white façades and huge, cage-looking windows were observed with admiration among Dubový's fellows from the GAMP. The leading chronicler of the GAMP, Branislav Kojić, acknowledged Dubový's complex as "the first monument of explicit Modernism in Serbia."[35] The completion and opening of the scientific complex in 1932, considered ultra-Modern by its contemporaries, made a great impact on the city's self-esteem during tough political times. The complex was thoroughly photographed and publicized in the daily press. As an homage to the project, the entire area of the expanding city close to the observatory was named Zvezdara, after the word "zvezda," meaning a star in the Slavic languages.

Even with being applauded as the Modernist breakthrough, the observatory complex demonstrated modernity rather for the site planning and adjustment to technological needs than for radical Functionalist aesthetics, as was the case with projects by Zagreb-based architects of the time. The sense of monumentality in Dubový's project could be traced back to Czech Purist Classicism – besides the already mentioned Antonin Engel, also to works by Alois Mezera in charge of the Czechoslovakian Embassy in Belgrade, designed at the time when Dubový was appointed for the project. Dubový compositional schemes and neo-Classical articulation, enhanced by bas-reliefs, were also attuned to Art Deco, steadily conquering Europe and the United States after the Paris show of 1925. The line between Art Deco and Modernism was hardly visible during the interwar development, as much in Belgrade as elsewhere around the world. It was only a few attempts by Serbian architects, such as those by Nikola Dobrović, to radicalize the notion of modern and bring it closer to Central European Functionalism

102 *National architectures in the unified nation*

than French Decorativism. The spirit of Modernist monumentality pursued through the variations on the Art Deco theme was a common ground in Belgrade through the late 1930s.

The significant shift toward Modernism in public architecture was first noticed in Hugo Ehrlich's project for the Yugoslav Union Bank in Kralja Petra [King Petar] Street, with Knez Mihailova the main retail spine of the old town. Erlich's layout was of the early Modernist origins from Vienna, like Viktor Kovačić's Stock Exchange in Zagreb, which he completed after Kovačić's death. The skeletal construction enabling the open floor plan of the main banking hall was lit from the flat glass lantern over the central aisle and simply clad in rich marble, the natural texture of which was the only decorative motive spread throughout the space. Although the use of visible modern materials – steal, glass and rubber – were allowed only in areas hidden from customers' eyes, it was a few rows of Wassily chairs, designed at the Bauhaus by Marcel Breuer, which made the central banking hall feel unprecedentedly modern, especially in the context of the exposed commercial architecture. Although Erlich collaborated with Adolf Loos on the project for Villa Karma more than twenty years earlier, he decidedly shifted from Historicism to Modernism only in 1928,[36] the year he received the commission in Belgrade after seeing the Exhibition of Czech architecture circulating throughout the country.

Erlich did not hide his frustration about dealing with "conservativism of nouveau-riche architectural establishment and building bureaucracy of Belgrade,"[37] yet a more explicit reason for complaint about these matters was had by young, Zagreb-based Josip Pičman, who won the competition for the Main Post Office and Postal Saving Bank across from the still-unfinished National Assembly in 1930.[38] The jury consisted of well-established architects of the older generation, Dragutin Đorđević from Belgrade, Janko Holjac from Zagreb and Jože Plečnik from Ljubljana, who, despite their mature age, recognized the potential of Pičman's boldly Modernist design characterized by an open-plan, skeletal structural system, transparent façades and light volumes. Allegedly, when King Aleksandar learned about the continuous glass surfaces to rise next to the National Assembly, he ordered that the façades be redesigned,[39] and a Russian-born employee of the Ministry of Buildings, Vasili Androsov, was invited to clad Pičman's skeleton with stone blocks chiseled from Jablanica granite,[40] The realization of weird compilation between Pičman's and Androsov's projects started in 1935, a year after the king was assassinated in Marseilles. In 1936, Josip Pičman committed suicide, unable to cope with the disappointment; besides the main post in Belgrade, a couple of more projects he received in architectural competitions failed in realization. The building wrapped in stone was festively opened in 1938 with an inscription recognizing Josef Pičman as the architect. His name was carved into a roughly polished granite block over the overwhelming colonnade above one of the entrances. Pičman was commemorated on an architectural element that was the antipode to the transparency he had intended to achieve.

Imperial Belgrade 103

A delicate political climate after the proclamation of dictatorship fueled anger about Serbian supremacy, yet King Aleksandar's involvement in decisions about architectural and urban development did not please the Serbian side either. The position of the Main Post Office across from the National Assembly was initiated by the king; although in collision to the broader urban vision about the cross-section of Price Miloš and King Aleksandar Boulevard. The edifice was longitudinally stretched along Takovska Street, continuing from Price Miloš Boulevard, in front of the second largest Orthodox church in the city, St. Mark's to be developed by the Krstić brothers, in that way blocking a visual connection between the St. Mark's and the Assembly and the Court, as had been anticipated by the Master Plan. Hiding the ethnically overloaded religious structure by the programmatically neutral Post Office – the underlying motive of the king's initiative – was understood by some public Serbian voices as an attempt at pleasing the Croatian and Slovenian, in other words the Catholic side.

There is no better evidence of how Belgrade interwar architecture shifted from Historicism to monumental Modernism than two masterworks by Dragiša Brašovan, the Air Force Headquarters and the State Printing Plant, commissioned at the critical moment between the proclamation of dictatorship and the assassination of King Aleksandar. As a tactical player in complex professional relationships, Brašovan was a maestro of "architectural syncretism,"[41] capable of pleasing the public eye as much as the professional judgment since winning the competition for the Ministry of Agriculture. He departed from eclectic Historicism towards decorative Modernism after Dobrović's success with the Terazije Terrace in 1929. Declaring that "all that has been done until now must be forgotten and architecture must start from the new beginning,"[42] he joined the GAMP the same year, when works of its members started being on display and noticed by developers.

The State Printing Plant was Brašovan's first large-scale Modernist project gained through the architectural competition of 1933 for a different location.[43] When the development moved from downtown to the newly cut boulevard of Vojvoda Mišić, an industrial alternative heading to Topčider, Brašovan altered the original composition of broken volumes into a monumental collage of cubes and prisms to fit into a new site against the hilly backdrop, a steep slope of Senjak facing the Sava River. This was the first time Brašovan experimented with asymmetrical forms, although still within the predetermined scheme. Some of his contemporaries found the result innovative, while the others, such as the leading voice in the Modernist breakthrough, Nikola Dobrović, attacked Bašovan's project as inconsistent, only shallowly attached to the principles of Modernism:

> The technical program gave Bašovan an opportunity to react more bravely and to play with the expressive means of contemporary architecture narrative. Instead, the architect struggled to integrate the various

differentiated programs and technological requirements into a single building. The division of the overall massing among many motifs and substructures and the separation of the composition is taken to the limit. Had been taken further this disunion would create an impression that the building mass comprised a bunch of independently conceived objects.[44]

Unquestionably, the engineering and technological achievements were the main attributes distinguishing the State Printing Plant from other contemporary realizations in Belgrade. It was the first building in Serbia to be conceived as an open grid plan fully executed from reinforced concrete. The structural skeleton was "veiled" in the collage of glass surfaces and embraced by "meshes" of horizontal and vertical strips of various widths. Its large scale, structural methods and modern materials – cement and steel conjoined with the program – were the main attributes, as was highlighted in the daily press:

The State Printing Plant is the biggest building ever built in our country but also in the Balkans. As the fourth largest printing plant in Europe, by its size and modern technologies, it shows the attempts of our government to meet the growing needs for books so evident in all regions of our country.[45]

To learn more about advanced printing technologies, Brašovan took a study trip to Germany where he saw works by the Expressionists, an experience he would use in the design for another large-scale public palace, the Air Force Headquarters, designed simultaneously. However, the State Printing Plant used modern technologies as a grounding narrative for explaining how illiterate peasantry might convert into nationally conscious citizenry, while the Air Force Headquarters (Figure 4.5) engaged formal symbolism in fostering an image of national strength and integrity. The powerful composition of expressive forms, literally evoking shapes of a plane consisted of solid and glass horizontals, cut through by a soaring vertical in the central axis, a triangular stairway shaft above the main entrance. The attributes of both monumental and the modern gained by means of expressive formalism were further boosted by shiny qualities of untraditional materials and anticipated sounds of elevators, radars and antennas.

The concept of just completed Air Force Palace in Zemun is fully successful for its purpose and function. During the design, the leading idea was that the building represents and symbolizes our air forces. Indeed, with its layout, the cast iron colonnades and the shiny beak it looks like a real plane [...] Two elevators run through the central tower reaching its top level with the meteorological station and the radio-communication center. A tall antenna reaching into the sky serves both

Figure 4.5 Brašovan's Air Force Headquarters (Photo Archive Miloš Jurišić)

a practical as well as aesthetical role. The building is certainly one of the most beautiful and the most monumental buildings in our country and a true representative of modern architecture.[46]

Located in Zemun's old core, this was the first seat of the Royal Yugoslav Army to be built beyond the boundaries of the hundred-year-old Serbian military center around Prince Miloš's barracks. Prior to the war, with 70 percent of the population being Croats, Zemun was culturally and economically tied to Zagreb rather than Belgrade. After the Serbian army took over the city in December 1918, Zemun became part of Srem District, one of the thirty-three territorial units of the kingdom, named after the ancient city of Sirmium. For the first time in its long history, Zemun was integrated into Belgrade metropolitan area in 1934, when the road and tram bridge over the Sava, named after the recently assassinated King Aleksandar, was put in use. As was observed in the daily press, "a vibrant atmosphere of fast-growing Yugoslav capital finally spread on the left bank of the Sava."[47] With the construction of the Air Force Headquarters, which started the same year, Zemun was included in an integrative national narrative on another level.[48] The symbolical plane's "beak," mingled with Baroque belltowers of both Catholic as well as Orthodox-Christian churches, started ruling over the skyline, which had been controlled by the Habsburgs for centuries.

The Kingdom of Serbia established an Air Force in 1911 for fighting in the Balkan Wars. The military airport and base for soldiers trained at French pilot academies were built in the suburb of Banjica, ten kilometers to the south of the main military headquarters. Another Air Force base was established in Novi Sad, the regional center of Vojvodina, predominantly settled by Serbs as part of the Austro-Hungarian defense in 1913. After Vojvodina became part of Royal Yugoslavia, the base in Novi Sad replaced Banjica as the county's main aircraft headquarters with the pilot academy. The further expansion of aircraft forces required centralization of the existing bases to be controlled from the new establishment somewhere in-between the two existing aircraft garrisons.

A large portion of Zemun close to the confluence of the Sava into the Danube was a marshy land to be drained and filled-in as a symbolic act of overcoming the previous border between the Ottomans and the Habsburgs that had separated South Slavs before the unification. It was anticipated to grow into a modern district named New Belgrade, the development of which started with the construction of first civic airport in the country, after WWII moved to the town of Surčin, ten kilometers to the west. After the opening in 1927, Belgrade Airport served flights to Paris, Bucharest and Istanbul, becoming a serious competition to the Orient Express, hosting fourteen international flights per day by 1937. The Air Force Headquarters was placed in the same neighborhood for a good reason: programmatically and aesthetically both programs pursued an image of the nation as belonging to the modernized world, as the entire new city on the left bank of Sava that New Belgrade should have become. A dream of national unity in progress was visualized as the Air Force Headquarters "beak" overlooked the airport, as was observed in the daily press of the time:

> On a clear spring day, from the beak of Air Force Headquarters one may enjoy observing planes taking-off and landing to Belgrade airport; moreover, all activities at the airport can be controlled from here.[49]

That was not all. On a clear day, the monumental corpus of the State Print Plant, sturdily anchored to the slope of Senjak, was also visible from the same spot of Air Force Headquarters. With these two governmental edifices by Brašovan, Belgrade's interwar Monumentalism finally extended the limits of eclectic neo-styles. Besides shifting towards the Modernist aesthetic, Brašovan also managed to extend an accustomed concept of historical urban limits and establish new spatial relations between the faraway topoi. By conceiving new referential points at the edges of the urban fabric, he framed what would be considered metropolitan Belgrade – a desired framework for the fast-rising city looking for an equal status among the European nations.

Monumentalizing the everyday

> History has not left Belgrade a developed center as in other European cities. Thus, there is no more important task than to finally build up and harmonize the central area of our capital in a consistent manner. We cannot give up this idea. This is the priority not only of the municipality but of the entire country that Belgrade becomes a representative metropolis.[50]

The regulation and embellishment of city center had been a goal pursued by politicians and urbanists since Emilijan Josimović's regulatory plan for Belgrade from 1867, yet the fast growth during the 1920s and 1930s raised the question of the city limits within which the comprehensive interventions would take place. The clash between the center and the periphery coincided with the social inequality and lack of opportunities, especially for the poor and newcomers from the countryside. The polemics on discrepancies between the development in the center versus the periphery grew on the political level, as well as among the ordinary citizens. Yet, the tensions between the center and the periphery reached far beyond the local Belgrade boundaries to the national level. Discontent about the amount of state funds put into the reconstruction of the capital city culminated in parts of the kingdom previously subjected to Austria-Hungarian authorities, originally more developed than the eastern regions. The harshest criticism came from Zagreb, the strongest economic and industrial city, put down to the secondary position instead of remaining the leading center of Yugoslavness as had been anticipated by the Illyrians.

Belgrade's municipal budget was used for street pavements, lighting, horticulture, benches, public monuments and fountains in the downtown area. Lacking the basic infrastructure such as street surfaces, water supply and sewage, inhabitants from the periphery insisted on allocation of the funds to projects in underdeveloped neighborhoods. With the extension of city limits, the new peripheral areas did not gain much for being administratively incorporated into the metropolis. The inhabitants from the periphery were overburdened with high city taxes while their neighborhoods stayed neglected and their living conditions remained at the poverty level.

The poor were being rapidly pushed from the center, clearing lots, whose real-estate value was dramatically increasing, for upscale developments accessible to a small percentage of citizens. In collision with monumental transformations of the civic core, the rising population consisted predominately of the poor, settled in unplanned, unhygienic "patches" mushrooming at the city edges. Belgrade was the city where more than 70 percent of people lived in poverty and only 23 percent of the housing stock in met hygiene standards as estimated by the statistic overview from 1932.[51] "Belgrade was the city of the poor, the city of hovels and back-yard huts, the city of chaotic and uncontrolled development, of bad infrastructure and illogical use of open spaces."[52]

Housing for the poor was addressed by the municipal authorities to an extent allowed by the unbalanced economy. The construction of the first housing complex for low-income families by Jelisaveta Načić was started in the lower Dorćol area in 1911. The project resumed as a sequence of modest pavilions to enclose the previously delineated urban block in 1922–1924. In the Master Plan, planners proposed few districts for low-income housing. Accordingly, the realization of workers' pavilions in Svetog Nikole [St. Nickola's] Street in 1929, Humska Street in 1930 and the social housing colony in Severni [North] Boulevard, from 1937 to 1941, financed from the municipal funds, were conceptualized by a renewed urban theorist and practitioner, employed at the municipal direction, Branko Maksimović.[53] Two gender-separated facilities for temporarily unemployed workers, the Women's and Men's Worker Shelters by Jan Dubový, from 1928, have been the most discussed examples of socially engaged architecture of interwar Belgrade, mainly for their Modernist outlook.[54] Dubový employed functional layouts, hygienic standards, clean lines, large openings and easy-to-clean finishes in both shelters. Maksimović insisted on the same values, yet Dubový's shelters were placed within the boundaries of the "građevinski reon" [urban area] defining the inner city. Consequently, they were incorporated into traditionally conceived street façades, obeying the rule of being well-styled in respect to their traditional-looking neighbors. Thus, Dybový's compositional schemes were neo-Classical, stylistically reminiscent of his Astronomical Observatory.

Certain social housing projects resulted from initiatives by the state government to improve the living conditions of its employees. For example, the Ministry of Transportation erected various types of apartment buildings for the workers and staff of the Yugoslav Railway. While the administration was placed in immense townhouses in the inner city close to the railway station in Savska Street, the housing colony for workers was pushed a few kilometers further away, to an unregulated slope of today's Prokop Station. The townhouses for administration performed monumentality with their size and massing rather than decoration. Their long, heavy street façades with small windows resembled military barracks, yet the massive silhouettes were highlighted with turrets and dormers inserted into a steep roof. On the other hand, the colony in Prokop consisted of one-story barracks of modest size with no sewage and running water, hence they reached a lower standard than those designed by Branko Maksimović. A recognizable effort on improving the living conditions of the poor was made by wealthy benefactors, the merchant family of Persida Milenković and factory owners Vlada Ilić and Đorđe Vajfert [Georg Weifert].

The process of "cleansing" the central zone of unhygienic dwellings and small business, dating back to the early 1920s, culminated in the following decade. The most frequent building type to replace hovels was the "multi-story rental apartment townhouse" built by motivated developers taking advantage of the government's program of ten-year tax exemptions and low-interest loans; both measures fashioned to boost the fast reshaping of the city.[55] "With a growing appetite for becoming rich overnight, most investments have gone into rental properties: the renting real-estate has become the most popular business, safe and effortless," complained a contemporary chronicler.[56] The building boom, however, had an impact only on a limited area delineated by circular route of tram No. 2 and lasted until the outbreak of World War II. After the war, the communist government confiscated the houses as the reminders of decadent pre-revolutionary bourgeois and turned them into collective property. Most original owners as well as wealthy tenants fled the country to leave space for the communist elite to settle in, hence the evidence of the pre-WWII social milieu remains unclear.

The task of the architects in charge was to envision a modern urban life of wealthy tenants but also to please the not-always-articulated aesthetic judgments of the nouveau riche. Their efforts resulted in the apartment scheme recognized as "beogradski stan" [Belgrade apartment], considered one the key features of Belgrade interwar architecture. The scheme refers to a spacious apartment with two entrances, one for family and guests, another for servants. The representational entrance with lobby opens into a large, centrally positioned hall for formal receptions called "salon" – the focal point toward which all other family rooms gravitate,[57] while the rear entrance leads to the kitchen, storage, bathroom and servant's room. The rental townhouses were usually extravagantly decorated. The leading names of Serbian Modernism, such as the Krstić brothers mastered the "Belgrade apartment" spatial configuration in projects whose stylistic features varied between Historicism and decorative Modernism to please the taste of investors. For example, around 1929, they completed two rental properties, Šojat House and Madam Jelinić House, both well-known for the implementation of Belgrade apartment layouts, yet incomparable from the standpoint of façade stylization. While Šojat did not feel comfortable about approving the Art Deco instead of the Historicist façades, Jelinić encouraged experimentation, so that the street elevation of her house reached a surprising level of abstraction. Krstićs composed the front façade for Jelinić simply from pieces of dark polished marble and greenish limestone set into Terranova plastering, the technique that had only recently begun receiving extensive attention in technical journals, manuals, handbooks and advertising brochures throughout Europe.[58] The asymmetrical collage of the ground floors was in sharp contrast to the precise ordering of the upper zone, the symmetrical composition of which was highlighted by abstract cornices and pilasters cladded in stone. The Art Deco époque sensibility culminated with a bas-relief – a heroic narrative reminiscent of Meštrović's heroes from the Kosovo Cycle incorporated into the granite and stone cladding of the entrance level – which would become a standard motif spread on street façades in the 1930s.

110 *National architectures in the unified nation*

The taste of developers quickly switched toward the Modernist style, yet the quest for monumentality was unchanged. Instead, the Historicist façades from the previous decade, plain and sturdy compositions lavished with the Art Deco details and rhetorical reliefs, were in high demand. The belief in French-Serbian friendship, rooted in common victories in the Great War, inspired many Belgrade intellectuals, including architects, to go for future training in Paris rather than other cultural centers of Europe. The architects were also introduced to new ideas through French architectural publications. French Modernism was a top-ranked topic among architects, yet it was the works by Robert Mallet-Stevens rather than the ideas by Le Corbusier that Belgrade architectural audience preferred to learn about.[59] Even the youngest and most progressive fellows hardly explored radical Functionalism coming from the Bauhaus and its circle, experimenting neither with bold forms nor with the new materials in search of transparency. The rental apartment townhouse, as the most common program of interwar architecture, did not challenge the compact sturdiness of the traditional urban blocks and regulation lines.[60]

A surprising exception from this pattern was a rental property of doctor Đurić at a demanding location in Prizrenska Street (Figure 4.6), designed by the leading voice of the GAMP, a French pupil, Branislav Kojić,[61] who managed to turn a narrow building lot and steep-sloped terrain into advantages for his design. Instead of dull differentiation between the street and rare façades, Kojić envisioned a dynamic composition of volumes consisting of overlapping plain surfaces, strip windows, horizontal lines of protruding balcony parapets, railings and roof deck overhangs. All three façades were considered equally important regarding the cardinal directions and topography, therefore there was no single point in which axiality played any role. The cascaded collage of bare geometric elements culminated at two angles: one opening toward the bottom of Prizrenska Street and the other, more geometrically pronounced, toward the Sava River, providing the occupants with unrestricted views of the future New Belgrade. Kojić's project was the first to acknowledge the potential of using the slope a few years after Dobrović's unrealized Terazije Terrace. The completion of Đurić's property coincided with the opening of the bridge with tram tracks to Zemun. As Kojić recorded in his writings:

> Before the bridge to Zemun was completed, the view of Belgrade had not been often observed from that side. The situation was that most of buildings on this slope were showing unfinished backs toward the fields of Zemun. Now, the views from the bridge while approaching from Zemun side point out to how the undefined gables are creating an ugly image of Belgrade.[62]

Kojić's project was the first to consciously challenge old practices of taking into consideration only the main street façades. The project for Đurić's

Imperial Belgrade 111

Figure 4.6 Kojić's Apartment Building in Prizrenska Street (Photo Archive Miloš Jurišić)

townhouse inspired a new building ordinance requiring all buildings to be presentable from all sides, which was to be put in effect in 1935.

The development of single-family villas took place in the upscale neighborhoods of Dedinje, Senjak and Topčider. The taste of rich clients varied between neo-Classicism and ethno-inspired Romanticism, only randomly slipping toward the Modernist concepts.[63] Evidence of what kind of Modernism appealed to rich clients was recorded in the first issue of *Arhitektura* [*The Architecture*],[64] established as the leading architectural journal in the country to promote Modernism. In the first issue, the photograph of Villa Milićević (Figure 4.7) by the Krstić brothers, displayed how the keen supporters of a new architectural climate in Belgrade invested in their upscale residences in Topčider. The villa's asymmetrical layout inventively

Figure 4.7 Brothers Krstić's Villa in Topčider (Arhitektura, vol.1, Ljubljana 1931)

incorporated into sloping terrain were the features attuned to Modernist thinking, yet the formal tune was far from the white unornamented abstract compositions associated with the International Style. The two-story volume of the villa was vibrantly articulated by deep horizontal grooves, the shadows of which made a dramatic enhancement visible from street level. The main entrance, accessible by a footbridge between the street and a monumental portico carried by free-standing caryatides, was flanked on both sides by elaborate stairs leading down to the garden. Despite the unusual concept, the stylization in the end made it up for a traditionalist-looking result. The opening issue of *Arhitektura* published designs of two more villas: one from Zagreb and one from Ljubljana, in a politically correct key representing all tribe nations: Villa Pfeffermann by Marko Vidaković and Vladimir Šubic's family house in Ljubljana's suburb of Vrtača. Conceptualized as a sequence of white prisms of different heights, mirroring the interior program lined up along the L-shaped footprint, the Zagreb counterpart demonstrated the openness of local investors for the radical Functionalism, while Šubič's house in Ljubljana showed off a tendency of infusing Classical as well as Mediterranean vernacular motives into the Modernist concepts, influenced by Jože Plečnik.

The development of Belgrade "reon" [zone] as it had been outlined in the regulatory plans was in harsh contrast to the periphery. Yet another, blurrier boundary defining "the city" was in use to point out to the most attractive area for commerce, banking and merchandise. Belgrade was deprived of projects for museums, art pavilions, galleries and performance halls, with only one single building, the National Theater, purposely designed to house a cultural institution of national importance. The only clearly defined public space was Theater Square in front of the National Theater. The acclaimed artistic events from the pre-WWI era, the Yugoslav Art Exhibitions, were installed in adjusted spaces of Kapetan Miša's Endowment and the Second Men High School. The lack of institutionalized cultural venues might be a reason why the growing middle class preferred the alternative culture and populist entertainment that went hand-in-hand with the spread of new technologies and mass media:

> In the decades following the Great War, middle-class citizens grappled to define the parameters of unified national culture but, at the same time, consumed leisure from beyond Yugoslavia's borders. They accommodated entertainment like film, jazz, and cabaret into their cultural palate because they interpreted it as a symbol of European metropolitan modernity.[65]

The first example of art pavilion to be built in Belgrade was designed for the art society Cvijeta Zuzorić,[66] founded in 1919 as an extension of older association of Serbian artists from 1898. The goal of the society was to help Belgrade grow into a cultural metropolis similar to its European counterparts by promoting a national culture of Yugoslavs. Cvijeta Zuzorić received a great support from the Art Department of the Ministry of Education, especially from writers and politicians Vladimir Velmar-Janković and Branislav Nušić, one serving as the secretary and the other as the head of the society. The two of them organized a fundraising campaign for the building, including an architectural competition announced in 1925. The first prize went to Branislav Kojić, just graduated from Paris École Centrale. The pavilion was to be erected behind Princess Ljubica's Konak [Residence], a reminder of the Balkan vernacular traditions fused into the speedily Europeanized Belgrade of the early 1800s. Vladimir Velmar-Janković was a strong supporter of ingenious folk culture, a possible reason why Kojić's design, characterized by low sloped roofs, deep eaves, arcaded porches and traditional material strongly referring to the vernacular forms of the neighboring Konak, won the competition. Kojić started exploring and documenting folk architecture and experimenting with vernacular forms soon after he moved back from Paris. There is no clear evidence about Kojić's connections with Le Corbusier there; however, the way he engaged the vernacular as a counterpart to the modern resonated with Le Corbusier's observations about the potential of the vernacular during his Balkan voyage.

The municipality came to the conclusion that the location next to the Konak was not adequate and finally granted a parcel of land for the pavilion in Lower Kalemegdan as part of the campaign that the fortress to be converted into the city's main leisure district. Moreover, the building was

114 *National architectures in the unified nation*

to be a theatrical framework for entering Lower Kalemegdan from the direction of Kraljevski Trg [Royal Square], historically the Ancient Forum. As soon as Kojić adjusted the earlier proposal to the needs of the new site in 1927, the head of the municipal authority complained about the vernacular forms, "reminding [him] of an oriental caravanserai." He argued: "I have never seen an art pavilion like this in any European city" and suggested that Kojić "make it in a neo-Classical or some other monumental style"[67] if he wanted to build. To meet the quest for monumentality expected for the program and to keep the construction going, Kojić resurfaced the façades into the neo-Classical composition (Figure 4.8) the only stylistically colored project in his entire career. The rest of the structure remained composed from distinct volumes integrated into the surroundings. Despite its stylistic cover, its image achieved the goal of becoming the center for promoting up-do-date art and architectural movements. This was the venue where two exhibitions of modern Yugoslav architecture took place.

The second cultural institution built in interwar Belgrade was Kolarac Endowment, still colloquially called Kolarac. Its benefactor, Ilija Milosavljavić-Kolarac, born in the village of Kolari, became one the wealthiest Serbian merchants of the nineteenth century, whose trust continued supporting national culture after his death. In respect to his will, the endowment initiated the construction of a cultural center and an independent university open to all social groups, but especially to the poor and marginalized. The ambitious program included the first competently designed concert hall, art gallery, conference room and classrooms, with the library for continuing education. The

Figure 4.8 Art Pavilion Cvijeta Zuzorić (Photo Archive Miloš Jurišić)

merchant had owned a large piece of property at a prime location, between Knez Mihailova Street and the Royal Square, a block away from Kapetan Miša's Endowment, around which the main campus of Belgrade University has been formed. Many young architects around the country submitted proposals in an open architectural competition for the Kolarac announced in 1928. The same year, the Exhibition of Czech Architecture traveled through the country, so that the submitted entries reflected an ongoing excitement of what was seen. The next issues of *Arhitektura* presented some of the Modernist-looking entries submitted for the Kolarac: Stanislav Rohrman's anticipating a grid-patterned façade with huge horizontal openings emphasizing the skeletal construction, and Milan Zloković's, proposing voluminous abstract white cube perforated only by a ribbon-window along the piano-nobile.[68] However, the executed edifice was neither positioned in accordance to the competition stipulations, nor executed according to any of the rewarded designs.[69] Finally the project was granted to fifty-five-year-old Petar Bajalović, previously discussed for the collaboration with Ivan Meštrović on the project for Serbian Pavilion at the Rome Exposition of 1911, since he proposed the construction in two phases to be finished at no debt. He pushed the concert hall to the back, and left the portion facing the square for shops and rental office spaces. Consequently, the main façade ended as the tripartite composition with an exaggerated, two-story high "base" and large shop windows, pleasantly decorated to attract renters. Fortunately, the shape and materials of the later completed concert hall met the standards of its European forerunners. As Bajalović recorded, "the walls of the concert hall, its gallery and the stage frame were all covered in walnut lumber from Caucasus for better acoustics."[70]

The beautification of what was defined as "the city" in the Master Plan was a common goal of the state and local governments, but was also supported by private investors: banks, insurance companies, business headquarters, commercial and professional associations, various clubs and societies. Branislav Kojić recorded in his well-documented memoires that more announcements for architectural competitions came from independent enterprises than from the governmental institutions.[71] The most desired for the development of commercial and office spaces and seats of headquarters were the parcels around Terazije. Besides Dobrović's Terazije Terrace, many visionary ideas of how Belgrade's most prestigious urban knot could look, were born by the leading architectural ateliers. A few months after Dobrović's victory, Branislav Kojić submitted a sketch for an immense high-rise at the crown of Terazije, where a shoddy Balkan-style tavern called "Albania" had existed for decades. Kojić not only respected the potential investor's appetite for square footage at the hot location, but he anticipated the overall public excitement about an American-looking skyscraper stuck in the middle of old core as a symbol of national commitment to progress and modernization:

> The sketch for Albania Palace has been not only one of the best Kojić's unrealized projects, but also the best attempt at grasping the spirit of the

116 *National architectures in the unified nation*

modern age. With its skeletal construction, open plan and daring form his proposal stood hand-to-hand with the counterparts from technologically more advanced countries. The fact that skyscrapers rarely existed even in European countries at the time and were mainly built on American continent emphasized the significance of Kojić's proposal.[72]

Kojić's sketch from 1930 never advanced toward realization; however, the idea of a skyscraper at the crown of Terazije would inspire a new developer a few years later. Meanwhile, Kojić received an offer to design the headquarters for the leading daily newspaper *Vreme* [*Time*][73] (seen in the background of Figure 4.9) at an extremely important spot between Terazije and the National Assembly, which would after World War II reconstruction grow into what is today known as Nikola Pašić's Square. Remembered as Belgrade's first skyscraper, the *Vreme* Headquarters was incredibly massive in comparison to the skeletal open plan and light façade of his previous design for Albania Tower, not to forget the American precedents, whose father William Le Baron Jenney had graduated from the same École Centrale, sixty-five years before Kojić. The *Vreme* monumental tone, with axially prearranged set-back massing, underlined by white marble cladding hooked with bolts, had little in common with the aesthetics of the Industrial Age, yet the noise of printing machines coming from the backyard certainly did; this aspect of modernity was not what the upper middle-class recently moved to deluxe apartment townhouses expected from this location.[74]

Figure 4.9 Terazije Square – the view toward Brothers Krstić's Igumanov Palace with the National Assembly and Vreme Headquarters in the background (Photo Archive Miloš Jurišić)

Defining a processional route from Terazije to the National Assembly and articulating visual connections between the two public spaces was initiated by the Master Plan of 1923, yet the realization of large-scale projects to frame the sequence and give it a representational character was subject to long-lasting negotiations between the city authorities and architectural profession. The final decision was reached following the voice of developers. Two immense corner-lots, both sharp-angled, one at on the south side of Terazije convoluting toward the Assembly and the other at the intersection between Dečanska and Vjakovićeva streets, oriented both toward Terazije and the Assembly, were the key projects to determine the architectural character of two intermingled, yet programmatically contrasted, urban foci.

When the polemics about Pičman's design for the Main Post Office was at its peak and its position attacked for the disrespect of the Master Plan, a lot on the opposite side from the Assembly, at the corner of Dečanska and Vjakovićeva, caught attention of one of the leading investors in the country, the Yugoslav Agrarian Bank. The bank, run by a board of trustees, yet strongly influenced by the state administration, accepted and perused the rule about organizing architectural competitions for development at prestigious locations, set by the UJIA. However, instead of being transparent, the competition, announced in 1930, was limited to invited participants from Belgrade, Zagreb and Ljubljana, most of whom had established their reputation as Modernists. Among the invited were Nikola Dobrović, the Krstić brothers and Milan Zloković from Belgrade, Edo Schön and Stjepan Hribar from Zagreb, and Vinko Glanz from Ljubljana. The jury granted the first prize to Edo Schön, at that time dean of the Technical Faculty in Zagreb, whose proposal was noticed for an exceptional layout underlining the acute angle of the building lot. Despite the jury's decision, the trustees were unsatisfied with Schön's bare, transparent façades considered, similarly to Pičman's Post Office, too radical for a location close to the Assembly. Since the architect was not willing to please the investor, the contest ended with an "ambiguous result," as a contemporary critic recorded.[75] In the end, the third-prize winners, the Krstić brothers, were asked to submit a more traditional-looking solution for the façade to better meet the bank's idea of how their financial power should be represented. The Krstićs proposed a new, Classical-looking, heavy curtain to be placed over their original layout, and by so doing received the job, which was realized straightaway during 1932 and 1933. Both Schön's and the Krstićs' proposals accentuated the acute angle, centrally positioning the main entrance at the angle's top; however, Schön's concept suggested a more elegant, trapezoid instead of a quarter-cylindrical form at the protrusion. The Krstićs' original proposal, suggesting a curvilinear façade with clean forms and wide window screens, accentuating the inner logic of structural elements, was in a radically Modernist mode. Yet, the realized façade was monumentalized by a gloomy Doric colonnade stuck onto the ground floor, heavy entablature and deep cornices, which even after the serious, post-WWII reconfiguration of Nikola Pašić's Square continued to stick out because of their robustness.

118 *National architectures in the unified nation*

Despite their belated affiliation with the GAMP (similar to Dragiša Brašovan, they joined the group in 1930), the Krstićs maintained a stylistic adaptability to the client's taste instead of pursuing the stubborn justification of International Style aesthetics. It was that adaptability rather than professional superiority that brought them the realization of vital projects at the most exposed spots of Belgrade central core. The Krstićs received the second-largest scale commission in the same area for the Igumanov Endowment based on positive public opinion about the Agrarian Bank, but also because of their realization of St. Mark's, the forms of which paid tribute to the medieval catholicon of Gračanica Monastery in Kosovo. It was a project for mixed-use development at the south-east corner of Terazije, to replace three small single-story houses owned by the Igumanov Endowment, whose board of trustees decided to erect a representational palace as a "dignifying monument to the people's benefactor Sima Igumanov to contribute to a modernized image of the capital city."[76] Igumanov was a merchant from Prizren in Kosovo, who, after gaining his fortune selling tobacco, started supporting monasteries and building schools for Serbian communities in the regions that were still under the Ottoman control. One of his main contributions was the establishment of Prizren Seminary, so he remained highly respected by the Serbian Orthodox Church. The Endowment appointed a board of experts, professor at the Theological Faculty Steva Dimitrijević and professor at the Technical Faculty Pera Popović, to coordinate the design process assumingly in the Serbo-Byzantine tone like that of St. Mark's. The Krstićs even submitted a Byzantine-stylized project appealing both to the trustees and the experts, yet as soon as the construction started, they managed to cut off the most explicit Byzantine elements from the original composition hoping for a more Modernist appearance. Their long-term supporter Pera Popović was furious, however the Krstićs' excuse only showed how confident they had become in maneuvering through a tough field of architectural commissions and realizations:

> We can understand why the Endowment originating from the Serbian south insists on the Serbo-Byzantine style for their palace, however, at the end, everything once being built goes only under the architect's name, and that is to stay forever.[77]

So, the Krstićs finally succeeded in executing the Modernist-looking public building, the ground floor of which, planned for shops, turned into a continuous, curvilinear glass surface instead of a heavy arcaded base. On the upper floors, each window vertical was framed with an arcade cut from white marble, the element that culminated with a monumental trifora at the curvature facing the intersection. This vague reference to the Byzantine heritage, alluding to the benefactor's ties to the Serbian Orthodox Church, challenged a stereotypical image of monumentality considered synonymous with Historicism. The edifice was observed as a theatrical doorway of Terazije framing the view toward the Agrarian Bank and the National Assembly in its background, the first large-scale edifice which finally gave a Modernist appeal to the focal point of urban communication (see Figure 4.9).

> We doubted that any of us, the contemporary citizens of Belgrade, would live long enough to see a respectable face of Terazije. What is still present today is a sequence of old-fashioned cantinas where Belgraders keep on dipping goulashes, baiting ćevapčići and enjoying other Balkan mezze-platters. That is why is so important to see how Terazije has started shaping its new, more presentable face. The Igumanov Palace will finally bring Terazije an image of a European metropolis while pushing away shabby looking restaurants such as Šiško and Albania.[78]

Although ambitiously planned, the contours of Terazije stayed asynchronous from the first expansion of Belgrade outside of the moat until the fever of large-scale commercial developments in the mid-1930s. A few earlier campaigns for the refurbishment of Terazije, including the competition for Terazije Terrace of 1929, resulted only in the transformation of horticultural arrangements, sidewalks, streetlights and benches, with a little effort put into the replacement of small-scale houses dating back to the 1800s. The substantial rearrangement of Terazije's street elevations would take place right before the outbreak of World War II.

The long-lasting ambition to compete the unbalanced vertical regulation and raise up the overall height culminated when the Mortgage Merchandise Bank expressed an interest in developing the northeast section of Terazije, at the mouth of Knez Mihailova Street leading to the fortress. The bank announced an architectural competition for its new headquarters in January of 1938, to which eighty-four entries were submitted.[79] Despite an intense debate over the design chosen for the final realization, caused by excluding the winning team from Zagreb from involvement in the execution, the immense structure was finished in October 1939. The credit for this success went to a local engineer, Đorđe Lazarević, who developed a concrete skeletal system that could stand hand-in-hand with daring constructions from technologically advanced countries such as the USA.[80] The validity of his achievement was assured after the structure survived a severe bombing by the Allies during World War II, when it had become a shelter for German military commanders.[81]

After the completion, the surprisingly tall structure aimed to persuade Belgraders that the Yugoslav capital had grown into a European metropolis. With the height of forty-five meters and immense 700-square-meter footprint, the thirteen-story construction became celebrated as the tallest and biggest building in the Balkans. The goal of monumentalizing the most exposed point of Terazije, stipulated in the competition, was finally achieved. Besides its height and scale, it was the design solution by Zagreb-based

120 *National architectures in the unified nation*

Branko Bon, taking advantage of the sharp-angled lot, that transformed the sight into a soaring backdrop enclosing Terazije. The prominent Belgrade architect and critic Ivan Zdravković commented in daily newspaper *Pravda* on the quality of juxtaposing the convex and concave surfaces in the design:

> The Palace of Mortgage Merchandise Fund Bank dominates Terazije like an American high-rise set at crown of the square. The entire structure lays on a powerful platform following the concave form of the regulation line through the first two levels. On the other hand, the upper floors shift into a dramatic convex surface. Modern architecture found its full expression here; although neither ornamented not sculpturally decorated, the building is serious and flirtatious at the same time. Besides its height, making it the tallest building in the Balkans, it is not only the number of floors, but rather the complexity of its concept which stands for its monumentality.[82]

While the city authorities and architectural professionals seemed satisfied by the long-awaited transformation of the city's core, the public perception of the project, especially during the first stages of construction did not go as smoothly. For a few generations the spot was one of the most popular gathering places of writers and poets, including Branislav Nušić in the Oriental-style cantina called Albania, criticized for its shabby appearance and unhygienic conditions, but also admired for a specific spirit and diverse, both bohemian and elegant clientele.[83] So, the demolition of this old structure and the considerable earthworks prior to the setting of the foundation stone for the bank provoked doubtful comments.

> During the foundation works which went as deep as 12 meters under the street level, various fossil bones, including a mammoth skeleton were found. Daily press announced that the mammoth died at the shore of Pannonian See. One day the construction site dawned covered in water coming from the broken water pipe, which was nonetheless explained as an event mysteriously linked to the dead mammoth. Moreover, upon reaching its full height, the structural skeleton started sinking, another creepy activity the pedestrians observed with fear and excitement.[84]

Adjusting to new building models, technologies and materials was an integral part of the modernization process, yet it triggered nostalgia for the old customs and the intimately shared settings. Two newly raised palaces on both ends of Terazije, the Mortgage Merchandise Fund Palace, nicknamed "Albania" after the old restaurant, and Igumanov Palace, along with the Agrarian Bank at the back, transformed the busiest public intersections from the intimate meeting places into abstract images of collective identification. Now distant and representational rather than commonly used, the palaces of commerce fixed onto the most exposed corners in the city shifted the way

Imperial Belgrade 121

Figure 4.10 Terazije Square – the view toward Albania Palace (Photo Archive Miloš Jurišić)

an interaction between people and architecture occurred at the everyday level. That was the price Belgrade needed to pay for pursuing an "imperial" image like the other cities with similar aspirations. The advantage Belgrade had lay in the fact that architects from all over the country participated in the competitions and juries for the prominent pubic locations. Despite the long-lasting controversies over the authorship, projects like "Albania" ended up being the most successful contributions to Belgrade's monumental skyline (Figure 4.10). The fact that the Croatian team won the competition while the Serbian team lead the realization, only contributed to its identity as truly a piece of Yugoslav architecture.

Notes

1 Anonymous, "Statistički pregled" [Statistic Overview], *BON: Beogradske opštinske novine – Belgrade Municipal Paper*, Belgrade, 1938: 962.
2 Predrag Marković, *Beograd i Evropa [Belgrade and Europe]*, Belgrade: Savremena administracija, 1992: 43.
3 Daily press commented on the received entries: Anonymous, "Generalni plan Beograda: ocenjivački sud počinje rad" [Master Plan of Belgrade: The Evaluation Jury Starts the Work], *Vreme*, vol. 2 (April 7, 1922): 3. An extensive study about the plan can be found in Zlata Vuksanović-Macura, *San o gradu: međunarodni konkurs za urbanističko uređenje Beograda 1921–1922 [Dream of the City: The International Competition for the Urban Regulation of Belgrade 1921–22]*, Belgrade: Orion Art, 2015.

122 National architectures in the unified nation

4 The ideas of transforming the fortification into a public park with a zoo dated back to the nineteenth-century regulatory plan by Emilian Josimović.
5 Although administratively unified, the two urban cores remained separated by the vacant land until the 1950s, when the area of today's New Belgrade was converted into an explicitly Modernist city, a symbol of the socialist man. After the new urban grid was laid onto the filled-in marshland, the authors of New Belgrade's original concept from the 1923 Master Plan were forgotten.
6 Turning Terazije into the entertainment district is discussed in Jovana Babović, *Metropolitan Belgrade: Culture and Class in Interwar Yugoslavia*, Pittsburgh: Pittsburgh University Press, 2018: 107–139.
7 Zlata Vuksanović-Macura, *Život na ivici: stanovanje sirotinje u Beogradu 1919–1941* [*Life at the Edge: The Housing of the Poor in Belgrade 1919–1941*], Belgrade: Orion Art, 2012: 28.
8 The term of Belgrade post-Academism was defined by Bogdan Nestorović, son of Nikola Nestorović, to highlight the legacy of his father. See Bogdan Nestorović, "Postakademizam u arhitekturi Beograda 1919–1941" [The Post-Academism in Belgrade Architecture], *Godišnjak grada Beograda*, vol. 20: 353.
9 The term "state-axis" comes from Ignjatović, *Jugoslovenstvo u arhitekturi*: 341.
10 The full name of the ministry was the Ministry of Agriculture, Forests, Mining and Waters.
11 Dragiša Brašovan (1887–1965) graduated from the Technical Faculty in Budapest and moved to Belgrade in the early 1920s. Although considered as the leading Serbian Modernist, he skillfully mingled a variety of styles at the beginning but also in the later phase of his career during the late 1940s–1950s.
12 Kadijević, *Jedan vek traženja nacionalnog stila*: 121.
13 Dimitrije M. Leko, "Nova zgrada Ministarstva poljoprivrede, voda, šuma i rudnika" [The New Building of Ministry of Agriculture], *Tehnički list*, no. 13–14 (1926): 193–202.
14 Dimitrije M. Leko was already known for the debate on national style during the competition for the royal mausoleum at Oplenac.
15 Zoran Manević, "Jučerašnje graditeljstvo" [Architecture of the Yesterday], *Arhitektura i urbanizam*, vol. 53–54 (1979).
16 Nikolai P. Krasnov (1864–1939) had been a municipal architect in Yalta, working on a few extensions of the summer residence of Romanovs. See Aleksandar Kadijević, "Rad Nikolaja Krasnova u Ministarstvu građevina Kraljevine SHS/Jugoslavije u Beogradu od 1922. do 1939. godine," *Godišnjak grada Beograda*, vol. 44 (1997): 221–255.
17 The contribution of the Ministry of Buildings's architecture department in the development of state-funded institutions is discussed in Snežana Toševa, *Graditeljstvo u službi države: delatnost i ostvarenja Arhitektonskog odeljenja Ministarstva građevina u srpskoj arhitekturi 1918–1941* [*Building in Service of the State: Work and Realizations of the Architecture Department of the Ministry of Buildings in Serbian Architecture 1918–1941*], Belgrade: MNT and DKS, 2019.
18 The project presented in Gordana Gordić and Vera Pavlović-Lončarski, *Ruski arhitekti u Beogradu* [*Russian Architects in Belgrade*], exhibition catalog, Belgrade: ZZSKGB, 1998:2.

Imperial Belgrade 123

19 Miodrag Jovanović, "Kralj Aleksandar i ruski umetnici" [King Aleksandar and Russian Artists], in M. Sibinović (ed.), *Ruska emigracija u srpskoj kulturi XX veka*, Belgrade: Folološki fakultet, 1994: 93–97.
20 Aleksandar Kadijević and Marina Đurđević, "The architecture of Russian emigrants in Yugoslavia in the period between the world wars," *Spatium*, vol. 3 (1998): 15–22.
21 Jovanović, "Kralj Aleksandar i ruski umetnici": 97.
22 This team was probably chosen because of their previous experience and expertise in courses they taught: Đorđević run the design studio focusing on large-scale public programs, while Nestorović introduced students to the theory of styles.
23 The two saints have been celebrated among most Slavic people as the forerunners of literacy and education.
24 Anonymous, "Osvećena zgrada Univerzitetske Biblioteke" [The Consecration of the University Library], *Politika*, vol. 22 (1926).
25 Dimitrije M. Leko argued against the altered site, but also about weak interpretation of the design for Charlottenburg. See Dimitrije M. Leko, "Nove zgrade Tehničkog fakulteta u Beogradu," *Tehnički list*, vol. 8, no. 5 (1926): 65–66.
26 Andra Stevanović was a member of the building committee deciding about Kostantin Jovanović's project for the Royal Academy.
27 Aleksandar Kadijević, *Estetika arhitekture akademizma, XIX –XX vek* [*The Aesthetics of Architectural Academism, Nineteenth and Twentieth Centuries*], Belgrade: Građevinska knjiga, 2005: 355.
28 Nikola Dobrović (1897–1967) gained international reputation as a pioneer of Yugoslav modern architecture at the time of Terazije Terrace competition. His early work was promoted by Theo van Doesburg, "Architectuurverniewingen in Servie", *Het Bouwbedrijf*, no. 7 (1930) and Kosta Strajnić, "Soudoba jihoslovanska arhitektura, Nikola Dobrovič, a jeho vyznam," *Architekt SIA*, vol. 29 (1930). The Royal Institute of British Architects (RIBA) granted Dobrović honorary membership in 1965.
29 Blagojević, *Modernism in Serbia*: 119.
30 Such as Miloš Perović, "Dobrović," special issue of *Urbanizam Beograda*, no. 58, (1980), and Miloš Perović and Spasoje Krunić, *Nikola Dobrović: eseji, projekti, kritike* [*Nikola Dobrović: Essays, Designs, Criticism*], Belgrade: AF, 1998.
31 Blagojević, *Modernism in Serbia*: 245.
32 Rostislav Svácha, *Architecture of New Prague 1895–1945*, Cambridge MA: MIT Press, 1995.
33 Jan Dubový, "Vrtarski grad" [The Garden City], *Tehnički list*, no. 1–3 (1925): 7–46; "Nešto o gradovima u vrtu" [Something about Cities in the Garden], *Savremena opština*, no. 4 (1926): 66–68.
34 The group was founded in 1928. Its program is kept in the Archive of the Institute of Cultural Monuments Belgrade and its mission explained in Branislav Kojić, *Društveni slovi razvitka arhitektonske struke u Beogradu* [*Societal Conditions for Development of the Architectural Profession in Belgrade*], Belgrade: SANU, 1979. Branislav Kojić was one of the founders. For discussion in English, see Blagojević, *Modernism in Serbia*: 57–71.
35 Branislav Kojić, *Društveni uslovi razvitka arhitektonske struke u Beogradu, 1920–1940*, Belgrade: Srpska akademija nauka i umetnosti, 1979: 169.

36 The Exhibition of Czechoslovakian Architecture had strong impact on Ehrlich's new course. The skeletal construction of the Yugoslav Bank could have been influenced by Oldřih Tyl's Fair, completed in Prague in 1925.
37 From Erlich's letter dated March 1, 1929, kept in the Building Archive of Belgrade. Quoted in Žarko Domljan, *Hugo Ehrlich*, Zagreb: DPUH, 1979: 158.
38 Marija Drljević, "Arhitektura Pošte 1 u Beogradu" [Architecture of Post Office 1 in Belgrade], *ZLUMS*, vol. 37 (2009): 277–296.
39 According to Dimitrije M. Leko, King Aleksandar ordered a new completion for the façade of the Main Post Office and picked the winning entry. See Saša Mihajlov and Biljana Mišić, "Palata Glavne pošte u Beogradu" [The Palace of the Main Post Office in Belgrade], *Nasleđe*, vol. 9 (2008): 239–265.
40 Jablanica quarry in Herzegovina was considered the best in the region. Ivan Meštrović often used granite from Jablanica for his architectural projects.
41 The sources for Dragiša Brašovan's architectural syncretism are discussed in Aleksandar Ignjatović, *Arhitektonski počeci Dragiše Brašovana, 1906–1919* [Architectural Beginnings of Dragiše Brašovana, 1906–1919], Belgrade: Zadužbina Andrejević, 2004.
42 Recorded by Brašovan's nephew Stevan Županski, *Dragiša Brašovan: Pionir jugoslovenske moderne arhitekture* [*Dragiša Brašovan: The Pioneer of Yugoslav Modern Architecture*], an unpublished text written in 1966, kept in the Library of Serbian Academy. Quoted in Aleksandar Kadijević, "Život i delo arhitekte Dragiše Brašovana 1887–1965" [Life and Work of Architect Dragiše Brašovana 1887–1965], *Godišnjak grada Beograda*, vol. 37 (1990): 154; and Blagojević, *Modernism in Serbia*: 180.
43 The architectural competition was announced for another location close to Kalenić Market. Yet, after the public debate, it was decided that the State Print Plant would be built in Vojvode Mišića Boulevard. See Anonymous, "Gde treba podići Državnu štampariju?" [Where Should the State Printing Plant Be Erected?], *Pravda* (June 22, 1934).
44 Nikola Dobrović, "Brašovan," *IT Novine*, no. 697–732 (1976–1977): unpaginated.
45 Anonymous, "Ministar građevina G. Krek pregledao sa novinarima novu zgradu Državne štamparije" [The Minister of Buildings, Mr. Krek with Journalists Inspected the New State Printing Plant], *Politika* (November 30, 1939).
46 Anonymous, "Zgrada koja daje utisak džinovskog aviona" [The Building Which Leaves an Impression of a Gigantic Plane], *Politika* (April 28, 1936).
47 Anonymous, "Zemun sve više postaje deo velike prestonice – tramvajske šine u Zemunu" [Zemun is Rapidly Growing into an Integrative Part of the Big Capital – the Tram Route to Zemun], *Vreme* (November 4, 1934).
48 Anonymous, "Zemun – Novi Beograd dobija još jednu palatu – zgradu Komande Vazduhoplovstva" [Zemun – New Belgrade Will Have Another Palace – the Air Force Headquarters], *Vreme* (April 5, 1934).
49 Biljana Mišić, "Hangar na Novom Beogradu: svedočanstvo prvog vazdušnog pristaništa u Beogradu" [The Hangar in New Belgrade: A Testament to the First Belgrade Airport], *Nasleđe/Heritage*, vol. 14 (2012): 95–114.
50 From a speech the president of Belgrade Municipal Office, Milosav Stojadinović, delivered at a conference about Belgrade and its suburbs in 1930. Quoted in Vuksanović-Macura, *Život na ivici*: 40.
51 Statistic data from Slobodan Vidaković, *Naši socijalni problemi* [*Our Social Problems*], Belgrade: Geca Kon, 1932: 198. The low number of apartments with

Imperial Belgrade 125

bathrooms demonstates the fact that even key central neighborhoods like Vračar, Kosančićev venac and Palilula were not supplied by the central sewage system until the 1920s. See Stojanović, *Kaldrma i asfalt*: 160.
52 Vuksanović-Macura, *Život na ivici*: 28.
53 Theoretical works on urbanism by Branko Maksimović, such as a multi-volume title *Urbanism through Centuries*, were well-known among European scholars.
54 Dijana Milašinović-Marić, *Arhitekta Jan Dubový's*, Belgrade: Zadužbina Andrejević, 2001: 36–39, recognizes the shelters as the first projects to allow Dubový to fully express the Modernist attitudes, right before his project for the Astronomic Observatory.
55 Vuksanović-Macura, *Život na ivici*: 30–35.
56 Danica Tomić-Milosavljević, "Razvitak grada Beograda 1919–1929" [The Development of the City of Belgrade], in *Jugoslavija na tehničkom polju*, Zagreb: Udruženje jugoslovenskih inženjera i arhitekata, 1929: 227.
57 Bogdan Nestorović, "Evolucija beogradskog stana" [The Evolution of "Belgrade apartment"], *Godišnjak grada Beograda*, vol. 2 (1955): 127–270. More recent discussions on "Belgrade apartment" include: Ljiljana Blagojević, *Moderna kuća u Beogradu 1920–1941* [*The Modern House in Belgrade, 1920–1941*], Belgrade: Zadužbina Andrejević, 2000: 38; Sanja and Đorđe Alfirević, "Beogradski stan" [Belgrade Apartment], *Arhitektura i Urbanizam*, no. 38 (2013): 41–47.
58 Emilia Garda, "Smooth, Hard, Clean, Perfect: Terranova, History of a Modern plaSter," *Proceedings of the First International Congress on Construction History*, Madrid, 2003: 965.
59 A lecture on Robert Mallet-Stevens's work were held in the Architecture Club in 1936. There is no evidence about any promotion of Le Corbusier's works and ideas before the constitution of Socialist Yugoslavia in 1945.
60 Even the most radical architects from this new generation, such as Momčilo Belobrk (1905–1980) never experimented with strip windows or transparent façade surfaces.
61 Branislav Kojić (1899–1887) was educated in France from elementary school through college. He earned a degree in engineering from the École Centrale des Arts et Manufactures in 1921. He left an immense opus of writings including his documented memoires about the architectural profession in Belgrade between the two wars: Branislav Kojić, *Društveni slovi razvitka arhitektonske struke u Beogradu* [*Societal Conditions for Development of the Architectural Profession in Belgrade*], Belgrade: SANU, 1979.
62 Kojić, *Društveni slovi razvitka arhitektonske struke u Beogradu*: 19.
63 The ultra-Modern concepts of Belgrade villas during the interwar period are discussed in Ljiljana Blagojević, *Moderna kuća u Beogradu 1920–1941* [*The Modern House in Belgrade 1920–1941*], Belgrade: Zadužbina Andrejević, 2000.
64 *Arhitektura: mesečna revija za stavbno, likovno in uporabno umetnost*, vol. 1, no. 1, (1931): 2–4.
65 Jovana Babović, *Metropolitan Belgrade: Culture and Class in Interwar Yugoslavia*, Pittsburgh: Pittsburgh University Press, 2018: 5.
66 Named after the Renaissance poet from Dubrovnik, considered neither Serbian nor Croatian at the time.
67 Recorded in Kojić, *Društveni uslovi razvitka arhitektonske struke u Beogradu*: 205–206.

126 National architectures in the unified nation

68 Zloković published the design in *Arhitektura*, vol. 1–2, no. 5 (1932): 143–145 to illustrate his article "Stara i nova shvatanja" [Old and New Apprehensions].
69 Noticed by Kojić, *Društveni uslovi razvitka arhitektonske struke u Beogradu*: 252.
70 Petar Bajalović, "Zgrada Kolarčevog narodnog univerziteta u Beogradu" [The Building of Kolarac People's University] *Arhitektura*, vol. 3, no. 1–2 (1933): 11.
71 Kojić, *Društveni uslovi razvitka arhitektonske struke u Beogradu*: 201. Kojić's statistics shows that thirty-two architectural competitions were initiated by banks, professional associations, pension funds, charity societies and churches in comparison to nineteen organized by governmental institutions.
72 Snežana Toševa, *Branislav Kojić*, Belgrade: Građevinska knjiga, 1998: 47–48.
73 Kojić developed plans for the *Vreme* Headquarters in early 1937. The construction started in June 1937 and was finished in October 1938. Toševa, *Branislav Kojić*: 93.
74 Mentioned in Boško Mijatović, *Dva veka Dečanske ulice* [*Two Centuries of Dečanska Street*], Belgrade: Službeni glasnik, 2009: 82.
75 Mate Baylon, "Javni arhitektonski natječaji izmedju dva rata" [Public Architectural Competitions between the Wars], *Čovjek i prostor*, vol. 22, no. 9 (1975): 10.
76 Marina Đurđević, *Petar i Branko Krstić*, Belgrade: RZZSK, 1996: 53.
77 Branko and Petar Krstić, "Sećanja" [Memories], unpaginated manuscript kept at the Institute for Cultural Monuments of Belgrade.
78 Anonymous, "Terazije menjaju izgled" [Terazije is Changing its Appearance], *Politika* (October 7, 1937).
79 The rules about architectural competitions for the entire country were published in *Tehnički list*. See "Pravila za raspisivanje natječaja-utakmica u oblasti arhitekture i inženjerstva" [The Rules about Announcing Architectural Competitions in Architecture and Urbanism],*Tehnički list*, no. 6 (1921).
80 Uroš Martinivić, "Đorđe Lazarević – doajen našeg neimarstva" [Đorđe Lazarević – the Doyen of Our Civil Engineering], *Izgradnja*, vol. 10 (1986): 10.
81 Marinko Paunović, *Beograd kroz vekove* [*Belgrade Through the Centuries*], Belgrade: Svetozar Marković, 1971: 1113–1114.
82 Ivan Zdravković, "Značajniji arhitektonski objekti podignuti u Beogradu u prošloj građevinskoj sezoni: Palate Hipotekarne banke Trgovačkog fonda" [Noticeable Architectural Realizations in Belgrade of the Last Season: Palaces of Mortgage Merchandise Fund], *Pravda* (January 28, 1940).
83 Milorad Ćirilović, "Sat ispred Albanije" [The Clock in front of the Albania], *Politika* (September 15, 1997).
84 Milica Ceranić, "The History and Architecture of 'Albania' Palace in Belgrade," *Nasleđe/Heritage*, vol. 6 (2005): 147–162.

5 Avant-garde Zagreb

The capital of wealth, business and commerce

During the last stage of long-lasting political negotiations on behalf of the proclamation of the autonomous Banovina Hrvatska (Banat of Croatia),[1] a respected Croatian economist Rudolf Bićanić observed that "Belgrade had been sucking state funds for the construction of immense public buildings more luxurious than we can find in reach Western European cities."[2] Indeed, the development of large-scale public and administrative buildings to house the centralized state government flourished in Belgrade after the constitution of Yugoslavia, while Zagreb cut down the earlier, pre-WWI aspirations of becoming the leading South Slavic national capital, and started focusing on profit-gaining and social programs: banks, factories, insurance companies, hospitals, educational facilities and housing. Instead of becoming the capital of a South Slavic state, as the nineteenth-century protagonist of the Illyrian Movement had anticipated, it remained a regional center merely associated with Croatian identity. The city was still identified as the national seat of Croats, with most of its cultural, educational and political institutions of national importance being already established and built before the unification. As a result, the interwar development primarily showed off the vitality of economic growth and social concerns, as the goals of searching for architectural nationhood lost their initial clarity.

The pre-WWI role of Viktor Kovačić as the father of Croatian architecture, however, did not fade. On the contrary, with the establishment of the Architecture Department at Zagreb Technical Faculty in 1919,[3] Kovačić gained a chance to educate the first generation of domestically trained architects. The professorship came after a long-lasting struggle to validate his Viennese diploma, but also coincided with a commission for the prestigious project for the Stock Exchange to become the most appreciated and largest realization in his entire opus.

The Stock Exchange was the most monumental public edifice of interwar Zagreb (Figure 5.1), recognized for its exquisite formal qualities, as well as for its power to articulate its immediate surroundings and a broader urban development to the east. As the strongest financial establishment of

128 *National architectures in the unified nation*

Figure 5.1 Kovačić's Stock Exchange with Meštrović's Art Pavilion in the vanishing point (National and University Library, Zagreb)

the country during the 1920s, the Exchange was capable of raising funds for the project and construction, depending neither on state nor municipal financial plans, in contrast to what was most often the case with representational developments in Belgrade. Although failing in ambition to become the political capital of South Slavs, Zagreb demonstrated strength as financial and economic capital; therefore, the city authorities together with numerous local investors supported an urban vision for developing New Zagreb with the Stock Exchange as its foremost visual reference. The golden age of Zagreb Stock Exchange lasted until the Great Depression, while its decline continued through the 1930s. Then the opening of the Stock Exchange in Belgrade took over the leading role in the country.

The disposition of Kovačić's masterpiece determined a layout of the new commercial district to be spread at the former Fairground, marking the gateway from the direction of the Lower City. The Stock Exchange Council, together with the municipal authorities and the leading urbanists and architectural professionals, had gone through a serious process of decision-making, prior to buying the land and as soon as the decision about the site was made and the parcel bought, the Council announced an invited competition with only five architects being asked to participate. Besides Viktor Kovačić, "the father of Croatian architecture," his Slovenian counterpart Jože Plečnik was also invited, yet he rejected the invitation due to his parallel engagement at Prague Castle. To insure that the choice of winning design was in the best public interest, the city officials invited an internationally recognized founder of German Werkbund, Herman Muthesius, to participate on the jury. Although the process of finding the right site and the best design solution included various voices in decision-making, Kovačić accepted the offer and continued working on developed plans in an extremely short period. He signed the contact in summer of 1921 and, after a few preliminary designs, completed the final project ready for execution in 1922.[4]

The trapezoid shape of the lot, and consequently the building's footprint, was determined by Kovačić's urban vision for the expansion of the city to the east into the area at that time named New Zagreb. The zone was imagined as a high-end residential district with a variety of public and cultural institutions of a representational nature. The central element of urban design was the diagonal avenue running between today's Trg Hrvatskih velikana [Square of Croatian Eminences] and Trg Žrtava fašizma [Square of the Victims of Fascism], visually connecting the spires of the main cathedral with an obelisk – the vanishing point of perspective placed in the center of public space furthermost on the southeast. Therefore, Kovačić's Exchange was set at the opening of the diagonal avenue to frame a vista toward the obelisk. In the best tradition of Wagner's appropriation of the Renaissance urban schemes, Kovačić imagined a symmetrical composition of two trapezoid-shaped edifices, one of which was the Exchange on the left side, to flank the diagonal avenue, today's Franje Račkog ulica [Franje Rački's Street] as the central axis of the Renaissance-conceptualized trivium, together with Martićeva and Draškovićeva streets.

The idea of an obelisk at the furthermost southeast square was never materialized. Instead, the Strossmayer Art Society, within the shield of Yugoslav Academy for Sciences and Arts, initiated a campaign for erecting a monument to King Peter I Karađorđević at the same spot, while the Stock Exchange was still under construction. Despite the seemingly patriotic intentions, the Society did not support a realization of a free-standing sculpture glorifying the king, but the construction of an exhibition pavilion to be named after him. The commission was granted to Ivan Meštrović, at that time serving as dean of the Art Academy in Zagreb and actively working on other commissions received from the Karađorđevićs. This was Meštrović's largest architectural realization, envisioned as a circular cella, surrounded by a heavy portico and topped with a shallow dome, the monumental neo-Classical composition that succeeded in completing Kovačić's urban scheme with Meštrović's aesthetic contribution, as if these two Viennese School of Fine Arts graduates had initially synchronized their designs. Neither Kovačić nor Meštrović were supporters of the imperialistic values, yet their monumental works in New Zagreb were attuned to the late nineteenth-century urban visions for Zagreb – the extension of the Green Horseshoe.

The analogies between Kovačić's Stock Exchange and Adolf Loos's Goldman & Salatsch at Michaelerplatz in Vienna were significant. In both layouts, the monumental entrance, emphasized by the Classically conceptualized elaborate portico in contrast to the sober façades, was placed at the cut angle of the intersection and opened toward the prominent public square. In the Zagreb counterpart, however, the processional movement toward and through the building, starting from the public square and continuing through the representational vestibule, ended with the dramatic rotunda reminiscent of the Roman Pantheon, where the busiest stock exchange activities were taking place. Covered with a double shell reinforced concrete cupola, twenty-one meters wide with the height extending through four floors and the only source of light coming from the glass oculus, Kovačić's Stock Exchange rotunda was to become the central shrine of commerce of the newly born country.

Kovačić and Loos met in Vienna in 1905 and developed their friendship through a vibrant correspondence and exchange of ideas. As was previously noticed, Kovačić had already submitted a design with the cut angle and Classically composed main façade, very similar to the later proposal for the Stock Exchange, at the competition for Russia Palace at Terazije Square in Belgrade in 1904, before Loos conceptualized his palace at Michaelerplatz. Although the jury, consisting of prominent architects, including Otto Wagner, granted Kovačić the first prize, the project for Russia Palace never materialized. Kovačić and Loos also shared a passion for the Chicago School – Louis Sullivan's work in particular. They were both strong and intractable individuals, probably a reason why they never worked together. Yet, they were both succeeded by a common Croatian associate, Hugo Ehrlich, who finalized their unfinished projects. Ehrlich completed the project for Villa Karma on Lake Geneva in 1906 due to Loos's disagreement with the client and finalized the interior design for Zagreb Stock Exchange after Kovačić's premature death in 1924.

The next generation of Croatian architects, most of whom were Kovačić's students, turned away from Viennese precedents in favor of more radical solutions, promoted at the Bauhaus and Le Corbusier's ateliers. The emergence of Modernism was tied to the Exhibition of Czechoslovakian Architecture in 1928, shown also in Belgrade and Ljubljana later that year. Yet, the Modernist breakthrough coincided with the foundation of the avant-garde art group Zemlja in 1929 and the redevelopment of Zakladni blok[5] [Foundation Block] in the same year,[6] after the public initiative for the beautification of this precious piece of property on the southwestern corner of Ban Jelačić's Square. By the time of Zagreb's rapid urban transformations in the mid-1880s, the deteriorating hospital complex of the Catholic order of Brothers Hospitallers of St. John of God was described as "the public shame" at the city's heart. After long-lasting negotiations between the brothers and the municipality, the old hospital was torn down and the money from the land used for the construction of a new, public-owned hospital at Šalata.[7]

The prime location of Zakladni blok dictated a new program – the mixed-use of business, rental apartments, commerce and leisure, defined through an architectural competition appealing to the young generation of domestically trained architects. None of the winning entries from the 1929 went beyond the initial ideas,[8] as most of the participants proposed compact megastructures over the whole property. Yet, instead of attracting a single developer for a monolithic project, as was originally anticipated, the municipality initiated a new allotment allowing possibilities for multiple investors, and accordingly different architects to work on partitioned projects. With no exception, the projects promoted the radical, Functionalist aesthetic, as if they mirrored the recently completed, Modernist-looking reconstruction of the Stern Building by Peter Behrens[9] on the opposite side of Ban Jelačić's Square.

The groundbreaking solution for Zakladni blok came from Drago Ibler,[10] previously employed at Behren's office in Berlin,[11] who proposed an unconventional design of two transparent slabs: the horizontal spreading along Gajeva Street in contrast to the high-rise at the convolute of Ban Jalačić into the main commercial Ilica Street. Originally Ibler's vertical accent could not be developed during the original building campaign because of the citizens' initiative to preserve the original hospital's chapel. Only after the establishment of communist rule, when the ideology of atheism helped for the chapel to be torn down, was Ibler's vision for the vertical landmark at the mouth of Ilica realized. Although the entire block was parceled into smaller lots, the feeling of "monolithic" horizontality, as in Ibler's proposal, was retained as a result of strict zoning codes imposed on individually designed buildings. In charge of particular buildings were the rising names of Croatian architecture such as Slavko Löwy, Antun Urlich and Stjepan Planić, whose radical Modernism in Zakladni blok would canalize the mainstream of Croatian architecture during the 1930s.

The last structure of the pre-WWII building campaign within the Zakladni blok and the first to break the strictly regulated height constraints was the Napretkova zadruga [Progress Cooperative] or simply Napredak [Progress] (Figure 5.2), at the back corner of Gajeva and newly cut Bogićeva Street. Ibler submitted a new proposal for this location: a set-back skyscraper, the skin of which was composed of juxtaposed glass and solid horizontal strips, laid onto a tall transparent prism;[12] however, it was not him but one of his students, Stjepan Planić,[13] who received the commission. Only a few years after the uniform row of buildings characterized by plain aesthetics, white surfaces, ribbon-windows and roof terraces had grown at the regulation lines of Petrićeva, Ilica and Gajeva streets, Planić's project for the Napredak from 1936 challenged the previously canonized aesthetics. His ellipsoid tower was rimmed with a robust cogwheel cornice and a necklace of wedged capitals underneath each of the teeth. The blue façades were dominated by vertical strips, delineating the window frames, onto which the wedged capitals were topped as their crowns. The entire corner resembled of an exaggerated fluted column, even though only the upper zone with apartments – the last four floors and the set-back attics – was protruding as a fully enclosed ellipse. On the other hand, the layout of lower levels with

132 *National architectures in the unified nation*

Figure 5.2 Planić's Napredak Collaboration (National and University Library, Zagreb)

shops and offices respected the regulation lines of a traditional urban block. The expressive convex corner helped the advertising logotypes of firms seated in the building – Napretkova Zadruga, 20th Century Fox Film and Siemens – to be easily noticed from Ban Jelačić Square, making a synthesis of the Classical and Modernist aesthetics attuned to the monumental manner spread through mid-1930s Europe. However, the main value of Planić's masterpiece relied on a unique and provocative double-coded syntax embracing Classicism, consumerism and industrialism under the same shield, a

Figure 5.3 Löwy's Skyscraper Radovan (Löwy Family Archive)

reason why the Napredak is still applauded as the most original aesthetic contribution of Croatian Modernism still waiting to be discovered by the international academic audience.

Although it challenged the vertical regulations proposed for Zakladni blok, Planić's Napredak was not the first Zagreb skyscraper. It was the mixed-use building Radovan (Figure 5.3) in the vicinity, named after its owner Eugen Radovan,[14] that is considered the first Modernistic-conceptualized Croatian high-rise. As sales representative of Bosh, Buick, Blitz and Opel factories, Radovan managed to purchase a high-end land parcel at the sharp angle of the intersection between Masarykova and Gundilićeva streets, yet right before choosing an architect, he learnt that a certain portion of his land was to be appropriated for widening of a public sidewalk. Since the lot was already too small, while the zoning codes limited the building height in respect to the cathedral on the Kapitol Hill, the municipality issued a waiver allowing Radovan to double the height of a new building at this location as a compensation for the loss. The rising young voices in the architectural profession supported by the daily press, stood for the idea of loosening the urban codes, which were considered outdated and conservative. A commentator from a popular daily newspaper lamented:

> Had some happier circumcenters unleashed the building height restrictions at least ten years ago, a new Zagreb would have grown into a city of immense six or more story high palaces instead of those little houses.[15]

It was a surprise when twenty-nine-year-old Slavko Löwy won first prize in the invited competition for the "tall house,"[16] as it started being called in press, still unsatisfied by the lost potential for an even greater height.[17] The fact that both the designer and contractor chosen for the construction were under thirty years of age fueled public enthusiasm about the arrival of new architectural forms and technologies. "Radovan will be the first building in Zagreb to prove the logic of high rise developments for the profitability of private investments on small and extremely pricey properties in the old urban core," highlighted Löwy in his article published in *Građevinski vjesnik*.[18] In order to prove the power of a new aesthetic, he proposed a dramatic visual statement at the intersection between Gundulićeva and Masarykova Street – a composition of two contrasting volumes; the lower, five-story-high horizontal tract was integrated into the street-façade with the neighboring Benedik Building, while the tower challenged the regulation lines both by its unprecedented height as well as the rotated volume opening towards the narrow intersection. Until the present, skyscraper Radovan has been recognized as the most "dynamic" urban landmark at the historically notable Masarykova Street,[19] which never managed to widen the pedestrian sidewalks as had been anticipated at the time of construction.

Radovan was constructed in only seventy-nine days, which was a remarkable accomplishment by the local constructors applauded in local press as another record to emphasize the pace of progress in Zagreb.[20] The first floors with retail spaces and offices, were entirely wrapped in glass, allowing interaction with the pedestrian movement through Masarykova and Gundulićeva streets. Each floor of the lower block facing Gundulićeva was a mixture of two- or three-bedroom apartment units, while the tower contained offices and studios for single professionals to whom "the architect granted the best double exposure" towards the intersection and the city's skyline.[21] The interiors were treated as "the state-of-the-art in residential architecture so that the building attracts the residents to stay inside and enjoy their apartments all day long."[22] The architect designed his own apartment on the top floor, with unobstructed views from the belvedere towards the Green Horseshoe, where he would reside until his death in 1996. The indoor and outdoor illumination were turned into architectural elements for the first time in Croatian architecture. Two continuous horizontal light strips wrapped the edges of the flat roof and the last-floor parapet delineating them as the top of an urban lighthouse. The vertical line of illuminated letters – "Bosch," "Buick," "Blitz" and "Opel" – accentuated the corner toward the intersection. The architect was in charge of marketing his masterpiece. Not only that he hired the "Specialized Enterprise for Industrial, Commercial, Technical and Advertising photography – Foto Donegani" to take a picture, but also demanded a night shot, emphasizing the illumination as the key compositional attribute.[23]

Although the first Zagreb skyscrapers bravely challenged the strict codes of vertical regulatory lines, they were still very delicately incorporated into the traditional urban fabric of the Lower Town defined by Građevni red [Building Ordinance] from 1909, slightly adjusted to meet modern needs during the 1930s. The mixed-use commercial and residential programs remained the most common type of development, initiated by private investors with growing interest in the Modernist aesthetics and Functionalist theories during the interwar period. At the same time, the new formal but also functional approach towards designing mixed-use properties within the traditional core gave birth to a new architectural type defined in literature as the "inbuilt" or "interpolated" rental building, recognized "as the most spread type of townhouses [...] which design process was fully controlled by the laws of capital and profit," as the designer of Napredak high-rise Stjepan Planić had observed.[24] They differed from Belgrade's "rental apartment townhouses" both stylistically as well as programmatically; the mixed-use townhouses with shops and offices combined with residences were far less present in Belgrade.

The earliest attempt at breaking the fixed patterns, the traditional street façades in the interpolated mixed-use projects was Drago Ibler's Rittig House in Ilica Street, yet his original proposal for this location, which had envisioned a U-shaped layout with an inner courtyard opening towards the main commercial street, thereby breaking the continuous street façade, was not approved.[25] The motive of setback street level, originally anticipated in Rittig House, would finally materialize in the project for an interpolated mixed-use building commissioned by Anna and Klotilda Wellisch in 1930 on their narrow parcel stretching from Martićeva on the south to Vlaška Street on the north – the realization to become celebrated as the first clear icon of Croatian Modernism, the first entirely unornamented, proportionally superb composition of abstract elements incorporated into the traditional street façade (Figure 5.4):

> Lacking any attached decoration, Wellisch House was a validation for the possibility of a new aesthetics, rooted explicitly on the beauty of proportions, rhythms, materials and colors [...] Still, the core of its perfection relies on the extraordinary proportion, achieved not purely though Ibler's design decisions, but also through his pragmatic fight with municipal administration to break the regulatory codes limiting the maximum height to only four floors.[26]

Figure 5.4 Ibler's Wellich House on the ad for Heraklit elements (Arhitektura, vol. 2, no. 6, 1932)

Parallel to the withdrawn line of glassed shop-windows overshadowed by a massive portico abutting the pedestrian sidewalk, Ibler broke the façade composition[27] with the roof-deck added to the original plans during the execution. Similar to the portico of the ground floor, the roof deck "façade" was conceived as a mounted colonnade as in Le Corbusier's Weissenhofsiedlung two-family residences. Instead of framing a wide panorama of Stuttgart cityscape, as was the case in Weissenhof, Ibler's roof-frame accentuated the view toward a specific building, Kovačić's Stock Exchange. The street elevation of the Wellisch house recalled the character of another masterpiece from Weissenhof, Mies's multi-family slab with layers of ribbon-windows interrupted by vertical lines of balconies with iron railings.[28] Besides the formal analogies, the entire organizational and structural concept was one of the earliest attempts of the open plan in the country as in the most advanced designs at Weissenhof. The skeletal reinforced concrete construction and prefabricated dividing walls and ceilings were considered the top technological achievement, allowing the flexible layouts of shops and apartments, as well as, the nonstructural façades with the continuous glass surfaces. A distributor of Heraklith insulated panels in Zagreb used photos of the newly completed building for commercial purposes stating that "Ibler used 26 000 pounds of [their] products for facades, nonbearing walls and concrete cladding."[29]

Despite tremendous investments in commercial developments in the central zone, the commissions of exclusively office buildings were rare. The first ultra-Modernist project for a company's headquarters was designed by the atelier of Rudolf Lubynski whose disciples turned from a stiff, slightly modernized academic tone to the upcoming Functionalist aesthetics. The Zagreb branch of Shell Company, run by Artur and Milan Marić, invited Lubynski's atelier to design their seat at the narrow parcel of land between the Foundation Block and Gajeva Street. Although significantly smaller in scale, the Shell project would become remembered as the earliest example of flexible workspace in Croatian architecture, the feature only anticipated in the competition proposals for Foundation Block run at the same time. The success of open plan in the office space corresponded to Lubynski's pioneering role in conceptualizing the original, "proto-Functionalist Zagreb-apartment residential floorplan." The use of a skeletal structural system allowed not only easily transformable, functional layouts but also helped in experimenting with "hanging façade screens" carried by cantilevers, a detail with no precedent among Modernist achievements in the region. Despite the narrow lot, Lubynski and his crew managed to create a vibrant shopping promenade incorporated into the layout of the ground floor, a covered path linking Gajeva and Praška streets. It was purely the quality of materials and details, with no decorative motifs, which contributed to the luxurious character of Marić Passage – as it has been called, still remembered as a hot spot of high-end consumerism.[30] Similar to its numerous turn of the century precedents in Vienna, Prague and Budapest, in addition to the older and more distant Parisian arcades, the imaginary of Marić Passage with its elegant shops has remained synonymous with the expending market economy and bursting modernization processes, "a symbol of the entire city, a new world in miniature."[31]

Numerous mixed-use interpolations built along the newly traced streets of the east section of Lower Town called New Zagreb during the 1930s, have remained the peak examples of interwar rental typology envisioned for the new middle class.[32] Despite the penetrating Modernist aesthetics, the new developments were tightly incorporated into the traditionally conceived urban fabric, with only a few examples provocatively challenging the predisposed regulation lines as a specifically Zagreb phenomenon. One of these was the immense retail-apartment development commissioned by two merchant families, Rosinger and Jungwirth, at the corner of Draškovićeva and Đorđića streets in the vicinity of the Stock Exchange, at a similar disposition as Ibler's Wellich building on Martićeva Street. Starting from the Stock Exchange, both Đorđića and Martićeva streets protrude like side arms of the trivium, with the central axis connecting the Stock Exchange with Meštrović's Art Pavilion. Therefore, both Ibler's Wellisch building in Martićeva Street and Vladimir Šterk's corner building in Draškovićeva Street were placed at the same distance from the Stock Exchange; their roof decks connected by an imaginary line running diagonally over the Stock Exchange's dome. Yet the boldness of the Rosinger & Jungwirth building by Czech-trained Vladimir Šterk relied on a striking detail of L-shaped cantilevered balconies, protruding at the street corner of each story, thereby provocatively hanging over the pedestrian sidewalks. The striking angle motive displayed new possibilities for reinforced concrete, yet it was even more revolutionary from an urbanistic point of view. The bare nature of details and rough materials resembled the "hard-core" Functionalist aesthetics of Czech contemporaries Oldřih Tyl and Ludvík Kysela; however, Vladimir Šterk added a new twist to the Functionalism to be displayed on Zagreb streets, a detail that was to be often repeated in the coming projects for corner buildings in New Zagreb in the 1930s.

Constituting the garden-city inspired suburbs was in most cases related to the urge of the wealthy to invest in larger residences and promote their openness toward the new aesthetics. Villa Pfeffermann (Figure 5.5)

Figure 5.5 Villa-Pfeffermann (Arhitektura, vol. 1, no.1, 1931)

designed by ČVUT-trained[33] Marko Vidaković north of the Old Town – the very first attempt at importing a Czech-inspired-Modernism in residential development – showed to what extent the investor's willingness to employ the radical design solutions played a key role in the emergence of the first Modernist realizations. Marko Vidaković, who organized and hosted the Exhibition of Czechoslovakian Architecture, was asked to design an ultra-modernist villa for the Pfeffermanns when the inspiring works by Czech architect Josef Gočár were still on display in Zagreb.[34] Villa Pfeffermann was envisioned as a sequence of white prisms of different heights lined up along the L-shaped footprint, while the outer composition corresponded to the interior program, thereby keeping up with the Functionalist ideas, as in Gočár's Villa Strand presented at the Exhibition. The abstract aesthetic – flat roofs and plain, white façades and ribbon-windows – has been applauded as the first experiment of this kind not only in Zagreb, but in the entire country; "the first domestic contribution to the International Style in general."[35] The advanced level of conceptualization and execution stood out in comparison to other two Modernist villas built simultaneously in Belgrade and Ljubljana, and published in the first issue of *Arhitektura* as the most representative case studies in the country:[36]the already discussed Villa Milićević by the Krstićs in Topčider and Villa Šubic in Ljubljana's suburb of Vrtača.

After the completion of Villa Pfeffermann in less than a year, the interest in similar-looking residences started flourishing among wealthy investors. The most remarkable cluster of small-scale residential buildings and villas inserted in greenery was developed in the outskirts, on the steep slope above the Upper Town, around the serpentine-cut Novakova Street, during the 1930s. Although strongly reminiscent of experimental housing projects such as Weissenhof in Stuttgart and Na Babe in Prague, Novakova Street neighborhood was not an experimental housing colony, but a piecemeal design strategy initiated by developers.

> The emergence of Novakova Street was not tied to experimentation; it was not just another event in the chain of the Werkbundsiedlungs elsewhere in Europe, but rather a product of real conditions […] Novakova Street emerged through a traditional dialogue between the architect and the client. There was no single architect in charge of the whole planning concept. Every landowner picked an architect of his choice, therefore the style of each building was unpredictable at the beginning. As the most appreciated names of the profession were not invited by the investors, the quality of realizations was mediocre, yet the overall impression of the settlement ended up being outstanding.[37]

As an urban ensemble, Novakova Street has become acknowledged for its overall appearance, yet its individually commissioned constituents lacked originality. The settlement was defined through one of the micro-regulatory plans for residential development in the attractive area north of the Upper Town, approved in 1930. Along the street profiles, the plan delineated twenty-one parcels, 200–280 acres each, to be sold to individual investors. Most buyers were German Jews moving to Zagreb away from the rising fascism, yet the lots were not planned for permanent residences but as rental investments. The building codes regulated the position of buildings on specific parcels, their size, height and number of apartments in the multifamily units. The Zagreb Commission for Façade Appeal – consisting of Hugo Ehrlich, Edo Schön, Stjepan Hribar, Ivan Zemljak and Vladimir Potočnjak among others – was in power to refuse any project they found displeasing. The outcome was a group of multifamily villas, built upon the strictly Modernist aesthetics, since every investor accepted this formal requirement. The willingness to deal with the new architectural trends could be explained by the small investors' backgrounds, as they may have been introduced to architectural Modernism or visited some of the Central European housing experiments prior to their settling in Zagreb.

After the crash of bank system in Zagreb in 1931, caused by the Great Depression, the small investors found apartment development and renting the safest source of survival.

> The low cost of building materials but also the low interest rates on mortgages helped construction jobs to flourish. Also, the modern way of building suits high expectations for gaining decent assets. Clear, rational layouts with flat facades do not require large amounts of money. The minimal investments resulted in maximum profit.[38]

In Novakova, the developers enthusiastically accepted and pursued the modern materials such as iron and reinforced concrete, along with skeletal constructive concepts allowing the flexible plans. Unornamented white façades with simple openings and balconies were easy and cheap to execute. Yet, any overly demanding form and expensive building element, such as continuous ribbon-windows or sliding panels, were avoided to minimize the costs. Finally, if someone dared to insert any condemned traditional element onto his façade, the Commission for Façade Appeal would veto such a detail.[39] While building on land parcels in Novakova Street, the investors and architect were preoccupied with financial security and led by pragmatic issues, yet despite their tiny ambitions, the cluster of residential properties turned into one of the most successful housing estates in interwar Europe.[40] Different from Weissenhofsiedlung in Stuttgart and Werkbundsiedlung in Vienna, Novakova did not rise as a preplanned unity of experimental designs by a recognized protagonist of the Modern Movement. It was rather an example of bottom-up micro-urban growth caused by the economic crisis. While the developers of the first two celebrated housing estates faced difficulties in the search for buyers, the individual, small investors of Novakova Street not only achieved a remarkable Modernist ensemble but created a reliable potential for their economic growth during the hard times of Depression.

The capital of social welfare

As the most developed industrial center, Zagreb started raising concerns about the status of working-class and low-income residents long before other cities in the country. Prior to unification, the social welfare services had existed mostly in parts of the country under Austro-Hungarian rule, and Zagreb, as the biggest regional center of the Habsburg southeast had been exposed to social movements and policies soon after their emergence in Vienna. Therefore, it was natural for the politics and future management of social welfare in the newly established Yugoslavia to be coordinated from the Croatian capital.[41] The pivotal event in constituting the uniformly organized welfare system on the state level was the proclamation of Zakon o socijalnom osiguranju radnika, ZOR [Workers Social Insurance Law] in 1922.[42] The acknowledgment of the law was followed by the establishment of the Central Workers Insurance Agency with its seat in Zagreb, given the task of implementing the law thorough the country, yet under the supervision of the Ministry of Health and Social Affairs from Belgrade. The idea of building the Central Workers Insurance Headquarters in Zagreb coincided with the proclamation of the law.[43] An open architectural competition for the building was announced in the same year as the law, in 1922, for a prominent site in the Green Horseshoe, between the main railway station and the Botanical Garden. The winner was Rudolf Lubynski, at that time considered an architect of the older generation, which could be a reason why he turned back to the Beaux-Art schemes in the Insurance Headquarters project. His robust, palazzo-looking edifice was completed in 1928, at the time when radical Modernism had penetrated into Zagreb's architectural academia.

Already in 1926, Drago Ibler opened the avant-garde-oriented architectural department at the Academy of Fine Arts with the aim of challenging the accustomed architectural practices. Yet, with his controversial entry in the same competition for the Insurance Headquarters he had started shaking the views of the previous generation. Although left with no prize, Ibler was recognized for his unconventional aesthetics as his compositional scheme consisted of clean setback slices forming an expressional trapezoid volume. A celebrated Croatian novelist, Ibler's contemporary Miroslav Krleža,[44] acclaimed:

> Ibler's structures grew up in accord to the elementary imperatives of our age: speed, practicality, simplicity, usefulness, brought all together into a puritan minimum of shapes. Huge, monumental blocks that carry within themselves certain similarities with distant Assyrian edifices, splendidly rounded forms of Roman Colosseum adjusted to the new needs of our time and needs.[45]

142 *National architectures in the unified nation*

Ibler's competition entry for the Insurance Headquarters, along with another unrealized competition proposal from the Institute for Epidemiology in 1924, became applauded as a fresh and progressive statement, resulting from Ibler's collaboration with Hans Poelzig during his stay at Dresden polytechnic. The politically engaged Krleža recognized Ibler as the herald of new age and social justice, while resentfully accusing Ivan Meštrović for his mediocratic spirit. It was at this time that Meštrović indisputably supported Ibler during the campaign of establishing the modern architectural curriculum at the Faculty of Arts.

The second largest Workers' Insurance seat in the country was to be constructed in Belgrade soon after the completion of its Zagreb forerunner.[46] It was imagined at the prominent location across from the main railway station, the key urban landmark opening toward Vračar district. The first prize in the architectural competition, announced in 1929 was awarded to Lavoslav Horvat,[47] at that time an unknown undergraduate student at Ibler's Academy, for an understandable reason. Horvat's entry bore a close resemblance to the recently finished Zagreb Headquarters, as it was similarly conceived as a traditional palazzo with an inner courtyard occupying the entire urban block at the just delineated Wilson's Square. The architect also took part in the development and realization of the winning entry for the Zagreb Headquarters while working in the bureau of Ludolf Lubynski from 1922 to 1926.[48] On the other hand, with a rising influence as the founder of new architectural school, Ibler received commissions for designing regional workers' insurance offices, known as OUZORs [Okružni uredi za Osiguranje Radnika – Regional Offices for Workers' Insurance] in Mostar (today's Bosnia and Herzegovina) and Skopje (today's Macedonia)[49] – the first public projects in Yugoslavia to explicitly comprise the aesthetics of the International Style.

The most innovative socially engaged concepts in Croatian interwar architecture sprouted from Ibler's circle and his curriculum at the Academy of Fine Arts. In 1929, only a few years after opening the program, Ibler was joined by some of his students in an initiative to constitute the avant-garde art group Zemlja [Earth]. He remained the chair of Zemlja until the group was prohibited by a police decree on April 6, 1935. The inspiration for establishing Zemlja came from the politically and socially engaged groups of artists Novembergruppe and Arbeitsrat für Kunst, who Ibler had met during his stay in Berlin after finishing the studies in Dresden. Upon his return to Zagreb in 1923, his interest in the social role of art and architecture grew into a passion, embedded in all spheres of his professional engagement. In the manifesto of Zemlja written for the opening of the First Exhibition in 1929, Ibler declared:

> We should live the life of our time,
> We should create in the spirit of our time,
> Contemporary life is intermingled with social ideas and the questions of collectivity dominate,

The artist cannot neglect the imperatives of a new society and stand aside from the collective,

Since the art is an expression of our perception of the world,

Since the art and life are the same.[50]

At the time of the opening, Zagreb had already built its identity as the most pronounced avant-garde intellectual center of the country. The concerns about social equality, workers' rights and wellbeing were fostered both by artist and architects, as well as the municipal government.

Zagreb went through two quite different periods of economic development between the two world wars: the first characterized by enthusiasm and liability of large investors, and the second, the period of recession after the collapse of banks in 1931.[51] However, the development of socially aware architectural programs continued after the collapse, despite the turbulent fluctuations in state budget, unstable economic policies and strong disagreements over the distribution of state funds. Besides the financial support gained through loans from English, French, American and German banks, a decent portion of governmental funds were spent on educational, medical and social care programs and facilities.[52] The aspiration for large-scale projects of public importance coincided with the penetration of Modernist ideas either from the associates of Adolf Loos or the followers of German Werkbund and the Bauhaus teachings.

The development of medical facilities had become a priority alongside the establishment of the workers' insurance network. A special contribution to health insurance and medical services in Zagreb was made by Dr. Andrija Štampar,[53] the professor at the Medical Faculty in Zagreb and also in service at the Ministry of Health and Social Affairs in Belgrade. Besides his unprecedented contribution to Yugoslav health policies and services, Štampar has been remembered as an activist in the World Health Organization, the creator of its constitutional act and the president at its first congress held in Geneva in 1948. Stances of the program Štampar fought for were:

1. The improvement of workplaces (standards for the minimum amount of light and air, limiting the pollution and chemical hazards).
2. The construction of hygienic workers' housing and improvement of the conditions of their everyday life.
3. Preventive health care (the system of community clinics and dispensaries).
4. The popularization of medicine and knowledge about diseases.[54]

The construction of the Public Health Palace in a very short time of only two years, 1925–1927, to house the School of Public Health was the pivotal event in establishing a broadly operating medical care system, affordable to all social groups. Later named the Institute of Hygiene "Anrdija Štampar," the public institution was originally founded through a generous donation of the Rockefeller Foundation, which explains the address at 4 Rockefeller

Street. The position of the Public Health Palace will determine the future development of medical facilities in its vicinity, serving a similar social mission: the spread of public awareness of preventive medical care.

In 1930, a few years after the completion of Juraj Denzler's[55] and Mladen Kauzlarić's early Modernist design for the Public Health Palace, Drago Ibler received a commission for the Institute for Hygiene in the neighboring block. At that moment finishing the Insurance Office in Mostar, Ibler ran into similar site constraints in Zagreb. As in Mostar, the sharp-angled land parcel was placed at the fork of Rockefeller Street and Mirogoj Road, yet a significant difference was the sloping terrain. Therefore, he conceived a L shaped composition of two abstract volumes: a strictly rectilinear four-story prism for administration perpendicular to Mirogoj Road and a lower, two-story horizontal wing for admissions and treatments, protruding as a semi-cylinder towards Rockefeller Street. The in-between area was leveled, divided into three separate green surfaces, buttressed by concrete walls and pavements. The horticultural design was conceptualized as an open "vestibule" in front of the discrete entrances into the functionally differentiated blocks. Like his just-completed Wellisch building, the main façade of the taller, administration building was composed as a precisely proportioned square, interrupted by a set-back portico at the entrance level, ribbon-windows on each floor and an open roof terrace covered by a horizontal slab. The lower wing for the patients was dynamic; it followed the logic of the slope with two sets of external stairs incorporated into the protruding semi-cylindrical volume. The precise delineation of various programmatic needs, easily readable through the external forms, together with the bold aesthetics, the advanced structural and new materials meant the entire project was recognized as the masterpiece of International Style – "an example of rare consonance, which explains Ibler's tendencies towards Europeanization of Croatian architecture."[56] On the level of socially engaged programs, this was the first Modernist complex in service of the public healthcare system to be erected in Zagreb.

The full penetration of Modernism was acknowledged in the competition stipulations and the choice of winning entries for other two medical facilities in Zagreb: the Jewish Hospital in Petrova Street and the complex of Foundation Hospital and Medical School Clinic on Šalata Hill, both announced in 1930 when Ibler worked on the Institute for Hygiene. The initiative for the construction of a Jewish hospital came from private funds of the growing Jewish community of Zagreb, considered the wealthiest in the country, while the second initiative resulted from the previously discussed sale of the Foundation Block at Jelačić Square, which filled the municipal budget with funds for the erection of a new prime medical facility.

> The Jewish Hospital planned to be a modest charitable institution that would meet the needs of modern medicine helping the members of Jewish community but also the other marginalized and poor unable to pay for

a hospital treatment. [...] The only valid principle in designing the hospital is efficiency. The mutual collaboration between the architects and user, in this case the physicians, is a requirement set by our time.[57]

The parcel designated for the hospital and owned by the Jewish community was recognized as too small to meet the necessary requirements, the reason why the construction was postponed until a better solution was found, which never happened. Another eagerly anticipated project for the Foundation Hospital and Medical School Clinic on Šalata at first looked promising. The project was developed by Le Corbusier's disciple Ernest Weissmann[58] and reflected some of the most advanced ideas in designing medical facilities in Europe of that time. The urban layout was conceived as a series of parallel pavilions, each dedicated to a specific type of medical condition and treatment – a scheme widely used in hospital designs after the revolutionary discovery that bacteria caused the spread of some deceases, so that the patients started being separated not only by gender but also by type of illness.[59] Weissmann was the first to introduce to Yugoslav hospital design new organizational schemes, engineering possibilities and advantages of prefabrication. His innovative approach came at the right political moment, at the peak of the government-initiated strategy to develop an advanced medical system throughout the country.[60] The leading requirement was the patients' hygienic exposure to the sun and air, thereby the design was grounded in the research on sun spectrum applicable in therapy, consequently the system of façade glass panels was a well-coordinated mechanical organism, figuratively exposing a delicate process of healing. Unfortunately, Weissmann's projects was never completed, despite his long-term involvement in the detailed plans.

Štampar's visionary initiative for preventive care included integrating sports and exercise into the everyday life of the broad population, resulting in various initiatives for development of sports facilities during the interwar period. The projects were numerous and ambitious, some proposed for the downtown area around the previously established Sokol Headquarters, while many more were envisioned in the protected green zones, large civic parks and along the banks of the Sava River. The Sokol Movement played a vital role in establishing new habits and promoting sports and recreation as a foundation of health and growth of the individual and the whole society. Initiated and found by a Czech art historian, Miroslav Tyrš, in Prague in 1862, the movement spread through the Slavic world. In 1863, the Sokol was found in Ljubljana as the first among the South Slavs. The significance of the movement for the growth of a Croatian national ideology was recognized when the Croatian Sokol was established in 1874. Then a monumental edifice for Sokol Headquarters was planned across from the National Theater, at Mažuranić Square, with the other urban landmarks along the Horseshoe. Around the headquarters, the extensions of Sokol sport facilities continued to be planned through the mid-1930s. The best remembered and recorded, although never executed, was Stjepan Planić's winning entry for the Sokol Stadium with gymnasium to host the rally of 1934 celebrating the sixtieth anniversary of Croatian Sokol at the irregular land parcel diagonal from Mažuranić Square, sadly abandoned because of the property issues. To emphasize the boldness of Planić's design, we should point out the new Sokol facilities realized around the same time in Ljubljana by Ivan Vurnik and in Belgrade by Momir Korunović, both experimenting with a unique emanation of a national style in the spirit of Czech Rondocubism.

The realization of Sokol Stadium was moved to another location, to Maskimir Park, where the beginnings of organized sports activities and manifestations dated back to the late 1800s. The turning point in promoting Maksimir as the center of Zageb's sporting life was the extension of the horse tram from the downtown to the entrance to the park's green promenade in 1892. Five years later, the first permanent construction, Sokol Velodrome, was built across the main entrance at the last tram stop. As well as hosting bicycle races, the Velodrome was imagined as "open center for all physical activities with athletic equipment, tennis and cricket courses placed in the central green area."[61] Until the outbreak of WWII, the development of sports fields in Maksimir was framed around the activities of Sokol and Hrvatski akademski sportski savez [Croatian Academic Sport Society] – HAŠK. Found in 1903, the HAŠK finally developed the first Zagreb soccer stadium in Maksimir when Zagreb bishop Antun Bauer granted a piece of land owned by the Catholic Church for that purpose in 1912. The HAŠK also gained rights to use the park's lake for sports training and water polo matches, the activities crowned in 1923 with the first international water polo game ever held in the country. During the interwar period, the HAŠK developed the Sports Park in Maksimir with fields and facilities for various sports, which would continue growing through the mid-twentieth century.

Despite the investments in large-scale projects for sports and recreation, Croatian criticism and historiography has recognized a low-budget shelter for the rowing club Uskok as the quintessential accomplishment of Croatian interwar architecture. The club did not qualify for financing from the municipal government, thereby relied on donations from its members, among whom one of the richest was involved in selling timber. The idea of building a shelter for boats was born soon after the club was established in 1928, thanks to enthusiasm of architect Anon Ulrich,[62] who had become a passionate rower during his college years in Vienna. Already as a student of the Kunstgeweverbeschule [Academy of Applied Arts] under the leadership of Josef Hofmann, Ulrich experimented with a similar program. The project for Uskok Club was an elaborated version of his graduation assignment, yet its brilliance lay in the contextualization, Ulrich's compromise to adjust to the Zagreb situation, respecting the restraints of the site while emphasizing the relationship between the building and the Sava River.

In Urlich project water was crystalized into architecture and granted her with sound and translucency. Following a requirement of the financier, the facades were made of clapboard, while the roof insulation was white to contribute to the best possible reflection of light.[63]

The main entrance into the building was from a deck hanging over the revetment, leading into the free plan utilized thought the modular skeletal system, a pile dwelling consisting of a longitudinal volume carried by pillars and partly spread into a two-story-high composition. Although small and built as a temporary construction, the Uskok Club has been remembered as a pioneering work, which anticipated the future of Croatian Modernism and crystalized its richest potential, providing a turning point for the Modernist aesthetic with a new dimension beyond the local boundaries. After its completion in 1931 "there was no way back," not only in the domain of sport programs, but in the architecture of the entire region. Its influence was such that Ulrich was awarded the first prize for the Tuberculosis Sanatorium on Avala Mountain near Belgrade, which was to become a custom model for the future, Modernist-conceptualized, small-pavilion cascaded scheme, adjusted to topography and landscape.

Prior to WWI, four higher educational institutions, covering the fields of theology, law, philosophy and medicine, existed within the shield of Zagreb University. The growth of the university during the 1920 and 1930s reflected the state government mission to cover new areas, but also to transform programs developed within the Austro-Hungarian political context to meet a new national agenda. All of the three newly formed academic institutions in Zagreb – the Technical Faculty, the Veterinary Faculty and the Agricultural and Forestry Faculty – managed to build modern edifices during the interwar period. Despite high expectations, the funds for construction from the central government were not delivered at the predicted pace, resulting in a construction delay until the mid-1930s.

Because of the high percentage of rural population, the country prioritized the role of agriculture for its economic growth, so the Ministry of Education first provided funds for the realization of Agricultural Faculty campus (Figure 5.6) in 1932, a few years before the other two. The project was chosen from the entries at the competition announced by the dean's office and chaired by Edo Shön.[64] "The most suitable for development since it had met most of the competition stipulations"[65] was the proposal submitted by a group of young architects Radna Grupa Zagreb [Work Group Zagreb] – RGZ, whose members signed the contract the day after the results were announced in fear that the funds for construction, finally approved by the Ministry of Education, would be redirected to some large-scale project in Belgrade. The ground was broken for construction only three month later, on a lot adjacent to Maksimir Park.

The project was signed by the entire group, however there is a reasonable assumption that the initial draft came from Ernest Weissmann, because

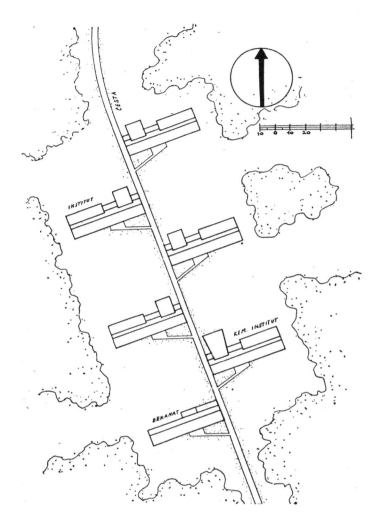

Figure 5.6 RGZ's Faculty of Agriculture (Tehnički list no. 20, 1933)

of a resemblance to his discarded project for the Foundation Hospital.[66] Weismann's enthusiasm for the realization of the Foundation Hospital was short-lived, as the developers started questioning his prefabricated structural system and the high cost of new building methods and labor engaged in the construction. It did not take him long to understand that the fight against the developers would not bring a positive outcome, so he turned his interest in a new direction, a radical theoretical platform to be promoted within the shield of the RGZ. Consisted of young architects, Weissmann's colleagues, the RGZ was eager to revolutionize the existing customs and practices, yet on a more concrete level that the previously established group, Zemlja. Although the RGZ and Zemlja shared similar political views, both demanding artistic engagement in service of social needs, their scopes of engagement were different. While Zemlja members embedded various artistic disciplines to demonstrate their leftist political platform and showed them mainly at art exhibitions, the RGZ was engaged in specific architectural projects and theoretical publications. Luckily for Weissman, the members of RGZ received the opportunity to probe their theoretical statements soon after he joined them.

Besides Weissman, other RGZ members, Josip Pičman and Josip Seissel, shared an enthusiasm about the social mission to be fulfilled with the project for new campus:

> Not only that our peasants lack modern technologies but also the knowledge to improve and multiply the results of his production. Besides the economic issues which burden our peasant, we have a long, pioneering work to enlighten people involved in the field of farmer's economy. Therefore, the construction of Agrarian-Forestry Faculty has arrived as the fulfillment of a long-lasting aspiration towards strengthening this crucial branch of our national economy. It is worth mentioning that this is the first faculty complex in Zagreb to be built explicitly in accordance to its needs. Until now, the high educational institutions have run their programs in the old existing buildings, originally designed for other purposes.[67]

The original urban layout proposed a hierarchized functional scheme with possibilities for growth and transformation. The site plan envisioned six parallel pavilions attached perpendicularly to the central communication spine oriented from the southeast to the northwest. The orientation was calculated in regard to optimum sun and light, but also in relation to the surrounding landscape of Maksimir Park and the communication paths to connect the complex to the rest of the city. Each of six "normal" or "prototypical" pavilions housed either separate departments in need of smaller classrooms and workshops or the central functions. They were clustered around the main administration building with the dean's office and library, the experimentation block with chemical laboratories and large amphitheater and the students' dormitory (domkomuna) with 150 beds and dining facilities, planned for a later phase. The concept of a prototypical pavilion resulted from the thorough analysis of single- or double-loaded corridor slabs in search of the most efficient dispositions of standardized classrooms, laboratories and workshops. The modular coordination and prefabricated method of construction, which Weissmann had already demonstrated in the project for the Foundation Hospital, were finally approved as the Modernist breakthrough, setting new standards for the domestic building industry. The quest for functionality and flexibility was affirmed through the structural system, the reinforced concrete skeleton and prefabricated ceiling manufactured in a domestic factory under the name Jugostrop [Yugo-ceiling].

The ground was broken for construction in the summer of 1933 and the first pavilion completed by early November of the same year. Josip Pičman and Josip Seissel became more engaged in the work on detailed planes and preparations for actual construction, but the funding from the Ministry of Education lacked consistency, resulting in delays and problems with the contractors. Only three out of the six originally planned pavilions were finished by the outbreak of WWII, so that the original concept of "live organism" – the urban composition which "organically" develops along the axial communication in accordance to the growing needs – was later abandoned. During the 1940s, the communication spine along which the pattern of pavilions was imagined for growth and extension was clogged by a newly designed centrally positioned administrative building.

The complex of Veterinary Faculty, the first higher educational institution in the country to be established after unification, was the first to be fully realized according to the pavilion scheme. After studying examples of modern veterinary schools in Europe, architect Zvonimir Vrkljan[68] proposed a symmetrical disposition of two U-shaped blocks of pavilions for teaching, research and experiments with animals, attached to each other by porticoes around the central courtyard. Although invited to develop the program for the new campus in 1935, the funds were finally received from the Ministry of Education in 1937, after numerous appeals sent to Belgrade officials. Only one pavilion was completed by the outbreak of World War II, yet, fortunately for Vrkljan's original project, nobody continued the construction during the war time and changed the vision, as was the case with the Faculty for Agriculture. Hence, Vrkljan continued realizing the rest of the project during two building campaigns in the 1950s and 1960s, maintaining the character of the original composition while improving the structural qualities and adjusting the materialization to the new economy. His modular approach to designing remained evident both through the logic of the reinforced-concrete skeletal system as well as in the subdivision of interior spaces and partitioning of façade surfaces. Despite its heaviness and traces of monumentality, especially in comparison to the RGZ's project for the Agricultural Faculty, Vrkljan's Veterinary Faculty turned into the most coherent large-scale campus in Croatia[69] due to the devotion to the original pavilion concept.

The decree of the state budget for the same, 1937/1938 fiscal year allowed a loan for another long-waiting project within the growing university, the Technical Faculty, to be taken from the Ministry of Education. With the Department of Architecture within its shield, it was natural for the project to be conceived by the architecture faculty. More accurately, the initial sketches and the first design came from the leading names of the first generation of architecture teachers, Hugo Ehrlich and Edo Schön, who had envisioned the campus in 1927, at the time the Technical Faculty in

Belgrade was under construction. Originally, the campus was envisioned for an older and bigger plot, to which the municipality awarded the Sokol. Fortunately, the dean managed to obtain a new parcel across the street when the funds were finally approved by the state government in 1937. By that time Hugo Ehrlich was dead, so the design was adjusted to the new location by Edo Schön in collaboration with his young colleague and teaching assistant Milovan Kovačević.[70] They proposed a composition of three parallel large-scale pavilions connected with a lower, transversal wing to spread through an immense urban block. The first pavilion was placed on the east regulation line to house architecture, civil engineering and geodesic studies. The developed plans for this, first-executed segment of the complex were attributed to Kovačević solely, nevertheless Schön still oversaw the design process together with Juraj Denzler, who supervised the construction. Denzler's influence was evident mostly in the development of elevations, which were originally to be clad in cut stone. Denzler's design for the Headquarters of Communal Municipal Services in 32 Gundulićeva Street, completed in 1935 – today the seat of Croatian Electric Company – was the most elegant Modernist in the Horseshoe urban core, wrapped in limestone on the upper floors and dark marble over columns on the street level. A similar rhythm and proportional relations between open and enclosed façade surfaces in Kovačević's project also shared a sense of monumental regularity evident in Dezler's slightly older design, a characteristic that could be credited to the strong influence of Adolf Loos on his Croatian disciples. Similar to the agricultural campus, the Technical Faculty was only partially competed according to the original plan, as the financing and construction were interrupted by the war and continued after the war according to the altered project. Nevertheless, its concept still shows the final step of the same trajectory – a deliberate attitude towards breaking traditional concepts in the design of higher educational institutions and bringing them closer to Functionalist ideas.

Along with the ambitious visions for the development of newly established higher educational institutions, waiting for the funds to be approved by the Ministry of Education, the campaign for constructing new elementary and high schools flourished on the local level, within the shield of Zagreb municipality. The compulsory elementary education in Croatia had been proclaimed in 1874, during the reign of Ban Ivan Mažuranić, and continued improving and developing as the foremost social agenda separated from religion. At that time, the school as a modern institution had no longer an exclusively didactic function as its program became far more open to public needs.

"School is the place where a child should be considered and developed as member of community in its entire psychological and social potentials,"[71] wrote Ivan Zemljak,[72] an employee of the Municipal Development Office, who conducted pioneering work on new methodologies and concepts for school architecture between 1924 and 1941. Like many South Slavs born

152 *National architectures in the unified nation*

in Austro-Hungary, Zemljak started his architectural studies in Gratz and continued in Prague after the beginning of WWI. After the return to Zagreb, he practiced in the bureau of Viktor Kovačić, until receiving the offer for a full-time job at the Municipal Development Office, where he, at first supervised new construction projects and later participated in urban planning decisions. Zemljak worked at the right place to initiate the construction of new schools and design them without going through trouble of competing with other colleagues. He also took advantage of the municipal government's willingness to support travel abroad, providing an opportunity for seeing the latest concepts and achievements in school architecture around Europe.

Zemljak made a breakthrough with the Elementary School Jordanovac (Figure 5.7), the project in which he experimented with the fusion between modern pedagogy and design, from the level of urban set-up to the detailed plans for built-in equipment and furniture. Built in 1930–1931, for the low-income neighborhood in the poorly populated area of Zagreb's western outskirts, the school was intended to contribute to children's wellbeing but also to the feeling of inclusion among members of the unprivileged community. The building was set on the top of a hilly land parcel owned by the city, at the spot where wind currents provided excellent natural ventilation, a desirable condition in times when tuberculosis was still widespread among children. The request for creating a healthy environment to support both the mental and physical development of the future generations was reinforced by additional open-air amenities: courtyard, roof deck, playgrounds, even a

Figure 5.7 Zemljak's Elementary School at Jordanovac (Arhitektura, vol.3, no. 12, 1933)

skating rink, surrounded by greenery. The school's layout was conceived as a symmetrical composition of clearly separated blocks for girls and boys, on both sides of the central hall, the space for gatherings, performances, indoor recreation and religious services. Each side wing consisted of six classrooms, two on each floor on both sides of the stairwells, in a way that every child could easily recognize the position of his or her classroom from the outside. The "projection" of inner functions onto exterior volumes was consistently performed by alternating their heights in elevations. Thus, the classrooms were placed in the tallest cubes above four corners of the mid-rise central hall, while the main entrance and axillary wings were the lowest. The shape and size of windows and casements also reflected various uses of the interior spaces, which along the bold aesthetics of abstract volumes, white undecorated façades and flat roofs, made an explicitly Functionalist character of the design. Together with Vidaković's Villa Pfeffermann, Jordanovac School was among the earliest realizations of this kind; unsurprisingly, both architects studied in Prague, thus were aware of the contributions of Czech Functionalism.

The second elementary school by Zamljak was built in a workers' neighborhood of Trešnjevka soon after the school in Jordanovac. Its symmetrical layout with strictly separated sections for boys and girls on each side of the centrally positioned space for gathering and exercise was similar to the organizational scheme of Jordanovac. Yet, instead of the compact scheme of Jordanovac School where all spaces gravitated towards the enclosed gymnasium, Trešnjevka Elementary School was composed as an open ensemble gravitating towards an open central courtyard with sand boxes, playground and swimming pool, around which the free-standing pavilions were connected by a U-shaped colonnade. Both educational facilities grew into the catalysts of public life in the unprivileged communities, providing the highest standards for intellectual development and social adjustment for children and their families. Their planimetric white volumes, flat roofs and unornamented façades perforated only by wide rectangular windows were the formal features by which Zemljak promoted the aesthetics of International Style in Croatian public architecture. The schools were first shown at the architectural exhibition, held in the Art Pavilion in 1932, and recognized as "the most successful realizations of all urgent needs expected from Modern Architecture."[73] A year later, Zemljak's work was presented in a special issue of *L'Architecture d'aujourd'hui*, dedicated to modern schools outside France, as the case studies representing Yugoslavia.[74] His architecture was included into a German edition of *Lexicon der Baukunst* published in 1937 and Albert Sartoris's book *Gli elementi dell'architectura moderna*, from 1941.

The care and control over high school education was assigned to the regional government of Savska banovina [Sava Banat]. After the proclamation of dictatorship in 1929, Yugoslavia was divided into eight provinces or banats, which respected topological and geographical characteristics, rather than the historical or ethic boundaries. Most of today's Croatia was

Figure 5.8 Steinmann's Second High School (National and University Library, Zagreb)

included in Sava Banat with the seat in Banski dvori in Zagreb, today the home of Croatian government, named after the longest river in Yugoslavia. The accessibility to secondary education was a strategic goal of regional governments, attempting to attract not only the students from large cities but also those from underdeveloped, rural areas. In the quickly expanding city, the building of a new high school originally named the Second Royal High School in Križanićeva Street (Figure 5.8), was initiated by the government of Sava Banat in 1930, with the construction competed in the next two years. The architect in charge of planning, design and supervision was Egon Steinmann,[75] one of the first graduates from Zagreb Architecture Faculty, and an employee of the Regional Government Technical Office since 1926.

The site was chosen in one of the fastest developing areas of Zagreb at the time, southeast from Kovačić's Stock Exchange, around the newly planned Square "N" (today the Square of Victims of Fascism) accentuated by Mešrović's Art Pavilion in the center. Steinmann respected the traditional regulation lines of the newly established urban block by enclosing it with a U-shaped footprint against the sidewalks of three streets, while the fourth side remained open toward a large garden with two small, free-standing houses for school administrators hidden in greenery. The composition and massing were traditional, rather more Classical than Modernist despite the unornamented aesthetics. The symmetrical organizational scheme with two identical L-shaped wings – one for girls and one for boys, culminated with the taller volume in the center, the gymnastic hall used by both genders. Later commentary noticed that "Steinmann mimicked the Ancient Greek educational philosophy by the logic of harmonious design, synthetizing both physical and spiritual culture important for young people."[76] The strictly symmetrical concept with monumental entrances under heavy porticoes certainly drew analogies to the Classical compositional schemes, while the stylization of façades with white undecorated surfaces, perforated only by various shapes of large windows, and flat roofs turned towards Modernism. Steinmann strictly divided communication paths regarding gender, as was required at the time, but also separated the students from the teachers. The entrances for students were placed in the rounded corners at the intersections between the main and perpendicular streets, thereby physically separating the northeast wing for the boys from the northwest wing for the girls. On the other hand, the teachers' entrances were centrally positioned, flanking the gymnastic hall and leading to the upper floors of this central volume containing the teachers' lounge, after-school classrooms, library, archive and administration offices. Despite the strict formal scheme of the layout, Steinmann demonstrated an explicitly Modernist approach to his design:

> If the school is a new home and, for majority of our children, a path towards moral and physical revival then the school needs to be close to nature, filled with air and sun, while its footprint needs to be horizontal. In this concrete situation, the ambitious program, the small construction site and the height of surrounding buildings determined the execution of the building in which every inch is going to be horizontal. The logic of horizontality, which is so well promoted by Modern Architecture, needs to be a logical consequence of inner functions and structures.[77]

The concerns for functionality and scientific approach towards health and hygiene were demonstrated though the disposition of classrooms oriented towards north, east and west while the communication corridors, illuminated and ventilated by natural air and light, were facing the courtyard with open playgrounds and greenery on the southern side. Steinmann's aesthetics was rather more Purist than Functionalist, influenced primarily by the French architectural scene of the mid-1920s, as he spent a postgraduate year auditing courses in drawing and decorative arts at L'Académie de la Grande Chaumiere in Paris. His long-lasting interest in the eternal values of Classicism, however, dated back to his college years in Zagreb, when he participated in the reconstruction of ancient heritage in Dalmatia under the guidance of professor Ćiril Metod Iveković, one of the founders of architectural conservation in Croatia.[78] The tendency towards strict formal schemes would remain the key characteristic of Stenmann's later works. The Regional Government Technical Office also initiated the construction of sports fields and an enclosed gym "in the very heart of the city, on the undeveloped field behind the school"[79] – the First Men's High School at Wilson Square. The project for new facility to serve two kinds of users simultaneously: the high school students and the members of Sokol's Club Zagreb,[80] was assigned to

Steinmann. In 1937, Steinmann completed the third interwar project serving the needs of secondary education, the Third High School in Kušlanova street, the Modernist forms of which still retained gleams of monumental Classicism.

One of the most controversial and provocative architectural competitions in interwar Zagreb, in which the workers' movement was significantly strong, was held in 1933 for the Palace of Labor. The competition inspired a number of left-oriented architects of the young generation, including Anton Ulrich, Milovan Kovačević and the members of RGZ, to participate. None of the competition proposals advanced towards realization since the proposed lot was given to another occupant. Consequently, two separate buildings: one for the Labor Exchange in today's King Zvonimir Street east from N Square, and another named the Workers' House for the Chamber of Labor and Workers Unions one block to the south at King Petar Krešimir Square. Although separated, the two buildings, in close vicinity to each other, spread the same political message: the further urban development of the Lower City should resolutely promote the social dimension of architecture.

The extension of Zagreb to the east was anticipated in the nineteenth-century plans defining the shape and program of the Horseshoe. In the original concept for the Horseshoe, Milan Lenuci envisioned an east–west avenue, today's Zvonimirova Street, to link the Horseshoe with Maksimir Park. The realization of the National Theater within the Horseshoe initiated the relocation of Fair Fields to the east, in the area between the future N and King Peter Krešimir squares. The Fair Fields were diagonally connected with the Upper Town by a road along the irrigated Medveščak Creak, later developed into the northwest–southeast avenue, today Franje Račkog and Prince Višeslav streets. The next relocation of Fair Fields was initiated with the post-WWI expansions of the Lower Town to the east, with Kovačić's Stock Exchange and urban ensemble in its front, becoming the monumental gate to the diagonal movement. The procession starting at Kovačić's trivium, continuing though N Square was finally completed with the execution of King Peter Krešimir Square regulated by Vladimir Antolić and Josip Seissel from 1935 to 1938. Together with urban and architectural regulation of the square, the horticultural design by Slovenian botanist Ciril Jeglič[81] has remained recognized as the last example of formal public park designs in Zagreb, in the same tradition as Lenunci's Horseshoe.[82] After the rise of radical Modernism during the 1930s and especially during communism, urban landscaping was narrowed down to greening of the leftover surfaces around free-standing edifices, while the traditional urban elements and compositional schemes started being considered retrograde. Although formal, the square with a park in its center intended to attract a broad populous, mainly by its various contents. The park was separated into a free garden in the south section, and a flower garden with children's playground on the north. The playground with the wading pool, swings and monkey-gyms was the first facility of its kind in Yugoslavia.

Avant-garde Zagreb 157

Figure 5.9 The State Trade Academy and the Workers Club at the King Petar Krešimir's Square (National and University Library, Zagreb)

The dominant position in the square was given to the monumentally formalized State Trade Academy by Zvonimir Vrkljan, the author of the previously discussed Veterinary Faculty, which contributed to a vibrant atmosphere at the square until it was converted into the Military Headquarters after WWII. Yet Radnički dom [Workers' House] (Figure 5.9) by Korka-Kiverov-Krekić atelier inserted into the northeast corner added a new quality to the public space by with its distinguishable shape and busy function. Its stressed convex layout was wrapped into a transparent glassed ground floor within a raster of piers, module-perforated façade surface of upper floors with ribbon-windows and a roof deck at the recessed top floor.[83] At the front facing the square, the sharp-angled lot was utilized to create the entrance hall with theatrical staircase leading to the amphitheater for workers' gatherings and performances. A similar theme of approaching the building from the sharp-angled side and continuing through a vestibule to the split-level audience hall, already recorded in Kovačić's Stock Exchange, become a signature feature of Zagreb public programs. The link between Kovačić's mid-1920s masterpiece and the later Korka-Kiverov-Krekić Functionalist realization is as strong from the prospective of broader urban design. While the first opened the path towards the development to the eastern part of Lower Town during the interwar period, the second gave it the final touch.

The concern for the social role of architecture was not limited simply to welfare programs and Modernist aesthetics. Rethinking the city as a catalyst of social life in modern conditions become the preoccupation of a young

158 *National architectures in the unified nation*

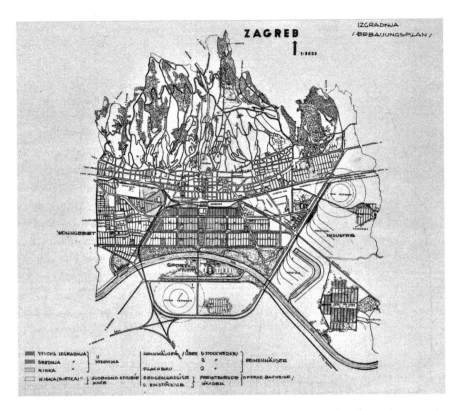

Figure 5.10 RGZ's Regulatory Plan of Zagreb 1932 presented at the CIAM meeting (City Museum of Zagreb)

generation of architects, trying to challenge the nineteenth-century urbanism that had primarily focused on extensions and the beautification of the city's core (see Figure 5.10). The pivotal role in prioritizing the social mission of urban planning was taken by Ernest Weissmann, who established important links with protagonists of the CIAM and its executive body, CIRPAK, during his stay at Le Corbusier's office. Despite close ties with Siegfried Giedion and José Luis Sert, his attitudes were even more radical, closer to Karel Teige's uncompromising leftist platform. His correspondence with Sert shows clearly to what extent the architect was excited about Marxism:

> The main problem lies in the fact that architects do not set architecture on Marxist basis, but rather work on the creation of a new, Machine Age style [...] The analysis of existing state of cities would help architects understand the true problems and take social and political responsibility, which would be the only way for architecture to overcome narrow formalism and get engaged into modern social programs.[84]

Together with his comrades from the RGZ, he probed the ideas on a real situation. As a part of preparation for the Fourth Congress of CIAM, RGZ members worked on detailed analytical maps of Zagreb, and submitted the material for pin-up at the National Polytechnic School Athens, where the Congress was opened and later on the cruise ship *Patris II*, where the discussions were taking place. The maps focused on the existing housing stock, transportation and infrastructure, and the relationships between the city and neighboring region, within which it coexisted. The group also analyzed and presented the causes of workers' slums in Zagreb, developed since the beginning of rapid industrialization and the growth of capital after WWI with the conclusion that:

> The social engagement of the municipality was not sufficient and was ill-managed. Instead of addressing the causes of workers' misery and solving it by planned housing programs, the municipal and state government welfare activities were directed towards establishing health institutions with insufficient capacity.[85]

Eleven housing colonies, including Cvjetno naselje [Flower Estate], the Railroad Colony and the First Croatian Savings Company were funded from the municipal and state funds and some private investors during the interwar period.[86] Yet the RGZ members were not satisfied with these results. Their sharp criticism of social conditions was illustrated in the maps and complemented by statistical data and graphs. A few months before the presentation in Athens they were presented to a domestic audience at the Zemlja exhibition "Kuća i život" [House and Life] in the Art Pavilion. Zagreb contemporary criticism applauded the braveness of the RGZ at a time of censorship and anti-communist sentiments growing out the central government in Belgrade:

> The RGZ made a radical breakthrough – it named liberal capitalism the main felon, which subordinated the public interests and the development of society to the interest of private profit. Architects are in service of profit as they used to be while serving the church and aristocracy; instead of healthy and wealthy life for everybody, they pay attention purely to formal aspect of architecture.[87]

At the CIAM meeting,[88] the RGZ members initiated a discussion about a more radical version of the later-signed Athens Charter which would have brought the social and political agendas to the forefront and challenge the technocratic visons for the future of cities advocated by Le Corbusier.[89] They stood for the abolition of private land ownership, yet in the final conclusions of the CIAM meeting developing in the Marseilles Resolution, they needed to accept a compromise that the free disposition of land ownership should remain under one condition: the individual interest should be subordinated

160 *National architectures in the unified nation*

to the public interest. The left wing of CIAM gathered together again in London in 1934, with an aim to prepare a more persuasive statement for the next congress, yet their opposition was stronger and more famous. Walter Gropius warned Siegfried Giedion about the radically leftist ideas of the young generation in the CIAM:

> It seems that the communist sympathizers in national groups have a secret plan to guide the congress into a different direction. As their initiative is strong, we must inconspicuously oppose this political danger.[90]

Ironically, both the most active and radical participants in the Yugoslavian branch of CIAM, Ernest Weissmann and Vladimir Antolić, did not continue the early enthusiasm about Marxism after the actual victory of Marxist ideology in Yugoslavia after WWII but ended up working for the HTCP (Housing and Town and Country Planning) at the United Nations in New York City.

Notes

1 Banovina Hrvatska [Banat of Croatia] was proclaimed in 1939, in an attempt to overcome growing tensions between Croats and Serbs in the kingdom. Banovina was the only autonomous political entity holding together all territories in which the Croatian population predominated.
2 Rudolf Bićanić, *Ekonomska podloga hrvatskog pitanja* [*The Economic Background of the Croatian Question*], Zagreb, 1938: 109.
3 For the history of Zagreb Architecture Faculty, see Zvonimir Vrkljan, "From the History of Zagreb Technical Faculty," *Arhitektura*, vol. 40, no. 1–4 (1987): 2–20.
4 All plans published and discussed in Krešimir Galović, *Viktor Kovačić: otac hrvatske moderne arhitekture* [*Viktor Kovačić: The Father of Croatian Modern Architecture*], Zagreb: Jutarnji list, 2015: 144–153.
5 "Zakladni blok" has been translated from Croatian to English either as the Endowment or the Foundation Block.
6 Discussed in Tamara Bjažić-Klarin, "Zakladni blok u Zagrebu, Urbanističke i arhitektonske odlike" [The Foundation Block in Zagreb: Urbanistic and Architectural Features], *Prostor*, vol. 18, no. 2 (2010): 322–335.
7 The municipality had bought the land from the brothers in 1883, yet the transaction was completed only after the long-lasting court trail in 1916. The money was redirected to the construction of a new hospital complex on Šalata Hill also known as Široki Brijeg [Wide Hill].
8 The wining proposals are published in Anonymous, "Futurističke osnove" [Futurist Plans], *Svijet*, vol. 15, no. 1 (January 18, 1930) and recently reprinted in Tamara Bjažić-Klarin, *Ernest Weissmann: Socially Engaged Architecture 1926–1939*, Zagreb: HAZU, 2015: 64.
9 The palace, originally named Elsa-Fluid Palace, was commissioned by Eugen Feller, a wealthy pharmacist, who had earned his fortune selling the rejuvenating "elixir" of the same name. In 1927, the property was sold to Otto Stern who invited Peter Behrens to replace the original secessionist façades with the up-to-date functionalist forms.

10 Drago Ibler (1894–1964) graduated from the Technical Faculty in Dresden and as soon as he returned to Zagreb started challenging the traditional climate with his Expressionist designs. Later, he become much more radical – both formally and on the level of architecture as socially engaged practice. He was a founder of the avant-garde group Zemlja and the avant-garde architectural program at the Academy of Fine Arts.
11 Peter Bahrens had met Ibler in Dresden and invited him to work for his office in Berlin until the return to Zagreb in 1923. Ibler was a student of a less influential Werkbund member, Martin Dülfer, included in the list of Werkbund members *Jahrbuch des Deutschen Werkbundes 1913*, Jena: Eugen Dieterichs, 1913. See Željka Čorak, *U funkciji znaka: Drago Ibler i hrvatska arhitektura izmedju dva rata* [*In the Function of Sign: Drago Ibler and Croatian Architecture between the Two World Wars*], Zagreb: Institut za povijest umjetnosti, 1981: 22.
12 Ibler's proposal was published on the cover of Zagreb magazine *Svijet*, vol. 21, no. 6 (February 6, 1936).
13 Stjepan Planić (1900–1980) was one of the most innovative and controversial architects in Croatian architecture, whose opus was characterized by brave syncretism between the Modernist, traditional and contextual. He graduated from Drago Ibler's school at the Academy of Fine Arts, became his collaborator and a member of the Zemlja Group. Besides his unorthodox designs, he also left significant theoretical works.
14 Anonymous, "Gradnja prvog zagrebačkog nebodera" [Building of the First Zagreb Skyscraper], *Jutarnji list* (October 10, 1933).
15 Ibid., 2.
16 Anonymous, "Gradnja visoke zgrade" [The Construction of the Tall Building], *Novosti* (November 11, 1933).
17 According to Löwy's own words "the building's height of only 35 meters hardly lets it hold such a loud entitlement." In Slavko Löwy, "Zagrebački neboder" [The Zagreb Skyscraper], *Građevinski vjesnik*, vol. 2 (1934): 40.
18 Ibid., 41.
19 Discussed in Darja Radović-Mahečić, *Slavko Löwy: sustvaratelj hrvatske moderne arhitekture tridesetih godina* [*Slavko Löwy: A Contributor to Croatian Modern Architecture of the 1930s*], Zagreb: IPU, 1999: 47–48.
20 Anonymous, "Za 79 dana izgradjen je prvi zagrebački neboder" [The First Zagreb Skyscraper Has Been Built in 79 days], *Jutarnji list* (April 29, 1934).
21 Radović-Mahečić, *Slavko Löwy*: 48.
22 Anonymous, "Najveću svjetleću reklamu imat će Zagreb" [The Biggest Light Logo Will Be in Zagreb], *Jutanji list* (September 16, 1934).
23 Darja Radović-Mahečić, "Apoteoza jednoj fotografiji" [The Apotheosis to a Photograph], in *Slavko Löwy*: 52–56.
24 Quoted in Radović-Mahečić, *Modern Croatian Architecture in the 1930s*: 161.
25 Ibler's original drawings were simply reversed in the later realization, so the U-shape arms that originally protruded onto the street were rotated 180 degrees, ending up oriented toward the courtyard, and these altered plans were realized under the architect's name. See Čorak, *U funkciji znaka*: 113–116.
26 Čorak, *U funkciji znaka*: 125. In footnote 143, Čorak presented the entire correspondence between investors and Ibler on one side and the municipal administration and various committees on the other.

162 National architectures in the unified nation

27 In the end, Ibler succeeded to increase the height to six floors plus the roof terrace instead of the originally anticipated four floors.
28 Despite weak evidence regarding Drago Ibler's visit to the Weissenhof exhibition in 1927, it was numerous publications circulating around Europe at that time and his connections with members of the German Werkbund that introduced him to the Weissenhof projects.
29 Anonymous, "Novodradnja Wellisch" [Newly Constructed Wellisch], *Gradevinski vjesnik*, vol. 2 (1932): 1.
30 Old Zagrebers still remember the refined atmosphere in Marić Passage after various shops, restaurants and services were moved in there in 1932. The passage was considered the "place to be seen while visiting hair stylist, barber, tailor or a hat-and-glove-boutique." The space retained its character until the end of communism, when the property was expropriated by the government. Along with the transition to a capitalist economy, the process of restitution of the pre-WWII ownerships took its toll. Most of the shops have been abandoned, and the pedestrian path neglected. Reported in Anonymous, "Marićev prolaz: nekada vrvio od života – danas zapušten i pun đubreta" [Marić Passage: Once Full of Life – Today Neglected and Full of Trash], *Večernji list* (February 20, 2015).
31 In Walter Benjamin's words from *The Arcades Project*, Cambridge, MA: Harvard University Press, 1999.
32 Darko Venturini, "Zvjezdane godine stambene izgradnje" [Stellar Years of Residential Architecture], *Arhitektura*, vol. 30, no. 156–157 (1976): 85.
33 ČVUT is the abbreviation of České Vysoké Učení Technické – the Czech Technical Faculty.
34 Dragan Damjanović, "Architekt Marko Vidaković, výstava Současná československá architektura (1928) v Záhřebu a počátky modernismu v chorvatské architecture" [Architect Marko Vidaković, Zagreb Exhibition of Contemporary Czechoslovakian Architecture (1928) and the Beginnings of Modernism in Croatian Architecture], *Umění*, vol. 62, no. 1–2 (2015): 79–91.
35 Darja Radović-Mahečić, "Letnjikovci i vile izmedju dva svjetska rata: avangarda i tradicija" [Summer Palaces and Villas between the Two Wars: Avantgarde and Tradition], in *Dvorci letnjikovci* (conference procedings), Varaždin, 2006: 352.
36 *Arhitektura: mesečna revija za stavbno, likovno in uporabno umetnost*, vol. 1, no. 1, (1931): 2–4.
37 Sanja Filep, "Kolonija vila Novakova ulica" [Colony of Villas Novakova Street] in Radović-Mahečić, *Modern Croatian Architecture in the 1930s*: 241. For further research on Novakova, see Sanja Filep, "Influences of Austrian and German Architecture on Croatian *Moderna* between the Two World Wars – Case Study Novakova Ulica", PhD dissertation, Stuttgart, 2000.
38 Tomislav Timet, *Stambena izgradnja Zagreba do 1954. godine*, Zagreb: JAZU, 1961: 182.
39 Zagreb architect Branko Siladin investigated the influence of the "Façade Commission" on realizations in Novakova and published an example of refused design in *Čovjek i prostor*, vol. 33, no. 10 (1986): 26.
40 Vladimir Šlapeta, "Novakova Street and the Problem of Stadtville in Central European Architecture," *Čovjek i prostor*, vol. 33, no. 10 (1986): 27–29.
41 The legislative system in the kingdom was neither centralized nor fully coordinated, despite various attempts at creating a synchronized, unique set of laws for the entire country. Historians have commented that there were at least six

different law systems operating simultaneously throughout the country. See Ivan Božić et al., *Istorija Jugoslavije* [*A History of Yugoslavia*], Belgrade: Prosveta, 1970: 446. Thus, the organization and management of social insurance and workers welfare from the central headquarters in Zagreb is not entirely clear.

42 Toma Milenković, "Privremeno radničko zakonodavstvo u Jugoslaviji od Prvog svetskog rata do donošenja Vidovdanskog ustava" [Provisional Labor Legislature in Yugoslavia from WWI until the Vidovdan Constitution], *Zbornik Zavoda za povjesne znanosti JAZU*, vol. 8, no 11 (1981): 109–232.

43 Vladimir Ivekovića, "Socijalno osiguranje u nas" [Social Insurance in Our Country], *Građevinski vjesnik*, vol. 9, no. 1 (1940): 1–4, 16–20, 30–32.

44 Miroslav Krleža (1893–1981) has been considered the most influential Croatian writer of the twentieth century. Besides numerous novels and poems, he wrote activist, left-oriented criticism against the petit bourgeois spirit and mediocracy.

45 Miroslav Krleža, "Slučaj arhitekte Iblera", *Književna republika*, vol. 2 (1924–1925): 170–173.

46 Zrinka Paladino, "Arhitektonski opus Lavoslava Horvata u Beogradu" [Lavoslav Horvat's Work in Belgrade], *Prostor*, vol. 20, no. 2 (2012): 311–327.

47 Lavoslav Horvat (1901–1989) enrolled on a newly established architecture program at the Academy of Fine Arts in 1926, as one of the first students of Drago Ibler. The life and work of Lavoslav Horvat are discussed in Zrinka Paladino, *Lavoslav Horvat: kontekstualni ambijentalizam i moderna* [*Lavoslav Horvat: Contextual Ambientalism and Modern Architecture*], Zagreb: Meanarmedia, 2013.

48 Horvat receive an offer to work in the office of Rudolf Lubynski after his graduation from the High Technical School in Zagreb in 1922. He stayed there for the entire construction period of the Central Workers' Insurance Headquarters.

49 Along with the headquarters in Zagreb and Belgrade, the commissions for workers' insurance offices in smaller towns across the country such as Mostar, Skopje, Leskovac, Slavonski Brod and Dubrovnik were also granted to Zagreb-based architects.

50 From the catalog of the first exhibition of *Zemlja*, Zagreb, 1929.

51 Tomislav Timet, *Stambena izgradnja Zagreba do 1954. godine* [*Residential Development in Zagreb until 1954*], Zagreb: JAZU, 1961.

52 Discussed in Alan Fogelquist, *Politics and Economic Policy in Yugoslavia, 1918–1929*, Los Angeles: Lulu.com, 2011.

53 The legacy of doctor Andrija Štampar is discussed in Vlado Puljiz, "Socijalna prava i socijalni razvoj Republike Hrvatske" [Social Rights and Social Policies of Croatia, 1900–60], *Revija za socijalnu politiku*, vol. 1 (2004): 3–20.

54 Quoted in Dražen Juračić, *Zdravstvene zgrade* [*Medical Buildings*], Zagreb: Tehnička knjiga, 2005: 35.

55 As a graduate from Zagreb Technical Faculty, Juraj Denzler (1896–1981) was strongly influenced by the first generation of his professors, primarily Viktor Kovačić. He would be remembered for his Viennese-inspired project for the Elektra Palace – the city infrastructures administration building, from 1933.

56 Radović-Mahečić, *Modern Croatian Architecture in the 1930s*: 123.

57 Viktor Altmann, "Gradnja Židovske bolnice u Zagrebu" [The Construction of Jewish Hospital in Zagreb], *Židov*, vol. 13 (1929): 7–10.

58 Ernest Weissmann (1903–1985) graduated from the Technical Faculty in Zagreb, and started a collaboration with Adolf Loos and Le Corbusier after his

164 National architectures in the unified nation

graduation. He was one of the most radical architects, a member of the Radna Grupa Zagreb, whose primary mission was socially engaged architecture. During WWII he fled to the USA and gained a position at the UN Housing and Planning Authority.
59 The "pavilion-scheme" dominated from the mid-nineteenth century until the mid-1930s, when a new "compact plan", inaugurated in the USA was accepted in Europe.
60 Tamara Bjažić-Klarin, "Health and Welfare Institutions 1930–31: Typifying, Standardization and Prefabrication," in *Ernest Weissmann: Socially Engaged Architecture 1926–39*, Zagreb: HAZU, 2015: 81–83.
61 Engineer Gustav Hermann was responsible for the construction of the velodrome. He wrote a report about the construction in Gustav Hermann, "Trkalište na drvenoj konstrukciji" [Race-field on the Wooden Construction], *Glasilo za sve sportske struke*, no. 5 (1898): 29–30.
62 Anton Ulrich (1902–1998) was a student of Josef Hoffmann, yet the influence of Adolf Loos is also evident, particularly in his proposals for row-housing for low-income families. His projects were noticed from a young age, yet his most successful realizations date to the period after WWII.
63 Vesna Mikić, "Klasičnost Ulrichova moderniteta" [Classical Quality of Ulrich's Modernity], *Prostor*, vol. 12, no.1 (2004): 92.
64 Edo Schön (1877–1949) graduated from the Technical Faculty in Vienna, after which he was briefly a collaborator of Max Fabiani. After returning to Zagreb he worked with Viktor Kovačić and later opened his own studio with Milovan Kovačević. He was among the first professors of Zagreb Faculty of Architecture, serving as the dean since its foundation.
65 Josip Pičman and Josip Seissel, "Poljiprivredno-šumarski fakultet u Zagrebu" [Agricultural and Forestry Faculty in Zagreb], *Tehnički list*, vol. 15 (1933): 281.
66 Bjažić-Klarin, *Ernest Weissmann*: 167.
67 Pičman and Seissel, "Poljiprivredno-šumarski fakultet u Zagrebu": 282.
68 Zvonimir Vrkljan (1902–1999) graduated from the first generation of students at the Technical Faculty. He left over seventy realizations and was also remembered for his pedagogical work and research in the field of prefabrication and standardization.
69 Zrinka Barišić Marenić, "Faculty of Veterinary Medicine Designed by Zvonimir Vrkljan: An Illustrative Example in the Context of Development Project for the Modern University of Zagreb," *Prostor*, vol. 12, no. 2 (2004): 167–177.
70 Milovan Kovačević (1905–1946) was a talented Serbo-Croatian architect, who suffered in a concentration camp during the Ustaša regime and died soon after the end of WWII with a few remarkable realizations left in Zagreb. He started his studies in Prague and finished at the Technical Faculty in Zagreb. Besides the project for the Technical Faculty, he has been remembered for a mixed-use development in Petrinjska Street from 1933.
71 Ivan Zemljak, "Écoles nouvelles en Yougoslavie," *L'Architecture d'aujourd'hui*, vol 2 (1933): 94–100.
72 Ivan Zemljak (1893–1963) studied first at Graz Technical University and after the end of WWI moved to Prague Technical Faculty where he graduated in 1920. He was involved in urban planning of Zagreb as well as in the design of school facilities.
73 Radović-Mahečić, *Modern Croatian Architecture in the 1930s*: 112.

Avant-garde Zagreb 165

74 Zemljak, "Écoles nouvelles en Yougoslavie:" 94.
75 Egon Steimann (1901–1966) was employed at the Technical Office of Sava Banat until the outbreak of WWII. Besides his most acknowledged secondary schools, he designed the Physical Institute at Marulić Square, the Orthopedic Department of Medical School on Šalata, the Post Office at the Railway Station and the Sokol Club. After the war, he focused mainly on research and design of industrial architecture.
76 Radović-Mahečić, *Modern Croatian Architecture in the 1930s*: 142.
77 Egon Steinmann, "Nova srednja škola u Zagrebu" [The New Secondary School in Zagreb], *Arhitektura*, vol. 2 (1933): 199–200.
78 Still a student, Steinmann wrote an article about the Roman amphitheater in Salona, in which reconstruction he participated as a member of Iveković's team.
79 Egon Steinmann, "Novogradnja gimnastičke dvorane" [The Construction of a New Gym], *Tehnički list*, no. 16 (1934): 2–4.
80 Ariana Štulhofer and Iva Muraj, "Srednjoškolsko igralište u Zagrebu" [Highschool Sports Ground in Zagreb], *Prostor*, vol.11, no. 2 (2004): 125–134.
81 Ciril Jeglič (1897–1988) was a Slovenian expert in botany, who gained his knowledge in landscaping at Hochschule für Bodenkultur in Vienna and later as an intern at Dahlem Charlotteburg Park in Berlin in 1929–1930.
82 Zrinka Barišić, "Trg Kralja Petra IV Krešimira: arhitektonsko-urbanistička i perivojna geneza" [Kralja Petra IV Krešimira Square: Origins of Layout, Architecture and Landscaping], *Prostor*, vol. 10, no. 1 (2002): 77–92.
83 Radović-Mahečić, *Modern Croatian Architecture in the 1930s*: 290.
84 From the correspondence between Sert and Weissmann from 1932. Quoted in Bjažić-Klarin, *Ernest Weissmann*: 183.
85 Vladimir Antolić, "Funkcionalni grad" [The Functionalist City], *Kultura*, vol. 1, no. 5 (1933): 363–368.
86 Darja Radović-Mahečić, "Socijalno stanovanje međuratnog Zagreba" [Social Housing in Interwar Zagreb], *Radovi instituta za povjest umjetnosti*, vol. 17, no. 2 (1993): 141.
87 Stevan Galogaža, "Problemi savremene arhitekture" [The Problems of Contemporary Architecture], *Literatura*, vol. 2 (1932): 90–95.
88 Together with Weissmann, the congress was attended by Bogdan Teodorović and Vladimir Antolić, who would remain the Yugoslav representative at the following CIAM meetings in Paris and London, because of Weissmann's withdrawal.
89 Ernest Weissmann, "Imali smo drugu verziju povelje" [We Had Another Version of the Charter], *Arhitektura*, vol. 37–38, no. 189–195 (1984–1985): 32–35. Weissmann wrote this article in form of a letter sent to the publishing board of journal *Arhitektura* a few months before his death in 1985.
90 From the correspondence between Gropius and Giedion from 1934. Quoted in Bjažić-Klarin, *Ernest Weissmann*: 225.

6 National Ljubljana

Tracing a Slovenian national capital

Before the constitution of the Kingdom of Serbs, Croats and Slovenes, Ljubljana had been the capital of the Austrian province of Carniola, with about 40,000 inhabitants, only half of which were ethnic Slovenes,[1] hence the city was not clearly defined as a Slovenian national capital.[2] Ljubljana was founded in Ancient Roman times as a military camp which expanded into the civil settlement of Aemona Iulia, a fortified city with four city gates, the main axes (cardo and decumanus), a forum, residential quarters and graveyards, whose traces are still visible today. According to some sources, the history of Slavic Ljubljana dated back to the 500s CE:

> In the sixth century after Christ, Ljubljana slowly converted into a central crossroad and the brave capital of Slavic people. We learn from history that the strength and exchange of this city was noticed: the geographic position of Ljubljana – situated between the Adriatic Sea and the continental countries – is so pleasing as if the city was the large gate through which the European roads from east to west and from south to north were passing [...] Celtic and Roman settlement Aemona was a rich trade center which has been evidenced in the city museum. During the great migrations, this settlement was destroyed, after which our ancestors Slovenians, while arriving to this wonderful province, founded a new city at the bottom of the Ancient fortification against the river, and named it Ljubljana.[3]

Most sources, however, link the development of medieval Ljubljana to the German noble family of Sponheim, which granted the city a charter and market rights in the twelfth century. The German name of Ljubljana – Leibach – was first recorded in the mid-twelfth century when the Slovenian Luwigana was also in use.[4] By the end of the next century, Ljubljana had become the capital of the Duchy of Carniola, possessed by Rudolf von Habsburg, and remained a part of Habsburg lands until the fall of the empire at the end of World War I. During the Middle Ages, the urban fabric consisted of three sections: one around the Stari trg [Old Square] inhabited by craftsmen, the second around the Mestni trg [Town Square] for trade and commerce, and the third around the Novi trg [New Square] where the nobility lived. Accordingly, the city was inhabited by merchants and craftsmen under the jurisdiction of the municipal administration; nobility under of the Lord of Duchy seated in the castle; and clergy under the Catholic ecclesiastical authority. Each portion was separately walled and mutually connected by gates. The older two communities, Stari trg and Mestni trg, were nestled underneath the castle on the east bank of Ljubljanica, while the newer quarters developed around the Sponheim property on the west bank. By the 1400s, Ljubljana became an important commercial center at the crossroads of trade communications between the core of Habsburg lands, Croatia, Italy and Hungary. The settlement was organized upon medieval customs of land division; the plots were narrow with all types of buildings placed on regulation lines so that rows of houses with shops were randomly interrupted by some public program such as the city hall, bishop's palace or church. At first, the town houses, containing shops or artisans' workshops, were made of wood, with gable roofs and bay windows facing the street.

The presence of the Habsburgs was a key factor in establishing the Roman Catholic Diocese of Ljubljana in 1461, with the Church of St. Nicholas becoming the cathedral. Less than a century later, Ljubljana developed a strong Protestant community and became a strong seat of the Reformation movement lead by clergyman Primož Trubar, thanks to whom the first two books in the Slovenian language, *Catechismus* and *Abecedarium*, were written, printed and distributed. At that time, Ljubljana also became an educational center where a Latin high school was founded, and the first printing shop opened. When the Reformation reached its peak around 1580, the Jesuit order arrived in the city, forcing many citizens to leave. Starting with the Jesuits, who established a Lyceum with four departments which would develop into a university, some other Counter-Reformation monastic orders such as the Capuchins and the Ursulines made a strong presence in the city because of the development of their adjacent educational institutions. With the arrival of Counter-Reformation, the city lost its vibrant, animated life, which would be resumed in the late 1600s, with the opening of modern economic exchanges and cultural institutions, also the establishment of several academies in the Italian fashion – for the sciences, the humanities, music and the fine arts. The first traces of the Enlightenment shaped the intellectual climate with figures such as the poet Valentin Vodnik and dramatist Anton Tomaž Linhart, whose comedy *Županova Micka* [*The Duke's Daughter Micka*] – the first stage play in the Slovenian language – premiered in 1789. Around this time the fortification walls were torn down, new streets laid in their place and new squares formed over the demolished civic gates. The streets and squares were named for the first time.[5] The wooden houses were replaced by brick mansions extending through two or three previous lots, thereby enabling the formation of wider street fronts, often embellished by arcaded porticoes.[6]

168   *National architectures in the unified nation*

The French Revolution, followed by Napoleon's wars, had a great impact on the city. From 1809 to 1813, Ljubljana was the capital of the Province of Illyria within Napoleon's empire, and as such would play an important role in establishing the South Slavic national ideology – the Illyrian movement, striving towards the liberation and unification of western South Slavs. During the short French rule, the Slovenian language was officially introduced in the administration, schools and newly established university. Although short-lived, this period had a strong impact on the modernization processes, continued even after the city returned to its previous status as an Austrian provincial center. The seeds of first manufactures occurred at that time, parallel to the growing role of the city as a trade center due to its position near Trieste, the leading Adriatic port.

The turning point in the transformation of Ljubljana from a provincial town into an engaging economic hub was the completion of the Southern Imperial Railway line Vienna-Trieste in 1857. As Ljubljana became a transit stop on the route, the position of the tracks and the railway station would determine the future urban development[7] between the station to the north and Ljubljanica River to the south. The newly formed quarters extended west to the Šempetrski most [Šempetr Bridge], while their development was controlled through the regulatory plan envisioned by a municipal building officer, Franc Pollak, in 1869.[8] The constitution of Krainische Baugesellshaft – Kranjska stavbna družba [Carniola Building Society] in 1873 influenced the development to the west and the northwest, between the present-day Cankarjeva [Cankar's] and Na Vrtači streets, since it was granted rights to parcellate and manage projects for new houses in those areas.[9] Until the final approval of the Regulatory Plan of Ljubljana in 1888, all new development in the city was controlled by the Bauordnung für das Herzogthum das Krain – Stavbeni red za Vojvodino Kranjsko [Building Ordinances for the County of Carniola], published in 1875. The rising building activity resulted from economic growth and influx of investments coming mainly from the German-speaking, rising middle class. Slovenian ethnicity fulfilled aspirations toward being more visible on the political scene after a Slovenian-speaking Peter von Grasselli was appointed as the župan [count] of Ljubljana from 1882 to 1896. Besides his role in reinforcing the public use of the Slovenian language, he also contributed to the foundation of the first Slovenian bank in the city. Three major municipal infrastructural systems were completed by the end of the nineteenth century: the gas system in 1861, the running water supply in 1890 and the electrical power plant in 1898, while the city was also endowed with a variety of cultural institutions and public buildings: the opera, the philharmonic hall and the museum. The first piece on the opera stage, in 1892, was an adaptation of the overture from Glinka's *Ruslan and Lyudmila*, named *Veronika Deseniška*, with artists from Vienna and Prague helping in its production.[10] In 1891, musical performances started being delivered in the newly completed venue, today's Slovenian Philharmonics, placed between the Ljubljnica River and

Kongresni Trg [Congress Square], yet neither orchestra nor musical pieces bore clear associations with Slovenian identity at that time. The same could be said about the Provincial Museum of Carniola, completed in 1885, which celebrated an integrated Slovenian and German culture simultaneously under the name of Rudolfinum. Although such impressive public institutions characterized many provincial centers of Austria-Hungary, Ljubljana started developing its particularly Slovenian character with the emergence of ethnically distinct societies: the Slovenian Matica, the Slovenian Literary Society, the Slovenian Art Society and the Slovenian Sokol, significant for the future recognition of the city as the capital of Slovenian nation. The key architectural event in the process of affirming of Slovenians as the *Kulturnation* was the construction of Narodni Dom [People's House], a prominent neo-Renaissance palace to house a variety of institutions involved in the promotion of their specific ethnic identity within the Habsburg boundaries, in a similar fashion to the Narodni Dom a few decades earlier in Zagreb.

Ljubljana drastically changed her face after the 1895 earthquake, which destroyed around 10 percent of building stock beyond repair; of 1,373 buildings Ljubljana had before, 145 were disastrously damaged. Guidelines, requiring wider streets and multistory structures, were adopted during the intense post-earthquake reconstruction campaign when the city started developing into what it has remained until the present.[11] Ljubljana's city council received a list of architects recognized by the Viennese authorities as the most adequate candidates to deal with the master plan. When Camillo Sitte learned that he was among the recommended planners, he sent a letter to the mayor of Ljubljana, Peter Grasselli, along with a copy of his book *City Planning According to Artistic Principles*.[12] Grasselli started advocating for Sitte's engagement, yet after his appointment ended in 1896, the new mayor Ivan Hribar redirected the planning priories and strategies. Hribar was the first Slovenian mayor of Ljubljana who insisted on the use of Slovenian language and history in street naming, as well as a more pronounced participation of native Slovenian community in decision-making. Upon his invitation, a Slovenian-born Max Fabiani received an invitation to submit a new version of the regulatory plan. Although attuned to the delicate, theoretically proved planning methods for highly aestheticized urban settings, Sitte's scheme was considered too generic and, as such, applicable to any Central European city. Fabiani's proposal, on the other hand, took into consideration a broader urban area to be appropriated for the rational expansion, and showed more sensitivity to the practical expansion of the city. Conforming to the historically concentric design of the city, with the castle in the middle, both Sitte's and Fabiani's plans directed views from all parts of the city toward the castle and proposed a radial system of streets outside the city center to complement the intrinsic fabric of the historical core. Stemmed from the existing shape of the city, following the motif of two streets underneath the castle's hill along the riverbanks, was laid the most important urban element embracing the entire newly defined city character: a thirty-yard wide and four-mile long

170 *National architectures in the unified nation*

ring road lined with trees – reminiscent of the Viennese Ringstrasse. Neither Sitte's nor Fabiani's ideas for Ljubljana's development were fully realized, yet many elements from Fabiani's proposal occurred in the approved regulatory plan of 1896. It would be in 1908 and 1924 when the previously anticipated schemes were developed into all-embracing urban plans, to serve as a basis for all future planning initiatives. A Slovenian-native, Ciril Metod Koch,[13] synthetized the urban visions (see Figure 6.1) after being appointed the architect of the municipal building office

Unable to probe his visions about Ljubljana's development, Fabiani published a booklet with drawings and explanations,[14] which would aid in his honorary doctoral title in urbanism from the Viennese Technical Faculty.[15] On the other hand, he succeeded in realizing the first comprehensively planed, large-scale public space in the newly regulated district between the railway station and the castle, known as Slovenski or Miklošićev Trg [Slovenian or Miklošić Square].[16] At the initiative of Ivan Hribar, a prominent banker and politician and elected mayor of Ljubljana in 1896–1910, Fabiani was invited to regulate the existing square in front of the monumental court house, to be completed for a special political occasion, a ceremonial visit of Emperor Franz Joseph in 1908. Along with urban design, enhanced by landscape arrangement by a Czech-born botanist Wenzel Heinitz, the entire area around the square became a

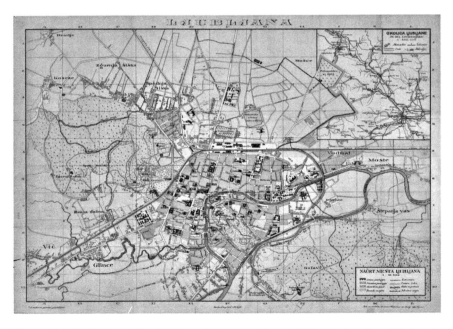

Figure 6.1 Ciril Metod Koch's Plan of Ljubljana from 1924 (National and University Library, Ljubljana)

construction field for many prestigious town palaces attuned to the up-to-date Secessionist trends in Vienna. Together with Fabiani's Bambergova Hiša [Bamberg House], which has remained celebrated as the key example of architecture in Ljubljana since its completion in 1907, two Vienna-trained Slovenians, Ciril Metod Koch and Josip Vancaš, left the most appreciated Secessionist realizations in the vicinity of Miklošić Square and contributed to the new programs which rapidly spread through Ljubljana at the turn of the century, such as banks, department stores, printing houses and multistory apartment buildings.[17] The new edifices were drastically larger in scale and height that the pre-earthquake town houses, while their architectural forms were attuned to the turn of the century stylizations in Vienna.

After WWI and the disintegration of Austria-Hungary, Slovenia became a part of the "three-tribe" kingdom and Ljubljana became a seat of the Slovenian national government. Despite its political subordination to Belgrade as the seat of centralized government, the city developed into a political capital of Slovenes, a unique symbol of their national consciousness during the period between the world wars. Slovenian intellectuals and politicians of the time sincerely believed in new opportunities leading toward the creation of a more pronounced national culture in the unified Slavic state.[18] As art historian France Stelè pointed out:

> After being a neglected provincial city of Austria, Ljubljana not only became the center of all Slovenes but also the third city of the new, large state. Both of those new roles imposed new responsibilities the city started dealing with. The needs of our city within its new position has become quite different. We suddenly must bring awareness to the fact that the cultural framework, previously established by the Austrian authorities, does not meet the new requirements.[19]

The main characteristic of the interwar development of Ljubljana was its rapid industrialization and the accumulation of capital in Slovenian banks. Although Slovenia was considered better industrialized than the eastern parts of Yugoslavia, it was still predominantly rural compared to the rate of industrialization in Western Europe and other parts of the Habsburg Monarchy. This was the time when the city reached its economic and commercial apex, changing from a provincial town with 45,000 people prior to WWI into an industrial and business center with 65,000 inhabitants in the mid-1930s. Major industries, which had been established during Austrian rule, expanded into multiple factories for timber, steal, textile, furniture, paper and glass production, manufacturing goods to be distributed through the rest of the country that was striving toward modernization.[20] The migrations from the countryside were tremendous, with the majority of newcomers employed in some of the industries, followed by jobs in commerce, administration and the army, while only around 500 inhabitants, at the outskirts, still depended on agriculture.[21]

With the rapid pace of urbanization, the old city core was quickly transformed from the pre-existing one- and two-story town houses into mixed-use urban palaces. The corporate sector took part in financing architectural and urban development far beyond the limits of specifically designated, private property borders. For example, one of the wealthiest Slovenian bankers and industry owners, Rado Hribar,[22] invested a considerable portion for public works on urban embellishment of the old core and new public buildings of national importance such as the National and University Library. Parallel to tremendous building activity within the private sector, the municipality invested much effort in infrastructure and reshaping the overall appearance of the city.[23] Besides the improvements and enlargement of the existing water supply and sewage, which had been put in service in 1890, the municipality worked on public transportation and the construction of roads to accommodate a growing number of cars.

The key task in defining a new architectural profile of Ljubljana, which would clearly acknowledge its role as the Slovenian capital, was given to Jože Plečnik, a Slovenian-born Wagnerschule graduate who had already gained a professional reputation around Central Europe. Together with Ivan Vurnik, also Slovenian, who graduated from the Technical Faculty in Vienna, Plečnik founded the faculty of Architecture, with the explicit aim of producing the first generation of Slovenian architects and promoting the ideas of national architecture, in 1919. The faculty was a part of newly founded University of Ljubljana, the first institution of that kind in Slovenia, within which all fields of technical studies were favored among the newly enrolled students, as a result of a broader political climate, promoting fast industrialization and modernization throughout the region.[24]

Although never fully realized, Plečnik's 1928 urban plan for Ljubljana[25] has remained a vital document for understanding the final city's transformation from a Dolga ves [Long Village] into a Velika Ljubljana [Great Ljubljana] in 1935.[26] Assuming an urban expansion and incorporation of adjacent small towns of Šiška, Bežigrad, Vič and Trnovo into a larger urban area, Plečnik envisioned a radial plan on a larger scale than Fabiani's earlier circular enclosure within the boundaries of the historic center. He also proposed new residential areas, defined the directions of the city's future development, and suggested new types of public buildings to be built both in the core of the city and in the new districts. The plan included a sequence of parks enriched by monumental structures as in the central public space of the main park of Tivoli with a memorial to King Aleksandar. He foresaw many grand public projects such as the Slovenian Parliament on the top of the hill, replacing the medieval castle; however, it was his small, but extremely effective, "micro-urban" projects that were to give Ljubljana a new identity as a Slovenian capital. Due to his engagement and influence, the entire development of the city during the 1920s–1930s the has been remembered as Plečnik's Ljubljana.[27]

The Viennese fathers and the Slovenian son – Jože Plečnik

Recognized for an extraordinary talent in drawing by teachers from the High School of Applied Arts in Graz, twenty-two-year-old Jože Plečnik entered the Academy of Applied Arts in Vienna, at the time when Otto Wagner was taking over the position of the head of Academy from Karl Hasenauer. Plečnik's fellows, including some of the most written about names of the Secession movement, such as Josef Hoffmann, remembered him as the best student in their studio, fully absorbed by his work and oblivious to everything else.[28] His final thesis project for a health resort dealt with a broad scope of architectural problems from the urban context to meticulous details of exterior design. Highly praised both by his professors and colleagues, the project was granted with a prestigious scholarship for a year of study through Italy and France in 1898. It was this exposure to Italian Renaissance and Baroque architecture that inspired Plečnik in revealing the genius loci of Ljubljana as the crossroad between the German and Italian spheres of influence to be transcended for the future of a uniquely Slovenian city. An opportunity to fulfill this ambition would not arise for another two decades, yet Plečnik's urge to affirm the Slavic roots emerged in his works in Vienna and Prague, realized from 1901 until the mid-1920s.

The extensive emigration of Jews and Slavs to Vienna from the eastern parts of Austro-Hungary during the last decades of the nineteenth century, perceived by old Viennese as "the eastern flood," had the effect of causing the already introverted Plečnik to stay away from Viennese public life. Yet, the rebellious projects he accomplished there during the 1900s, the Church of Holy Spirit and Zacherl House, could be understood as an artistic reaction to this hostility. The bold character of designs, especially Zacherl House,[29] built steps away from St. Stephan's Cathedral, were commented on by Plečnik in a letter to his brother:

> When my building finally gets completed, you must see it. There will be nothing like it in Vienna, no matter what other people think or say. I would like for you to see it and make your own opinion about all this effort for the sake of Slovenia. This building is the testimony of my background, and I want my country to know that it is an entirely my conception, born out of difficult times when artist frequently find it impossible to work.[30]

Both conceptually and stylistically, Zacherl House was the most radical architectural statement in *fin de siècle* Vienna, completed prior to Looshaus at Michaelerplatz. Like Loos, Plečnik disregarded the decorative Secessionism, at that time the style overwhelmingly spread through most cities of the empire. Both architects strived toward sober architectural answers to the escalating social and political tensions, while most of their colleagues covered them up by simply reinventing the opulent ornamental mode from the previous century. The refusal to participate in the ongoing games in the profession prevented Plečnik from exploring his talent in his native Ljubljana as an young architect.[31] The strong presence of Max Fabiani, whose architecture was firmly based on the prevalent Secessionism, both in Vienna and Ljubljana, blocked Plečnik's efforts to receive any commission in Ljubljana prior to the constitution of Yugoslavia. The reason for Fabiani's animosity could be Plečnik's disrespect for Secessionism, as he believed that the style was inappropriate to the Slovenes – the Slavs of southern Europe – yet it is more likely that Fabiani was threatened by Plečnik's undisputable talent and ensured he stayed invisible in Ljubljana as long as possible. After ten years of practice on several commissions in Vienna, received primarily through his strong ties to the Catholic Church, Plečnik started struggling there. Upon the invitation of his Wagnershule fellow, Jan Kotěra, he moved to Prague to teach at the Academy of Fine Arts. Due to the long-lasting execution of the Church of Holy Cross he made short trips from Prague to Vienna, yet he stayed detached from his Slavic compatriots because of uneasiness to clearly define a political position about the Habsburg authorities at the eve of WWI. While he was invited to participate in the cultural affirmation of the South Slavic ideology, fought for by his Croatian colleague from the Academy of Fine Arts, Ivan Meštrović, Plečnik neither accepted nor refused the invitation.[32]

His experience teaching in Prague was fundamental in developing a teaching philosophy for a new, national architecture program, established as the Department of Architecture at the Technical Faculty in Ljubljana, in 1919. Plečnik moved to Ljubljana and joined the faculty upon the invitation by Ivan Vurnik, after Vurnik's friend Max Fabiani had refused the same offer.[33] The question is if Plečnik would have arrived at the same decision had he succeeded in inheriting a place at the Viennese academy after Otto Wagner's retirement in 1912. Despite Wager's intentions to leave his position to Plečnik, along with an approval gained from the rest of the professors and colleagues, the Ministry of Education in Vienna did not allow Plečnik to be appointed.[34] The reasons lay both in the architectural radicalism of Plečnik's early designs in Vienna, and in his exclusively Slovenian, anti-elitist background, not suitable for reinforcing an image of the shaking empire. However, Vurnik regretted inviting Plečnik very soon after Plečnik joined the faculty in Ljubljana. Although sharing a similar passion for the creation of a Slovenian national architecture, the two architects developed conflicting visions of how it should look. In contrast to the previous argument by the Viennese authorities against Plečnik's radicalism, Vurnik considered Plečnik's approach too conservative for a nation in the making.

Upon his arrival to Ljubljana, Plečnik was still little-known there, yet he soon established a keen friendship with the director of the city planning department, Matko Prelovšek, and art historian Franc Stelè. As later noted by respected Plečnik scholar Damjan Prelovšek:

In the mid-twenties [these] three men presided over the destiny of Ljubljana. [...] Many of their ideas were developed spontaneously and without official approval, while they gathered around a glass of wine in the working-class inn Pri Kolovratu. At first working with the gardener Anton Lap, Plečnik planted a few trees or repaired a neglected corner with old blocks of stone found in the city's warehouses.[35]

Upon settling in Ljubljana, Plečnik became preoccupied with comprehensive visions for the city as a Slovenian capital, and although his most ambitious ideas would not materialize before the mid-1930s, he very soon become involved in small-scale urban interventions. His interest in micro-urban designs was manifested in works he led in the design studio with his students on three vital urban locations. These early urban projects were first published in the college's periodical *Lučine* in 1928, and soon executed in the short span of only three years. Plečnik could not hide his excitement about the quick realization of his first works in the homeland, after his long-lasting exclusion from the domestic architectural circle. Although almost sixty years old, the most fruitful part of his career was still to come. In the next fifteen years, until the outbreak of WWII, he accomplished an enormous number of designs of various scales and programs, and, as importantly, made an unprecedented impact on the future of the architectural profession.

The first urban designs included the remodeling of St. James Bridge [Šantjakobski most] and its expansion to Zois Street, the French Revolution Square with its connection with Vega Street, and, finally, paving of the immense surface of Congress Square (Figure 6.2). Plečnik inserted a sequence

Figure 6.2 Plečnik's reconfiguration of the Congress Square (Ethnographic Museum, Ljubljana)

of sculptural accents: monuments, free-standing columns, pyramids and fountains into each of the treated public spaces, alluding to the universal language of Classicism, Renaissance and Baroque, all of which he had explored during his field studies through Italy. His inclinations toward antiquity were emphasized by the fact that Ljubljana was established as the Roman city of Emona, with remains of spolia still evident throughout the urban fabric. The restauration of archeological remains and incorporation of ancient sculptural fragments into the contemporary design was Plečnik's vital strategy for pointing out the connection of Slovenian identity with the ancient Mediterranean realm. Another layer of symbolism Plečnik added was a design for the Monument to French Illyria, a granite obelisk erected in 1929, for the celebration of the 120th anniversary of Napoleon's constitution of the Province of Illyria, with Ljubljana as its capital city.[36] For that event, the historical square, at which the announcement of the proclamation of Illyria had been read in the Slovenian language, was renamed after Napoleon and remains the French Revolution Square today.[37]

Along with the realization of small urban projects, Plečnik worked a new version of the master plan, focusing primarily on the underdeveloped northern areas across the railroad tracks. Despite the troubled history of his relationship with Max Fabiani, he did not ignore the previously approved post-earthquake plan, but respected, for the most part, Fabiani's original vision for the developments within the inner ring.[38] Thus, the already defined street regulations and the positioning of main public spaces, parks and squares in the downtown area, remained almost untouched in Plečnik's plan. The main difference brought by Plečnik was the regulation of Šiška and Bežigrad and their integration with the old core.[39] Fabiani had already treated the area of Bežigrad in an appendix to his master plan from 1898,[40] yet Plečnik suggested a noticeably different concept for broader scope of the northern districts, reminiscent of Ebenezer Howard's visionary proposals for the Garden City reform.[41] As spread though the European architectural academia only during the 1910–1920s, Howard's ideas were unknown to Fabiani when he envisioned the plan. In line with Howard's schemes, Plečnik proposed a "fan-like" network of radial streets cut through by straight avenues leading towards the city and linking the new neighborhoods to the very precisely chosen spots in the old urban fabric.[42] What differed in Plečnik's scheme was the emphasis on main axial avenues, the containers of public programs of the new neighborhoods.[43] Primarily residential, the northern neighborhoods were of low density with semidetached and detached family houses sunk in greenery. At its very end, the entire northern zone was flanked by a wider radial avenue – the peripheral ring, "placed among trees and at least half a thousand vegetable gardens, providing the greenery always needed in a modern city."[44]

Svetokrižki okraj [Holy Cross District] was the most elaborately considered portion of the plan for Bedžigrad (see Figure 6.3). It was conceived within a conical area on the northeast aligned with the railway

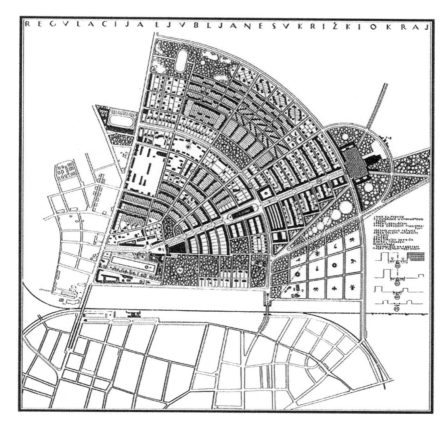

Figure 6.3 Plečnik's plan for Svetokriški okraj (Muzej za arhitekturo in oblikovanje – MAO, Ljubjana)

tracks, for which the city council ratified the development strategy in 1929, followed by regional government approval the following year.[45] The mixture of various housing typologies intended to provide comfort for the incoming population still fluctuated between the rural and fully urban way of life. The nature of future urban fabric conceived as a collage of carpet-looking patterns was to be diverse and full of contrasts in each of the blocks.[46] The main motive was the central avenue embellished with squares and public buildings, yet its symbolical importance as the urban spine lay in the fact that it was to connect the old municipal cemetery of St. Christoph at its beginning and the newly established Cemetery of the Holy Cross or Žale at its end. Plečnik provided designs for both memorials — the reconstruction and reuse of the old St. Christoph's and a new architectural and landscape designs for much larger Žale, the monumental, still functioning civic graveyard, considered one of the peak points of his entire career. Passionate about turning the area of St. Christoph's into a significant urban landmark

178 *National architectures in the unified nation*

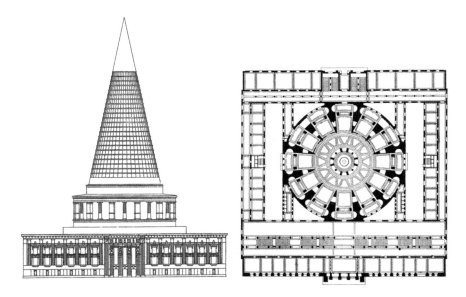

Figure 6.4 and 6.5 Plečnik's project for the Slovenian Parliament (Plečnik House)

of national importance he proposed for a central national memorial, the Temple of Glory or the Slovenian Pantheon – a shrine which would have commemorated remarkable figures from Slovenian history, like the German Walhalla – to be placed there. Yet, Walhalla and similar nineteenth-century national memorials around Europe put emphasis primarily on the power of nationalism as a secular religion, while Plečnik's intentions were to closely tie the shrine with the Catholic Church practices. Despite Plečnik's enthusiasm for the project, which he shared with his students, who took an active part in the design process,[47] the Slovenian Pantheon was never realized. Instead, he was invited to submit a project for Catholic seminary for the same site.

The project for the Slovenian Pantheon was later translated into an even more grandiose vision for the national shrine, the Cathedral of Freedom (Figure 6.4 and 6.5), the name given by Plečnik to the project for the Slovenian National Parliament.[48] Conceptualized as an exaggerated cone inserted into a four-story-high square pedestal, the layout of the Cathedral of Freedom recuperated the scheme of Schinkel's Altes Museum, repeating even the motive of Classical colonnade continuously spread over the entrance façade. The main difference was the way Plečnik accentuated the central rotunda, the space for assembly gatherings, by overstating the dome, twisting its geometry and turning it into an immense conical tower. This design decision had to deal with Plečnik's intention to place this visual landmark at end of Šubićeva ulica [Šubić Street] and its opening into the National Park, better known as Tivoli Park, so that the Cathedral of Freedom could dominate the downtown skyline, competing only with Ljubljana Castle at the top of the hill. Originally Plečnik wanted to place the parliament in the reconstructed castle, as he had done with Hradčany in Prague, yet it required radical alternations of the inherited remains. The idea of radically changing the layer of medieval history did not find enough support among Plečnik's colleagues,[49] thus the castle was preserved in a more traditional way and converted into the city museum. Plečnik was simply seduced with the visual attractiveness of the elevated site and its connections to the rest of the city; in a similar fashion Camilo Sitte understood the values of the castle in his post-earthquake master plan – as the focal point toward which all vistas would have gravitated. The Cathedral of Freedom also never advanced toward realization. It was considered dated by the time Slovenia reached the point when the construction of Parliament was supported in Socialist Yugoslavia.[50]

Linking the urban nodes of specific historical importance was the key strategy of Plečnik's urban interventions, both on the macro and micro levels, a skill he had gained through his exploration of the Renaissance and Baroque urbanism in Italy and also through an immediate exposure to Camillo Sitte's teachings and works in Vienna. As was previously mentioned, Sitte had submitted a plan for Ljubljana after the earthquake, later recognized as unreasonably generic to be applied to the specific case of Ljubljana. What was understood as generic in the plan was Sitte's approach toward the contextual enhancement, the way of linking new public projects done by the Habsburg authorities, into a coherent urban physique, as he had done in many municipal cities over the empire. "By focusing on the purely visual status of landmarks and public buildings, Sitte reinforced their institutional presence as public monuments";[51] moreover, he tried to root these institutions deeper into the urban experience. Similarly, Plečnik's main design method was the connecting of new public projects with old historical landmarks, yet within the new political framework of the South Slavic country, within which the political and cultural institutions he envisioned were the explicit showcases of Slovenian national emancipation.

There was another set of urban principles Plečnik derived from Sitte: the Classical schemes for conceptualizing public spaces, making them mutually connected and flowing into one another.[52] His urban designs aimed to enhance the experience of strolling through vibrant as well as serene pedestrian paths. As Peter Krečić pointed out:

> Plečnik saw the city as an organism, whose character and pulse are experienced by walking through its streets and squares and observing it both closely and from the distance. [...] For Plečnik a city's layout was like a story or like a musical theme with the beginning, middle and the end.[53]

180 *National architectures in the unified nation*

Figure 6.6 Plečnik's regulation of Ljubljanica River, Tromostovje and the Arcade in background (photo Tanja D. Conley)

Plečnik's urban interventions were connected to his own pedestrian paths[54] such as the route along the Ljubljanica river, conceived as a sequence of picturesque embankments, elaborately sculptured bridges and a lock. In 1930, he was invited to take part in the deepening of the Ljubljanica, yet the results were far beyond an engineering project – his approach was rather sculptural than pragmatic (see Figure 6.6). He turned the riverbanks into the promenades accentuated by a variety of masonry patterns of rustically cut or polished stone, fashioning small walls, theatrical stairways, arcades, balustrades, free-standing columns, benches, widened observation platforms and galleries on different levels. Plečnik used specific kinds of trees and greenery for a broader compositional scheme; he delicately inserted weeping willows next to more mature horse chestnut trees to provide an effect of opening and framing the vistas along the path. The highest aesthetic effects were achieved at the connections between the embankments and new bridges, Šuštarski most [Shoemaker's Bridge] and Tromostovje [Triple Bridge]. The primary function of bridges was elevated to another level; they became public places extending into squares on both sides of the Ljubljanica. Furthermore, Tromostovje defined the edges of the irregularly shaped Prešernov trg [Prešern Square] and highlighted the position of the existing Prešern's statue. Along the right bank it developed into a dramatic Greek stoa with a "Berninian"-looking colonnade to serve as a semi-enclosed market. Today called Plečnik's Arcade, the market remained the only realized segment of a more ambitious vision for the New City Hall complex – a large, mixed-use development with various retail and office spaces and a bigger central market fused with municipal offices and halls. Plečnik envisioned the equestrian statue of King Petar I Karađorđević at the main steps connecting the central public courtyard with the main entrance of the New Town Hall. The immense complex was to be spread from the main city cathedral, St. Nicolas, to Kopitarjeva ulica [Kopitar Street], on one side ending with the Dragon Bridge over Ljubljanica and on the other with Krekov trg [Krek Square]. From here the monumental staircase would have led to the top of the hill, with the Slovenian Parliament at the reconstructed Ljubljana Castle as the apex of the processional movement through the city.

The second pedestrian route Plečnik beautified was more explicitly rooted in his immediate strolling experience, starting from his house in Trnovo with the end at Congress Square, he had already elaborately furnished with his students in 1928. His house was next to the church of Trnovo, so he made a semicircular paved podium in front of the church as the point of departure. For the crossing over the Gradaščica river, Plečnik designed an arched bridge with railings composed of expressive vase-shaped balustrades and accentuated at their ends with massive pyramids; this was the threshold, dividing the predominately suburban Trnovo district from the central zone. The path led over the bridge to Emona Street, along which the most archeological findings from the ancient times were excavated, ending with French Revolution Square with Plečnik's monument to Napoleon as its focal point. At this spot, at the crossing of Revolution Square with Vega Street, the remains of both ancient and medieval Ljubljana overlapped. Plečnik freely incorporated the historical remains into new parapet walls topped by cut-off pyramids and pedestals with busts of notable Slovenians. The busts portrayed notable musicians as a part of celebrating the sixtieth anniversary of the Music Society established in 1872 with its seat in Vega Street. The pedestrian route finished at Congress Square, further developing into Zvezda park [Star Park]. The path was supposed to end at the never-realized South Square connected to Zvezda Park through grand propylaea leading to a monument of the assassinated King Aleksandar Karađorđević.

The most symbolically overloaded historical spot of Ljubljana, the joint between French Revolution Square and Vegova Street, turned into the site for the key national institution confirming Slovenian identity, the National and University Library (Figure 6.7). Plečnik accepted an invitation to work on the project in 1930, when the site for the library was chosen and approved by the authorities. The structure was to occupy the urban block spreading from the mouth of Vega Street on the southwest corner and the Novi trg [New Square] on the northeast side, where the Baroque palace of Prince Auersperg had once stood before it was destroyed by the earthquake. The question of erecting the library became critical after the foundation of Ljubljana University in 1919 and Plečnik was enthusiastic

182 *National architectures in the unified nation*

Figure 6.7 Plečnik's National and University Library (photo Tanja D. Conley)

about designing it "as a temple of learning and human wisdom, essential for the healthy development of Slovenian people and their independence."[55] At the time he accepted the engagement the expectations about the size of the program were growing, both from the rectorate of Ljubljana University and the professional community. The prominent scholars of Slavic studies Franc Kidrič and Ivan Prijatelj outlined the general vision, aiming for the building to house one million books and be sufficient for educating the nation for the next hundred years. Plečnik accepted a broad scope of the programmatic requirements, yet only to the point it fit into his already developed visions for the library. The project, developed in 1930–1931, was published in the Ljubljana journal *Dom in Svet*, and in a separate booklet, *The Design for Ljubljana University Library*,[56] accompanied by an affirmative introduction by France Stelè.

Plečnik's concept was an homage to an older Central European precedent, the Munich City Library by Friedrich von Gärtner,[57] yet some other elements of design were reminiscent of Wagner's unrealized project for Vienna University Library, as pointed out by Peter Krečič:[58]

As we see from the lifts and his placing of the books in concrete cells, easily accessible but fireproof, Plečnik adopted the functional parts almost literally from Wagner's project for the Vienna University Library of 1910. Wagner's internal arrangement seemed to him so appropriate that he evidently saw no need to study other modern libraries as Kidrič and Prijatelj has envisaged when outlining the project. Plečnik only moved away from the principles of his teacher in the reading room, which Wagner believed should not exceed 4.7 meters in height, as a higher celling would have an unfortunate effect on the users.[59]

The analogies between functional solutions for book storage were inspired by Wagner, yet Plečnik's design was far more traditional than the twenty-year-older Viennese precedent. The leading idea Plečnik conveyed was of the Baroque palazzo, with a dramatic entrance and staircase cutting through the inner courtyard toward the main reading room. Flights of stairs, composed as a grandiose axial promenade flanked by a row of monumental columns on each side, arose to the point at which the entrance to the reading room is enhanced by a small cupola outlining the moment of mental preparation before immersion into the world of research and intellectual contemplation.

> These are the great staircase and the colonnade of the first floor peristyle, the famous symbolical path from the banality, rumors and rush of the every-day life to the consecrated silence of the spiritual, from the darkness of ignorance to the brightness of knowledge and erudition that is revealed in the great reading room.[60]

Climbing the theatrical stairwell climaxed at the reading room, the elongated rectangular volume, monumentalized by an enormous ten-meter-high ceiling and huge windows on both narrow sides opening toward vistas of the city. While the stairwell was heavy, dark and solid, the reading room was airy, delicately illuminated through two floor-to-ceiling windows and the clerestory light above the open book shelves on two narrow galleries flanking the central aisle. The entire procession toward the reading room was a "metaphorical path of the student rising slowly from the darkness of ignorance toward the light of wisdom."[61] The reading room recalled the sober and bright spirit of early-Christian basilicas. Its elongated shape and amplified height were similar to those sacred spaces, as were the coffered ceiling, the clerestory light over the "nave" shedding light onto the reading desks, and the two continuous window-screens on both ends of the "nave," carrying out the role of apsidal zones. As the central temple of knowledge, the task of which was to overcome routine boundaries of the everyday and bring a reader into the realm of transcendental experience, Plečnik's reading room succeeded in fusing the inherited images of Slovenian Catholicism with the modern concept of nationhood as a secular religion.

The exterior features embraced an opposite symbolical tie; instead of the allusions to sacred architectural precedents from the Catholic world, the library exterior followed the scheme of Roman Baroque palazzos, the urban nodes from which the wealthiest families and clergy navigated the realm of secular power. Following a typical palazzo scheme, the tripartite façade composition was separated into a robust, light-gray granite base; a vibrant upper-floor zone wrapped in much lighter brick and white marble blocks; and the smooth, marble-cladded top with cornice. The piano nobile was differentiated by a larger size and different shape of windows, while the remaining fenestration pattern repeated a dynamic and protruding form of "elbow"-shaped openings. The main character of all, consistently conveyed façade screens was rooted in tectonic qualities of various masonry patterns. The exception was radical forms of two large glass surfaces on the narrow sides of the main reading room: in front of each Plečnik placed an exaggerated Ionic column with bronze volutes, as if he had anticipated what would become one of the most admired elements in architectural Postmodernism, promoted parallel with the rediscovery of Plečnik's architecture to the world audience in the early 1980s. Overall, the mannerist façades were intended to respectfully replace the still-remembered monumentality of Prince Auersperg's residence, but also to monumentalize its high role as the pivotal institution for the development of Slovenian national program. The building's link to the past was confirmed through the continuity of palazzo typology in both instances, yet unraveling and remembering the past for sake of the nation's future was affirmed more literally with another architectural detail: Plečnik enriched the already dramatic nature of the library's façades by inserting ancient spolia into their textures. Similar methods of façade weaving had been introduced by Plečnik's Central European forerunners, first through Gottfried Semper's theory of Bekleidung and later through Otto Wager's practical reiterations of the same theory seen on the majority of his projects. Linking Semper's theories to Plečnik's architecture cannot be understood as simply arbitrary. The Slovenian disciple did not only inherit the manner of textile references learned through his immediate teacher, Otto Wagner, but rather dug into the origins of architectural production as it had been authentically explained by Semper especially in architectural details of "tying" either different materials or structural elements.[62]

Together with Jan Kotěra in Prague and Viktor Kovačić in Zagreb, Plečnik inspiringly transformed the legacy of Otto Wagner[63] and Wagnerschule into an individual architectural script recognized as the beacon of national identity. While Kotěra and Kovačić followed Wagner's revolutionizing spark in search for a perpetually transforming Modernism, Plečnik on the other hand, retained devoted to the constancy of universal Classicism. In the end, their work achieved extraordinary individual qualities, at the same time unquestionably linked to Wagner's design strategies. This was noticeable on various types and scales of urban and architectural designs, from a broad level of master planning all the way to the execution of peculiar architectural details and furniture design. Plečnik's contribution to Wagner's legacy stood out because of the number of designs and the widespread territory over which they occurred. He used to practice in four major cities of the declined Habsburg Monarchy – Vienna, Prague, Ljubljana and Zagreb – and in Belgrade as the capital of the expanding Slavic state. A high level of appreciation for the inherited urban setting and cultural context was the preoccupation of the leading voices on the Viennese architectural scene, Camilo Sitte and Otto Wagner, that highly influenced Plečnik's work. Their influence was visible both in Plečnik's large-scale urban visions for Prague and Ljubljana, and the ways he positioned single architectural designs in regard to their urban surroundings. Often considered Mannerist because of their link to Michelangelo's urban solutions,[64] Plečnik context-driven designs more likely fluctuated between Otto Wagner's and Camilo Sitte's teachings. "In functional questions to which he had no answers Plečnik always relied on Wagner."[65] Otherwise, he followed his own imagination by questioning Wagner's rigid schemes. Even when he tried to imitate a manner of Otto Wagner while schematically dealing with large urban arrangements, there was no monotony and repetition of standardized elements, but rather a play of various patterns contributing to the diversity of each block. Plečnik's urban projects were achieved thorough a piecemeal process, with a high level of sensitivity for every micro-situation within the larger vision. Like Sitte, Plečnik considered designing the city as an artistic endeavor, in which every view and every perspective reveal a thought-through correlation between buildings and public spaces. Plečnik's urban design strategies were similar to Sitte's, yet their political motives for designing according to artistic principles were opposite. While Sitte's designs reinforced an image of the imperial order, Plečnik believed in promotion of Slavic national identities to be achieved by artistic script, coming from "the will for art" of the architect in charge. Although mainly focused on conceptualizing the idea of national architecture, Plečnik never considered its roots in vernacularism, but searched for its affirmation through the continuity with Classical traditions. It would be hard to prove to what extent Plečnik's architecture was explicitly Slovenian, yet it was certainly the best example of continuous devotion to the Wagnerschule. Despite his tremendous role in constituting the identity of Slovenian architecture, Plečnik was in the first place a Central European architectural phenomenon.[66]

The Slovenian father and Slovenian sons: Plečnik's rivals and disciples

When Plečnik came to study in Vienna in 1895, the Wagnershule was considered the leading center of European modernity, but by the time Ivan Vurnik[67] enrolled at the school seventeen years later, "Wagner was no longer at the peak of his creativity."[68] Differently from Plečnik, Vurnik was born to an affluent family, which insisted on a broad humanistic education for their children. Since enrolling at the Technical Faculty in Vienna, Vurnik became close to Max Fabiani.[69] Opposite from Plečnik's case, Vurnik and Fabiani never became enemies, even when one turned into a Slovenian nationalist, while the other remained loyal to Austrian imperial politics. Both Plečnik and Vurnik considered themselves as heralds of a Slovenian national idea, yet their takes on how it can be architecturally manifested were in conflict. Vurnik was the first to take steps in the foundation of a national school of architecture within the newly established University of Ljubljana, yet most credit for the "birth" of Slovenian architecture went to Plečnik who joined the faculty upon Vurnik's invitation. Plečnik saw himself as a supreme executor of the will-to-art's universal calling sprung onto the nation at a given moment, while Vurnik, on the other hand, considered architecture as an intellectual endeavor in service of the nation. Vurnik's vision of how the architectural school should contribute to the national development was written in form of a manifesto,[70] while Plečnik almost never wrote about architecture, neither about his works nor his teaching philosophy, leaving us mostly with letters to his brother and memories of his disciples to decipher how he thought. The ambiguity of the relationship between Vurnik and Plečnik was evident not only in opposite ways of manifesting the idea of Slovenian national architecture in realized projects but also in the divergent approaches to teaching in two parallel-run studios and seminars, one called Vurnik's and the other Plečnik's.

Vurnik was, unlike Plečnik, attracted to the National Romanticism as it had occurred among Hungarian, Polish, Finnish and some other Eastern European national groups at the turn of the century. During his military service as an Austria-Hungarian soldier in World War I, which he spent erecting war memorials in Serbia and Bulgaria, he took a chance to study the folk art and architecture of the Balkans. After the war and settling in Ljubljana, his early works were bursting with colors and forms inspired by folklore as in his most famous work, the Cooperative Bank, built in 1922.

> The ornament on the façade of the Cooperative Bank results from the simplification of grape motif, which was taken from the interior painting of the ground floor banking hall. [...] The painting design of interior done by Vurnik's wife Helena, demonstrated a strong *fin-de-siècle* influence. Given her background and education under Rudolf Jettmar at Vienna Art Academy, who was also a Polish descent, she also did not represent a typical Viennese Secession.[71]

Employing vibrant decoration reminiscent of Slavic heritage bore a special, anti-Germanic message, after Slovenians finally became recognized as a legitimate European nation, liberated from the long-lasting dominance by the Habsburgs. At this moment, Vurnik's attempt at creating the Slovenian national style coincided with the search for finding the roots of a common, South Slavic and even broader pan-Slavic national expression. The façade of the Cooperative Bank was painted in the blue, white and red of the new Yugoslavian as well as the Czechoslovakian flag. A similar national euphoria occurred among Prague architects, such as Pavel Janák and Josef Gočár, previously involved in the movement named Czech Cubism. After the constitution of Czechoslovakia, they experimented with a new style, Rondocubism, which substituted the universal, abstract forms of Cubism with folk-inspired geometric motifs, pointing to specificities of a particularly national script to be achieved by modern architectural means.[72] It was Gočár's Legio Bank in Prague, designed at the same time as Vurnik's Cooperative Bank, which became celebrated as an architectural symbol of Czechoslovakian independence. Vibrant colors and allusions to wooden architecture in both cases stood out as the declaration of a new area of architecture for the people, among which the voice of peasantry counted as equal within the social stratigraphy. Although inspired by folklore, the means of architectural articulation in two projects were almost incomparable. While Vurnik's façade attracted as a plain surface of decorative painting abstracted from kilim-motifs of the Slavic south, Gočár's, on the other hand, was a tridimensional composition of conjoined elements, resembling nicely curved, yet robust woodwork from the northern Slavic cottages.

The Sokol Hall in Tabor Square (Figure 6.8) was Vurnik's next project, built in 1923–1926, in which the exterior resembled vernacular wooden architecture, yet instead of paint and colors, as on the Cooperative Bank, it was texture and plasticity boosting its vividness. "Some surfaces are bordered by a stylized rope patterns, perhaps twisted columns, which can be found

Figure 6.8 Vurnik's Sokol Club at Tabor (Archive of Tabor Sport Club)

on Serbian medieval churches of so-called Morava Group,"[73] known for the textile-inspired decorative patterns that were the source of inspiration evident in works of Serbian architect Momir Korunović. Yet, while Korunović linked the textile patterns of the Morava style to decorative elements of late-Byzantine architecture, in his Sokol Hall Vurnik employed the modern transformation of Gothic elements in search for a national authenticity. The central gymnastic hall contained an atmosphere of sacred space, achieved by the construction of ceiling and light lanterns cut into it, and forms in accordance with the organic logic found in nature, as had been proposed by Bruno Taut's Alpine architecture and the Expressionist fellows, as well as by the Czech Cubists. Despite certain references to Gothic architecture and elements reminiscent of Central European Expressionism, Vurnik was explicitly against the imitation of foreign historic styles. Moreover, he believed in the potential of an original South Slavic expression that would overcome "the exhausted longing of the Western culture," a statement strongly resonating with the writings of Ljubomir Micić and his Zenithism circle from the same time. According to Vurnik's own words, his design strived toward "the completeness of emotions in which the Slavic Orient finds its expression in a decorative manner."[74]

The construction of a new Sokol hall in the Tabor area resulted from rising enthusiasm about the foundation of Yugoslav Sokol with its seat in Ljubljana, a special political role in integrating South Slaves as a single nation into pan-Slavic "commonwealth." Along with Miroslav Tyrš's original motto: "With Sokol toward freedom, with Sokol toward Slavness, with Slavness toward humanity," a new maxim "Who is a member of the Sokol that one is a Yugoslav" was promoted. Established in 1862, soon after the initial foundation of the Sokol in Prague, the Slovenian branch was the oldest in the country. The newly constituted Yugoslav Sokol organized the first gathering in Ljubljana in 1922 and for that occasion a big stadium with a capacity of 50,000 was built from the state budget and bank loans.[75] Before the unification Slovenes, Croats and Serbs had participated in Sokol meetings under separate national banners, a reason for discontent about a new Yugoslav program of the Sokol, especially in Croatia, where the Catholic Church was its biggest opponent.[76]

It was an employee of the Ministry of Buildings Momir Korunović who was appointed the main supervisor of all projects for Yugoslav Sokol societies around the country, after his study stay in Prague, during 1921, when he had explored designs of the Sokol's facilities and the post offices. Korunović was an active member of Sokol society himself, and realized Sokol buildings in smaller towns in Serbia, Macedonia and Bosnia, from 1924 until the mid-1930s. The centralization politics after the proclamation of dictatorship caused the seat of Sokol to be moved from Ljubljana to Belgrade, with Korunović being appointed to design a new headquarters as well as a stadium for the second Yugoslav gathering of 1930.

Korunović's architecture was recognizable for heavily colored façades with flamboyant decoration including the Modernist distillations of Morava decoration: "knitted" or twisted elements around arches, bifore, trifore and quadrofore windows, roses and oculi, along horizontal cornices. This has been associated with the idea of a Serbian national style, the Serbo-Byzantine, a further development of turn of the century designs by Branko Tanazević and Dragutin Inkiostri Medenjak. Korunović's architecture, like Ivan Vurnik's, grew from similar Expressionist traditions, moreover they might be directly inspired by Czech Rondocubism, yet it is unclear to what extent they mutually influenced each other. Although Korunović visited Prague in 1921 and possibly saw Gočar's Rondocubist drawings, none of his textile-inspired colorful designs were developed before Vurnik completed the Cooperative Bank and the Sokol Hall. Korunović's nationally engaging architecture that referred explicitly to Serbian medievalism, might be an obvious manifestation of Serbian pretentions for cultural domination, yet the architectural methods Korunović used were rather distributed from than imported to Slovenia.

Vurnik's shift from the folklorist to the ultra-Functionalist phase was sudden. In 1925, he visited the International Exhibition of Modern Decorative and Industrial Arts in Paris, presenting the Cooperative Bank. Although not explicitly revealing an attitude on Le Corbusier's and Melnikov's pavilions at the exhibition, the fact that he saw the radically different structures not only on paper, but the real sites had some impact on his future shift towards radical Modernism. The same year two different curricula, Plečnik's and Vurnik's, started running in parallel at the Technical Faculty, with Vurnik's being considered the herald of a new age. Vurnik's manifesto about the leading principles of "his" national school sounded radically Modernist, pointing to the logic of construction and the truthful use of materials as the key attributes of a good design:

> The school wants to be contemporary – in other words it wants to educate the people who will be able to build in the way the contemporary life demands from us. That way, the creation process needs to be in the first place careful, constructively right and simple. The beauty is the best achieved by the right use of materials. Yet, the foremost ideal of the school is not a simple constructivism – but that idealism which has been the leading force in all ages of the healthy art development.[77]

Vurnik strongly believed in the value of humanistic education, especially the studies of boarder historical traditions, which was missing in the teaching curriculum of his competitor Plečnik. He was intensely involved in the studies in modern urbanism as a social discipline, being the first in the country to start teaching the science of city-making. He was also the first to develop a workers' housing colony in Slovenia, a project for the municipally financed

190 *National architectures in the unified nation*

neighborhood in the city of Maribor developed from 1927 to 1929, attuned to the experimental housing projects in Central Europe at the time:

> Like most participants in the International Congress on the Construction of Workers' Dwellings in Vienna of 1926, Vurnik was also an advocate of better living conditions of workers to be gained in smaller houses with garden access and flexible floor plans.[78]

His garden-city concept of parallel pavilions with plain façades and horizontal iron-bar railings bore Modernist features, yet the sloped roofs were still reminiscent of Slovenian traditional architecture. Only in his next design, the sports complex in Radovljica, did Vurnik employ the bold aesthetics of white plain façades and flat roofs exposing the structural possibilities of reinforced concrete, as the first clearly Functionalist achievement. The reason for his sudden move toward Functionalism could be understood through the lens of his frustration with Plečnik:

> He needed to redirect himself into areas his competitor had neglected and find his own place under the local sun. [...] His inability to follow Plečnik in the same field and means of his design preoccupied Vurnik until his death. Despite the strengths of his Functionalist architecture, one should not forget that he as a creator suffered from auto-frustration. More than being bothered by the post war conditions, he was vexed by feeling he would always be the second best. [...] He must have been very sad realizing that Slovenia was too small for two Plečniks.[79]

Since establishing his school in 1925, Ivan Vurnik consciously opted for the precepts of modern architecture, along with some of Plečnik's graduates who also decided to plunge into Modernist waters.[80] Despite the unusual, "counter-path" in development of Plečnik's architectural philosophy in regard to history and Historicism, the very first unornamented, volumetrically treated design in Ljubljana, the villa for actress Marija Vera completed in 1929, came from Plečnik's "classroom."[81] An even more pronounced departure from Plečnik's formal code was evident in the works of another student, France Tomažič,[82] one of the first to graduate from the Ljubljana school in 1924. At first, Tomažič worked on supervising Plečnik's projects in Ljubljana while he was away in Prague and at the faculty as his teaching assistant, yet in 1930 he started own architectural practice and "from a former loyal assistant transformed into one of Plečnik's most fervent critics."[83] It was through Plečnik that he received a commission for Villa Oblak (Figure 6.9) in 1931, which was to become one of the most appreciated works of interwar Modernism in Slovenia. Although his initial idea for turning toward Modernism was a social mission of new architecture to meet the needs of the underprivileged, the success of Tomažič's design

Figure 6.9 Tomažič's Villa Oblak – panorama (Muzej za arhitekturo in oblikovanje – MAO, Ljubjana)

relied on the willingness of a wealthy merchant to show off his sudden business success in an unorthodox way.

> Villa Oblak plays the same role in the architecture of Slovenia as Mies's Villa Tugendhat in the Czech Republic. Both were above averagely luxurious, they represented the reaches of state-of-the-art technology, and both were built as wedding presents.[84]

Undeniably, the abstract geometry, planimetric volumes, flat roof and subtle juxtaposition between the interior rooms and porches demonstrated the imperatives of a new age in Tomažič's design. The open plan with no bearing walls in which spaces flow from one to another provided an abundancy of natural light, sun and air. The southern exposure and the connection with garden met the needs of the user, according to the architect's own words:

> [A] true friend of nature and flowers to whom the garden and the house are the same. The house is no longer an enclosed box but presents a part of ordered natural setting as the man's place of being. The house encourages the felling of happiness and lightness and makes the dweller perceive a sense of freedom. Here, one can breathe freely and live his life to its fullest.[85]

However, the concept was based on a strict partie, a linear assignment of square-shaped basic modular units – a procession of interconnected rooms, onto which half modules were added on both sides like a diagram of the Romanesque cathedrals subdivided into bays of the nave and side aisles following a simple 1:2 proportional system. The strict modular scheme was spread through the elevations, a fixed grid of concrete rectangular frames, some of which were filled either by windows or solid surfaces while the others remained unclosed. The linear flow of rectangular compartments of the main façade was interrupted by a different subdivision of the original modular unit at the large porch in front of the main entrance, the already puzzling scale of which was highlighted by an oversized concrete arch performing as it had been a truss holding the flat roof. It might be due to his formal training by Plečnik that Tomažič could not liberate his open plan beyond the rigidly aligned structural system of concrete frames; however, the aesthetic of Villa Oblak anticipated a fusion of Modernism and Classicism which would incarnate – like the reincarnation of Plečnik's architecture – through a certain manner of Postmodernist designs in the 1980s.

Tomažič was a key figure in establishing a Modernist initiative named the Club of Architects along with the program of its mission and activities, which included presentations of the works of its members both at the exhibitions of Yugoslav architecture in Belgrade as well as at international gatherings. However, it was another name from the first generation of Plečnik's students, Dragotin Fatur, who took the promotion of Modernism to another level with the foundation of the first architectural journal in the country to "unite contemporary architects of Yugoslavia and direct their work toward a common aim."[86] In only four years of its existence, until 1934 when it stopped being issued for financial reasons, the journal *Arhitektura* put together a collection of plans, photographs and theoretical contributions that shaped the discourse of Yugoslav Modern Architecture – "a close communion between social and material means in a single union, the only one that could provide prerequisites for the emergence of great, contemporary architectural culture in our lands."[87] Projects, realizations and writings on contemporary architecture were arriving from all over the country, yet the involvement of local, Ljubljana-based architects was predominant; along with Plečnik's disciples and the internationally trained architects, the students who graduated under Vurnik such as Stanislav Rohrman and Herman Hus were strongly present. Earlier in 1931, another Slovenian Modernists team, Peter Behrens, Ivo Spinčić and Jože Mesar, had published a book titled *Stanovanje [Housing]*, an introduction to latest modern theories including Le Corbusier's "five points." Their contribution to the spread of modern doctrines was presented and reviewed in the opening issue of *Arhitektura*.

Even though almost all young architects from Slovenia, either Plečnik's or Vurnik's students, along with those who graduated from abroad, became the promoters of Modernism, the presence of Plečnik's legacy was obvious at least until the establishment of socialism after the end of WWII. For example, in the works of Vurnik's graduate Stanislav Rohrman, previously educated in Prague, the fluctuation between the Modernist aesthetics spread through Europe in the 1930s and Plečnik's influence was evident, even though he had never been Plečnik's immediate pupil. Rohrman's architecture turned from explicitly Modernist – seen in design of the Hotel Slon [Hotel Elephant] in downtown Ljubljana from 1938, whose bare white surfaces over the curved volume are reminiscent of the International Style – to sturdy Classical compositions such as the mixed-use Mayer Palace at Prešern Square adjacent to the Triple Bridge, the forms of which respected Plečnik's stylization of its surroundings.

A similar juxtaposition between the Modernist and the Classical, more precisely the Plečnikian, was noticed in the works of another key protagonist of Slovenian interwar architecture, Vladimir Šubic,[88] mentioned earlier for the realization of his family villa in Ljubljana's neighborhood of Vrtača from 1929, the first design in which this fusion was obvious. Šubic was a decade younger than Ivan Vurnik, so by the time he started serving in the Austro-Hungarian army during World War I he was halfway through his college education, which was a usual scenario for the students born in the last decade of the nineteenth century in the dual monarchy. After the war, he enrolled in the German branch of Prague polytechnic and obtained the title of architectural engineer in 1922. Upon his return to Ljubljana he at first worked for Tönnies Contractor Company,[89] which had started experimenting with concrete as a modern material prior to World War I, and was later appointed advisor at the building department of Ljubljana's municipality in 1926. Most of his work years, however, he spent as the head of Building Department of the Pension Fund, abolished after the establishment of the communist regime after WWII. Tragically, it was not only the institution that was found an enemy of "the socialist people's will," but also its chief architect. Šubic was arrested "based on clandestine denunciation" and sent to prison to "work for the benefit of the society."[90]

Šubic was close to the group of architects promoting Slovenian Modernism, yet he personally had no clear inclinations toward the social mission of modern architecture. Nevertheless, the first large-scale project he developed for the municipality office was the affordable housing complex with public amenities named Meksika in Njegoševa Street, adjacent to today's medical complex. The housing crisis after the Great War resulted in numerous attempts at creating new models for low-income families. The most explored have been attempts by Viennese authorities to meet the needs of the impoverished, resulting in the construction of large-scale residential complexes at the outskirts of Vienna, such as Hof Sandleiten and Karl-Marx-Hof, known as Red Vienna.[91] When the municipality of Ljubljana initiated the construction of an "urban apartment block" for its employees in 1922, Šubic submitted a project similar to the simultaneously developing Viennese Hofs – the concept based on the Roman insulae typology, revitalized during

194 *National architectures in the unified nation*

the late nineteenth- and early twentieth-century urban sprawl through continental Europe. The Meksika was designed after Šubic's trip to Vienna as a huge, enclosed block with inner courtyards – the scheme only partly realized since the municipality did not manage to buy a neighboring lot as had been originally anticipated. Besides the massive residential program, the Meksika included a variety of public and user-oriented functions, from huge retail spaces on the ground floor to the communal baths, laundries and spaces for social gathering. The Modernist agenda was also spread onto architectural forms cleansed from external decoration, yet relying on the spirit of Classicism, which later criticism defined as the "vocabulary of social pathos."[92]

By the time the Meksika was completed in 1927, Šubic had won an architectural competition for the Workers' Chamber at the intersection of Mikološičeva and Čufarjeva streets – as part of the system of workers chambers of the Kingdom of Serbs, Croats and Slovenes established in 1921 in an attempt to meet the rising needs of the fast-emerging urbanized population, with seats in Ljubljana, Zagreb, Split, Sarajevo and Novi Sad. In some cities like Zagreb the workers welfare system was tied to the communist network even though the state government had proclaimed any affiliation with communism illegal. The argument linking the radical modern forms and the leftist politics could be examined in the already discussed Workers' House in Zagreb, built under the leadership of the communist leader Božidar Adžija. Šubic was, on the other hand, closer to the high-end bourgeois social status than to the communist political orientation. The Classical formal code of the Meksika was to some extent reduced and schematized, while the design of the Workers' Chamber turned into a more flamboyant, Plečnik-inspired creation, due to the exposed position on Miklošićeva Street leading from Prešern's Square to the railway station. The character of forms: window frames with exaggerated keystones, elaborate beams over each portal and figural decoration, were the starting point from which we can follow the further influence of Plečnik on Šubic's compositional patterns and detailing. Yet, it was the concept of the main interior space, the gathering chamber (Figure 6.10) in which Šubic replicated the spirit of sacred spaces, namely the early Christian basilicas, as Plečnik would do. This building presented a turning point after which Šubic applied and developed similar formal solutions at the Apartment Palace of the Pension Fund and the Apartment Palace of the Chamber of Commerce, both realized in Ljubljana's downtown in 1928.

However, there is no better example of how Šubic synthetized his enthusiasm about the technological basis of modernity with Plečnikian modernized Classical language than the Nebotičnik [Skyscraper] (Figure 6.11) at the intersection of Slovenska cesta [Slovenian Road] with Štefanova ulica [Štefanova Street]. The project started when the Pension Fund, where Šubic was employed, gained funds to erect a building in the rapidly developing city

Figure 6.10 Šubic's Workers Chamber (Muzej za arhitekturo in oblikovanje – MAO, Ljubjana)

center, with a goal to develop a mixed-use program with high-end residences and offices, along with large retail spaces on the first two floors. The civic legislations restricted the building height at five stories, however Šubic proposed a much higher structure. His idea was accepted thanks to Plečnik's involvement and expert advice suggesting that "the right thing to do would be to erect an imposing corner building of decent height to create a pleasing emphasis of the intersection, both for the aesthetic and economic reasons."[93] After being asked for an advice on the matter, Plečnik reinforced the argument with a rough draft of an eight-story high-rise to dominate the intersection and continue further into a five-story slab along Štefanova Street. The final proposal by Šubic went beyond the height suggested by Plečnik; his Nebotičnik was executed as a twelve-story high structure, topped with a glass-cube attic and "tempietto" holding a lightning rod. The top added another few floors to the original height making it the ninth tallest building in Central Europe, built according to the newest advancements in the reinforced concrete skeleton system. According to memories of civil engineer Stanko Dimnik, in charge of the structural calculus, Šubic was preoccupied with forms and symbolism of the American skyscraper since the time of the Chicago Tribune competition of 1922, yet instead of the American steel frames, he was eager to explore the possibilities of reinforced skeletal constructions more relevant to the European continent.[94] The laying of the

196 *National architectures in the unified nation*

Figure 6.11 Šubic's Nebotičnik (Muzej za arhitekturo in oblikovanje – MAO, Ljubjana)

foundation stone had a special meaning for the city. At the day of the foundation ceremony, a copper casket containing a parchment, on which a verse by the Slovenian poet Oton Zupančič was inscribed, was set into it. "Our grain be in its bed and our crop under a safe roof," the poet's text stated. Besides the height, which made Nebotičnik a new urban symbol, the construction and technological innovations like elevators, the central heating ventilation and hot water supply were also seen as proof of national prosperity.[95] As a new city landmark, Nebotičnik was accentuated by a large sculpture – the statue of Genius by Slovenian celebrity sculptor, Lojze Dolinar, placed on a console of tall pilaster at the edge with the neighboring building.

> This female creature in not a genius in its modern sense: it is not a figure representing an exceptional capacity of mind [...]. It is the genius loci, the guardian of the place the heavenly messenger, the faithful companion: Angelus – the silent Angelus. Does his silence announce something? [...] It perhaps speaks about the border between the Nebotičnik and the rising metropolis, or about the border with an infinite space which open beyond our comprehension. Where Vladimir Šubic was, we still have to arrive.[96]

Although the original intention of the sculptor was not to commemorate Šubic's tragic death as a victim of the communist regime, as the commentator of Šubic's work, Janko Zlodre, poetically concluded, the Nebotičnik certainly symbolized the impetus of young Slovenian capitalism pushing Ljubljana into becoming a modern, large city. The attributes inseparable from the spirit of capitalism such as the new technologies, speed and efficiency, safe and secure investments, modern management and the division of labor, time for entertainment and leisure, were personified through the forms of Nebotičnik, a reason why the soon-to-arrive communist ideology needed to defame its protagonist. Šubic's formal articulation was classy, elegant and, to some extent, decadent. What was missing in his appropriation of Plečnikian modernized Classicism was Plečnik's sincere religiosity, instead of a simple search for pleasure in architectural forms. Surprisingly, together with the strong Plečnikian influence, relevant to almost all Šubic's works except for the early project for the Meksika, the last floor of Nebotičnik was finished with a strongly accentuated tier of arcaded windows, the vibrancy of which evoked the expressive forms of Czech Rondocubism from the time of Šubic's studies in Prague.

The construction of the tallest building not only in the city, but the entire country,[97] was a source of national pride, as it preceded both the first skyscraper in Zagreb, Löwy's Radovan, as well as Belgrade's Albania, both discussed in the previous chapters. From the stylistic point of view, three "skyscrapers" touched onto the very essence of the differences in the architectural settings of the three capital cities during the interwar period. Ljubljana could not help showing Plečnik's influence even through the works of those architects who leaned toward a more explicit Modernist path, and Belgrade kept on pursuing the spirit of Monumentalism imbedded into the newly arriving Modernism, Zagreb was the city that most categorically shifted toward the radical features of what would be later recognized as Central European Functionalism. On the other hand, the idea of modernization, radical urban transformations and the representation of power among the newly rising entrepreneurs worked the same way not only within the boundaries of Yugoslavia but in any portion of the rapidly changing Western world. Yet there was another quality that tied the Yugoslav skyscrapers together; all three were specific urban landmarks accentuating the tactical corners at intersections of special visual importance in the stylistic genres characterizing each of the cities.

Plečnik played a vital role in the genesis of the Slovenian architectural school and had enormous influence on the entire generation of Modernist architects that emerged on the Slovenian scene from the early 1930s through most of the twentieth century. Besides his immediate graduates and his first assistant, the previously discussed France Tomažič, there was an entire generation of Slovenian architects who continued absorbing Plečnik's legacy through the pedagogical guidance of Edvard Ravnikar, Plečnik's most celebrated student and collaborator on the project for National and University Library. In Ravnikar's early works, the similarities with Plečnik's architecture were undeniable, most obviously in the design for the Modern Gallery of Ljubljana, which was, after Plečnik's library, the largest cultural institution in Ljubljana built explicitly for the promotion of a Slovenian national program. The project was initiated by Izidor Cankar, one of the most influential art historians of interwar Yugoslavia, also serving as the ambassador in Argentina, who chose young Ravnikar based on his reputation of working with Plečnik. Ravnikar received the commission in 1936, in the middle of the project for the National Library, yet the reason he started working on the gallery only in 1939 was not caused by any obligations to Plečnik, but Ravnikar's decision to leave Slovenia and spend six months working and learning from Le Corbusier[98] at the time of Le Corbusier's involvement in the urban vision for Algiers. However, with the Classical, axially organized composition and the relief-like façade cladding, Ravnikar's gallery had little in common with anything he might have seen in Paris, on the contrary, it counted on familiarity with a recognizable, Plečnikian fusion between the Classical and the Modern. After being appointed as professor at the Faculty of Architecture in 1946, Ravnikar shifted toward an explicitly Modernist idiom, yet stayed devoted to Plečik's persistency to not only preserve but emphasize Slovenian cultural values and "physiognomy."[99] Even after he developed a critical distance from his fellow and mentor and started searching for new means to translate lessons from the past into more persuasive modern statements, his tone of addressing the historical continuum was not opposing Plečik's intuitive and transformative stance while dealing with the universally relevant architectural precedents. "There are no direct historical references in Ravnikar's architecture, but the past is present in a deeper sense."[100] In the architect's own words:

> Tradition is no sterile perseverance, but rather a certain flexible connection that searches in the past for points of reference rather than for dried-out examples [...] it is an arrow pointing towards the future. Architectural thinking needs to recognize tradition, what came before, however, seen through one's own eyes.[101]

Ravnikar's syncretism paved a specific path for Slovenian architecture of the twentieth century, "a performative step forward compared with the general, doctrinal modernization of Zagreb, Belgrade and Sarajevo immediately after WWII,"[102] a reason why he has been often compared to outside-the-mainstream Modernist figures such as Carlo Scarpa and Alvar Aalto. Despite the departure from Plečnik's Classicist script, Ravnikar and the next generation of Slovenian architects educated under his guidance would never neglect the importance of tectonic qualities, the power of materiality, and sensibility in regard to the urban context in the case of each new architectural artifact built in Ljubljana until the present day. Despite the attempts of his contemporaries and the younger generation of his students to challenge the "retrograde" aesthetics he kept on pushing forward during the exciting times of accelerating Modernism, Pečnik's influence was indisputable. As his long-lasting opponent Ivan Vurnik finally admitted, there was no room for another authority of Plečnik's scale in Slovenia of his time. Even those who were not his immediate disciples, such as Vladimir Šubic, could not help being seized with "the exceptional role of professor Plečnik's 'voice' in the sphere of building and his authoritative function. Since the failures were out of question one should keep mouth shut and continue to serve."[103]

Notes

1 At the beginning of the twentieth century, Trieste had the largest Slovene urban population. The number of Slovenes in Trieste was 57,000 in comparison to Ljubljana, which had only 20,000. Carole Rogel, "In the Beginning: The Slovenes from the Seventh Century to 1945," in Jill Benderly and Evan Kraft (eds.), *Independent Slovenia: Origins, Movements, Prospects*, New York: St. Martin's Press, 1994: 15.
2 A different assumption that Ljubljana was associated with an idea of the Slovenian capital after 1848 is explained in James Gow and Cathie Carmichael, *Slovenia and Slovenes: A Small State and the New Europe*, Bloomington, IN: Indiana University Press, 2000: 11.
3 Valentin Krisper and France Stele, *Prestonica Slovenaca – Bela Ljubljana u rečima i slikama* [*The Capital of Slovenia – White Ljubljana in Words and Pictures*] Ljubljana: Gradska opština Ljubljana, 1929: 3.
4 The names of the city appear in a document related to the medieval castle on the hill – Castrum Leibach. Peter Štih, *Castrum Leibach: The First Historic Mention of Ljubljana and the City's Early History: Facsimile with Commentary and a History Introduction*, Ljubljana: City Municipality of Ljubljana, 2010.
5 Vlado Valenčič, "Ljubljanska ulična imena nekdaj in danes" [Ljubljana's Street Names Then and Now], in *Ljubljanske ulice* [*Streets of Ljubljana*], Ljubljana: Geodetska uprava, 1980: 8–18.
6 Nace Šumi, *Po poti baročnih spomenikov Slovenije* [*The Baroque Monuments of Slovenia*], Ljubljana: Zavod za varstvo naravne in kulturne dediščine, 1992.
7 Vlado Valenčič, "Gradbeni razvoj Ljubljane od dograditve južne železnice do potresa leta 1895" [Urban Development of Ljubljana from the Construction of Southern Railway until the Earthquake in 1895], *Kronika*, vol. 9, no. 3, (1961): 135–144.

200 *National architectures in the unified nation*

8 Discussed in Jože Suhadolnik, "Arhitektura in urbanizem v Ljubljani v drugi polovici 19. stoletja, 1849–1895, in arhivsko gradiv o Zgodovinskega arhiva Ljubljana" [Architecture and Urbanism in the Second Half of the 19th Century, 1849–1895, and Archival Sources of the Historical Archive of Ljubljana], *Kronika*, vol. 48, no. 3 (2000): 108.
9 Ibid., 110.
10 Ties between Ljubljana and Prague were particularly important for the early formation of Slovenian cultural identity in the city.
11 The surveys of modern urban development include: Aleš Vodopivec, *Arhitektura Ljubljane*, as a special issue of *Arhitektov bilten*, Ljubljana: Mestni muzej, 1978; Breda Mihelič, "Koncepti mestne podobe u razvoju Ljubljane" [Concepts of the City Image in the Development of Ljubljana], *Sinteza*, no. 58/60 (1982): 25–27; Breda Mihelič, *Urbanistični razvoj Ljubljane* [*Urban Development of Ljubljana*], Ljubljana: Partizanska knjiga, 1983.
12 Vlado Valenčič, "Prvi ljubljanski regulacijski načrt" [Ljubljana's First Regulation Plan], *Kronika: časopis za slovensko krajevno zgodovino*, vol. 15, no. 2 (1967): 74–83.
13 Ciril Metod Koch (1867–1925) studied in Graz and Vienna, where he graduated from the Academy of Fine Arts. Upon his return to Ljubljana in 1893 he gained a position in the municipal office working on urban planning issues. He was also a highly appreciated Secessionist architect, with his building Mali Nebotičnik [Little Skyscraper] of 1903 being one of Ljubljana's landmarks.
14 Max Fabiani, *Erläuterungs-Bericht zum Entwurfe eines General-Regulierungs-Planes der Stadt Laibach*, Vienna, 1895. The brochure was bilingual, written both in German and Slovenian.
15 Fabiani received the first honorary doctorate in urbanism from the Technical University in Vienna in 1902 and "became the Emperor's counsellor for architecture and history of art in the same year. Between 1910 and 1917, he worked as a lecturer of ornamental drawing where he was promoted to professor of composition in 1917." Breda Mihelič, "Maks Fabiani and Urbanism in Vienna at the Turn of the 19th Century," *Urbani izziv*, vol. 19, no. 1 (2008): 131.
16 The square was named after Slavic philologist Franc Miklošić (Franz Ritter von Miklosich), who had served in the Upper House of Austrian Parliament, arguing for the national rights of Slovenians during the Revolution of 1848.
17 Marija Režek Kambič, "Meščanska stanovanjska arhitektura v Ljubljani 1870–1914: pozni historizem in secesija" [The City-dwelling Architecture in Ljubljana 1870–1914: Late-Historicism and Secession], *Arhitektov bilten*, vol. 45, no. 203/204 (2015): 56–62.
18 Discussed in Ervin Dolenc, *Med kulturo in politiko* [*Between the Culture and Politics*], Ljubljana: Inštitut za novejšo zgodovino, 2010: 21–24.
19 France Stele, *Grad Ljubljanski – Slovenska akropola* [*The Castle of Ljubljana – the Slovenian Acropolis*] Celje: Mohorjeva Tiskarna, 1932: 17.
20 For the modernization processes in the interwar period, see Žarko Lazarević, "Družba in gospodarstvo med obema vojnama: Vprašanja ravni modernizacij" [Society and Economy between the Two World Wars: The Level of Modernization], *Zgodovinski časopis*, vol. 67, no. 1–2 (2013): 110–134.
21 Mojca Šorn, *Življenje Ljubljančanov med drugo svetovno vojno* [*The Life of Ljubljana Citizens before WWII*], Ljubljana: Inštitut za novejšo zgodovino, 2007: 25–27.

National Ljubljana 201

22 Rado Hibar was wealthy enough to buy a medieval castle, Strnov – severely reconstructed and landscaped in the seventeenth century – as his residence. He invested a large amount in modern reconstruction of the historic site before he moved in there with his family. As one of the wealthiest people in pre-WWII Slovenia, Hribar was killed by communists after their victory in 1944, and the castle was confiscated.
23 Šorn, *Življenje Ljubljančanov med drugo svetovno vojno*: 19–20.
24 Lazarević, "Družba in gospodarstvo med obema vojnama": 120–121.
25 Jörg Stabenow, *Jože Plečnik: Städtebau im Schatten der Moderne*, Wiesbaden: Vieweg, 1996; Ian Bentley and Đurđa Gržan-Butina (eds.), *Jože Plečnik*, Oxford: Oxford Polytechnic, 1983; Đurđa Gržan-Butina, "Ljubljana: Master Plan and Spatial Structure," *Sinteza* (1984): 58–61.
26 Šorn, *Življenje Ljubljančanov med drugo svetovno vojno*: 17.
27 The phrase comes from Plečnik's friend, art historian France Stele, "Plečnikova Ljubljana," *Kronika slovenskih mest*, no. 4 (1939): 227–232.
28 Marjan Mušič, "A Letter from Josef Hoffman to Marjan Mušič Dated January 10, 1952," in *Veliki arhitekti* [Great Architects], Vol. 3, Maribor: Založba Obzorja, 1968: 145.
29 Plečnik received the commission from industrialist Joahnn Zacherl, who he met through their mutual devotion to the Catholic faith. A recent monograph on the building: *Josef Plečnik Zacherlhaus Geschichte und Architektur Eines Wiener Stadthauses*, published in Vienna in 2016, was edited by the surviving members of Zacherl family.
30 A quote from Plečnik's letter to his brother, published in Peter Krečič, *Plečnik: The Complete Works*, London, Academy Editions, 1993: 38.
31 Plečnik's refusal to deal with the indecent power games Fabiani played to gain numerous commissions in Ljubljana at the turn of the century is discussed and documented in Marjan Mušič, *Jože Plečnik*, Ljubljana: Partizanska knjiga, 1986: 116–118.
32 Meštrović was very enthusiastic about Plečnik joining the Yugoslav Committee, yet Plečnik was vague about the matter. From the correspondence between Plečnik and Meštrović kept in the Museum of Architecture – Ljubljana: Plečnik's Collection.
33 Fabiani was still loyal to the imperial authorities of the pre-Great War period.
34 The true reason why Plečnik was not appointed lay in the fact that Prince Ferdinand had "entirely different plans for the school after Wagner's retirement [...] he opted for Léopold Bauer." See Damjan Prelovšek, "The Life and Work of Jože Plečnik," in François Burkhardt, Claude Eveno and Boris Podrecca (eds.), *Jože Plečnik, Architects 1872–1957*, Cambridge, MA: MIT Press, 1989: 48–49. Also discussed in Krečič, *Plečnik*, 47–48.
35 Prelovšek, "The Life and Work of Jože Plečnik": 71.
36 Prior to the design of the obelisk in Ljubljana, Plečnik employed the same symbolism during the reconstruction of Prague Castle. In Prague, however, he dealt with a monolithic piece of stone, transported to the site with patience and dignity, similar to Domenico Fontana's relocation of the ancient obelisk to the center of Vatican Square during the reign of Pope Sixtus V.
37 Peter Krečič, "Plečnikov spomenik Napoleonu in Iliriji" [Plečnik's Monument to Napoleon and Illyria], exhibition catalog, Ljubljana: Arhitekturni muzej, 2013: 1–11.

202 *National architectures in the unified nation*

38 During his visit to Ljubljana in 1914, Plečnik obtained a copy of C. M. Koch's drawing of the master plan for Ljubljana, developed from Fabiani's. See Đurđa Gržan-Butina, "Ljubljana, Master Plan and Spatial Structure" in Bentley and Gržan-Butina (eds.), *Jože Plečnik*: 28.
39 The master plan with a zoomed-in section of the regulation of Bežigrad was first published in the monthly periodical *Dom in Svet* in 1929. See Jože Plečnik, "Študija regulacije Ljubljane in okolice" [A Study for the Regulation of Ljubljana and its Surroundings], *Dom in svet* (1929): illustration 4.
40 Fabiani's plan for Bežigrad from 1898 is published in Marco Pozzetto, *Max Fabiani: Ein Architekt der Monarchie*, Vienna: Edition Tusch, 1983: 37.
41 There is an argument that Plečnik's plan recalls only Howard's geometry while still owing more to Raymond Unwin's Garden City ideas. See Damjan Prelovšek, *Jože Plečnik, 1872–1957: Architectura Perennis*, New Haven, Yale University Press, 1997: 268.
42 Plečnik intended to dig the railway tracks underground and open a possibility for smother transitions between the old city and new northern districts. See Prelovšek, *Jože Plečnik*: 270.
43 A similar argument is found in Stabenow, *Jože Plečnik*: 70.
44 From Jože Plečnik's "Študija regulacije Ljubljane in okolice," quoted in Gržan-Butina, "Ljubljana: Master Plan and Spatial Structure": 30.
45 Prelovšek, *Jože Plečnik*: 271.
46 Stabenow, *Jože Plečnik*: 64–66.
47 A very Plečnikian project for the Slovenian Pantheon, characterized by a triangular bell-tower at the front façade and robustly treated wall surfaces, was drawn by Plečnik's famous disciple Edvard Ravnikar in 1932. See Krečič, *Plečnik*: 93 and Bogo Zupančič, *Plečnikovi student i drugi jugoslovanski arhitekti v Le Corbusierovom ateljeju* [Plečnik's Students and other Yugoslav Architects in Le Corbusier's Atelier] Ljubljana: MAO, 2017: 32. The same drawing is attributed to Plečnik in Prelovšek, *Jože Plečnik*: 302.
48 Plečnik's unrealized project for the Cathedral of Freedom found a special place as a national symbol on the new Slovenian banknotes issued during the fight for independence from Yugoslavia.
49 The term "Slovenian Acropolis" was first used by Plečnik's colleague, art historian Franc Stelè, who in his publication *Grad Ljubljanski – Slovenska akropola* pointed out the historical value of the medieval remains. Although very supportive of Plečnik's early ideas, Stelè would soon become alarmed by Plečnik's radical approach toward the reconstruction of historical landmarks. Krečič, *Plečnik*: 111.
50 The Slovenian Parliament was built as the assembly of the Socialist Republic of Slovenia, one of six entities of the Yugoslav Federation, after the project of Plečnik's student, Vinko Glanz, from 1954 to 1959.
51 Andrew Herscher, "Stadtebau as Imperial Culture Camillo Sitte's Urban Plan for Ljubljana," *JSAH*, vol. 62, no. 2 (2003): 222.
52 Prelovšek, *Jože Plečnik*: 274.
53 Krečič, *Plečnik*: 111.
54 Dušan Grabrijan, "Lik Plečnikove Ljubljane" [The Face of Plečnik's Ljubljana], *Naši razgledi*, no. 4 (1957): 80–82.
55 Prelovšek, *Jože Plečnik*: 253.
56 Jože Plečnik, *Projekt univerzitetne biblioteke Ljubljanske*, Ljubljana, 1933.

57 Krečič, *Plečnik*: 128.
58 Published in Otto Antonia Graf, *Master-drawings of Otto Wagner*, Vienna: Otto Wagener's Archive, 1987: 110–111.
59 Prelovšek, *Jože Plečnik*: 254.
60 Marko Mušič, "The National and University Library in Ljubljana – the Intersection of Time and Cultures," *LIBER Quarterly*, vol. 14, no. 2 (2014).
61 Krečič, *Plečnik*: 128.
62 Semper's influence on Plečnik is discussed in Prelovšek "*Jože Plečnik*: 118–121.
63 Clifford A. Pearson, "Finding the Roots of Modernism and Multicultural Cities in Central Europe," *Architectural Record*, no. 10 (2000): 75.
64 Stabenow, *Jože Plečnik*: 64–66.
65 Prelovšek, *Jože Plečnik*: 271.
66 Lukeš Zdeněk, Damjan Prelovšek and Tomáš Valena (eds.) *Josip Plečnik: The Architect of Prague Castl*, Prague: Prague Castle Administration, 1997.
67 Ivan Vurnik (1884–1971) studied at the Technical University in Vienna under the supervision of Karl Mayreder, a leading voiced of urban planning, one reason why Vurnik himself become involved in urbanism, along with his role as the founder of the Faculty of Architecture, after returning to Ljubljana.
68 Andrej Hrausky, "Some Remarks on Vurnik's Co-operative Bank," *Arhitektov bilten* (1994, special issue): 73.
69 Historian Marko Pozzeto recorded that Fabiani let Vunik attend architectural events to which other students were not permitted. See Marko Pozzetto, "Ivan Vurnik and Technische Hochshule in Vienna," *Arhitekturni bilten* (1994, special issue): 53–58.
70 Ivan Vurnik, "Vurnikova šola za arhitekturo," *Dom in svet*, vol. 40, no. 1 (1927): 29–31.
71 Hrausky, "Some Remarks on Vurnik's Co-operative Bank": 74.
72 For national connotations of Rondocubism See Rostislav Svácha, *The Architecture of New Prague, 1895–1945*, Cambridge, MA: MIT Press, 1995: 140, 194–198; also Benešová, "Rondocubismus", *Arhitektura ČSSR*, vol. 28 (1969): 303–317.
73 Damjan Prelovšek, "Decoration in Early Vurnik's Architecture," *Arhitektov bilten* (1994, special issue): 70. For the classification of Serbian medieval architecture, with the Morava Group being the last, see Gabriel Millet, *L'ancien art serbe: Les églises*, Paris: E. de Boccard, 1919.
74 Vurnik, "Vurnikova šola za arhitekturo": 30.
75 Vladimir Vilman, "Prvi ljubljanski stadion" [The First Ljubljana Stadium], *Kronika*, vol. 56 (2008): 85–98.
76 The Zagreb bishop wrote a proclamation in the church bulletin from 1921: "If you want your daughters and sons to get away from God let them join the Sokol. You Christians who see the savor in Christ, with your strong faith, together with your priests', you would never let your children to join Sokol society." Discussed in Ljubodrag Dimić, *Kulturna politika Kraljevine Jugoslavije 1918–1941* [*Cultural Politics in the Kingdom of Yugoslavia, 1918–1941*], Belgrade: Stubovi kulture, 1998: 429–430.
77 Vurnik, "Vurnikova šola za arhitekturo": 29.
78 Sanja Špindler, "Stanovanjska soseska 100 let po Vurniku" [Housing Neighborhoods One Hundred Years After Vurnik], *Urban Challenge Journal* (2016, special issue): 111.
79 Prelovšek, "Decoration in Early Vurnik's Architecture": 73.

204 National architectures in the unified nation

80 Stane Bernik, *Slovene Architecture of the Twentieth Century*, Ljubljana: Mestna galerija, 2004: 87–88.
81 A work of Plečnik's pupil Marks Strener.
82 France Tomažič (1899–1968) was involved in most of Plečnik's projects until his shift to the explicitly Modernist path. Besides Villa Oblak, he was involved in design of a few housing and public programs during the 1930s. Right before the outbreak of WWI he worked on a new urban vision for Ljubljana attuned to the CIAM theoretical platform.
83 Andrej Hrausky, "Functionalism and Arch," *Oris Magazine*, vol. 13, no. 69 (2011, online edition).
84 Ibid.
85 France Tomažič, "Stanovanja in hiše" [Flats and Houses], *Dom in svet*, no. 1–2, (1935): 83.
86 Dragotin Fatur and Rajko Ložar, introduction to the first issue of *Arhitektura*, vol. 1, no. 1 (1931): 1.
87 Ibid.
88 Vladimir Šubic (1894–1946) was born and raised in Ljubljana and trained at the Technical University in Vienna and Graz. He continued training in Prague at the German section of the Technical Faculty after WWI.
89 Gustav Tönnies was a Swedish-born factory owner from the nineteenth century whose firm greatly contributed to the development of the infrastructural systems of Ljubljana.
90 Janko Zlodre, "Vladimir Šubic, Architect-builder or about the Petrified Angel," *Vladimir Šubic – arhitekt*, vol. 22, no. 111/114 (1992, special issue): 3–4.
91 Eve Blau, *The Architecture of Red Vienna 1919–1934*, Cambridge, MA: MIT Press, 1999.
92 Tadej Glažar and Janez Koželj, "Catalogue – the Meksika," in *Vladimir Šubic – arhitekt*: 52–56.
93 Bernik, *Slovene Architecture of the Twentieth Century*: 250, also discussed in Glažar, *Vladimir Šubic – arhitekt*: 85.
94 Zlodre, "Vladimir Šubic, Architect-builder or about the Petrified Angel": 29.
95 Sonja Ifko, "Recent Slovenian Architecture," *Architectonic IV*, no. 2 (1995).
96 Zlodre, "Vladimir Šubic, Architect-builder or about the Petrified Angel": 35.
97 Lazarević, "Družba in gospodarstvo med obema vojnama": 130.
98 Discussed in Bogo Župančič, *Plečnikovi študenti in drugi jugoslovanski arhitekti v Le Corbusierovom ateljeju* [Plečnik's Students and Other Yugoslav Architects in Le Corbusier's Atelier], Ljubljana: MAO, 2017.
99 Aleš Vodopivec, "Edvard Ravnikar's Architecture: Locally Adjusted Modernism," in Aleš Vodopivec and Rok Žnidaršič (eds.), *Edvard Ravnikar: Architect and Teacher*, New York: Springer, 2009: 16.
100 William Curtis, "Abstraction and Representation: The Memorial Complex at Kampor, on the Island of Rab, 1952–53, by Edvard Ravnik," in Vodopivec and Žnidaršič (eds.), *Edvard Ravnikar: Architect and Teacher*: 36.
101 Ravnikar's original writings published in Nataša Koselj: "Tradicija napredka," [The Tradition of Progress], PhD dissertation, Ljubljana, 2003: 18, 137.
102 Boris Podrecca, "Cladding the City: Edvard Ravnikar's Architecture," in Vodopivec and Žnidaršič (eds.), *Edvard Ravnikar: Architect and Teacher*: 56.
103 Zlodre, "Vladimir Šubic, Architect-builder or about the Petrified Angel": footnote 9.

Conclusion
National and urban architectures within the Yugoslav cultural space: the role of architectural historiography

Since the collapse of Yugoslavia in the civil war of the 1990s, architectural historians in the region have been probing the question of correlation between architectural development and the rise of national ideologies. The nature of themes slightly varies among Serbian, Croatian and Croatian scholars. The most often discussed topic in Serbian research has been the idea of national architecture, its correlation to shifting ideologies and the formation of cultural identities. On the other hand, Croatian scholars have tended to connect the emergence of their architectural modernity to the Central European context, in the first place to reestablish the "natural" ties to Vienna. Slovenian historiography has remained preoccupied with the opus of Jože Plečnik ever since the pivotal rediscovery of his work through the exhibition at the Centre Pompidou in 1986, at the eve of the country's dissolution anticipating Slovenian independence. Even when the architects had not paid attention to the ideological implications of their work, the forthcoming interpretations often tied them to some ideological explanation depending on the shifting national politics. Initially, Yugoslavia and Yugoslavness hoped for synthesis into a unique national body – the concept abandoned during communism in favor of separate national identities, which consequently boosted the delineation of architectural histories. Intriguingly, the most comprehensive studies on the coherent Yugoslav space, recently developed by a group of international scholars, address the communist period during which the national fragmentation became a political imperative. However, the uniqueness of Yugoslav architectural production has not been recognized because the national boundaries were separated but, on the contrary, because of the openness of the country towards the Third World and its capability to challenge the rigid division between the Eastern and Western blocs during the Cold War. The forces of modernization conjoined with the specific communist economy relying on loans from the International Monetary Fund blurred the intentions of the political elites to fragmentize the Yugoslav into the separate national cultures.

Originally, the foundation of the disciplines of archeology, museology and accordingly the art and architectural history coincided with the constitution of nation-states[1] and the formation of modern national narratives both among Serbian and Croatian intellectuals. Even before the domestic researchers became aware of the importance of architectural history for finding the national roots, the foreign scholars, mainly French and German travelers, collected material and wrote about the region, yet their studies focused on regional rather than national classification of the architectural heritage. Alongside defining the broader historiographical discourse, the academic programs focusing on the origins of national past were established between the 1870s and the1890s by the Slavic-born individuals educated, with almost no exception, in the German-speaking academic centers. In Serbia, Mihajlo Valtrović[2] and Dragutin Milutinović,[3] both trained in Karlsruhe, were the pioneers of recording sacred architecture from the medieval past built prior to the Ottoman conquest.[4] They conducted field trips through the regions of Serbia recently taken over from the Ottomans, followed by the presentations of recorded drawings and the analysis of the visited sites, which inspired new attitudes about the concept of Serbian national architecture. In 1882, Valtrović became the first chair of the department of Serbian archeology at the Faculty of Philosophy and the first director of the National Museum when the institution split from the National Library. At the same time, Dragutin Milutinović started teaching history of architecture, design studio, structures and the foundations of Serbo-Byzantine architecture at Belgrade University. Although he initiated the future path of discussions on the nature of the Serbo-Byzantine idiom in contrast to the generic Byzantine style examined at German architecture schools, his realized and unrealized projects showed an ability to cope with a variety of the nineteenth-century Historicist references, in most cases unrelated to the Serbian medieval heritage. Only at the turn of the century would another generation of architects, mainly professors at the Faculty of Architecture, start a wider theoretical debate about the notion of national architecture rooted both the medieval-sacred and vernacular heritage. The movement was inspired by the research and writings of Carlo Inchiostri, born to an Italian father and a Slavic mother, who settled in Serbia in pursuit of his Slavic origins and changed his name to Dragutin Medenjak Inkiostri. Considering the Serbo-Byzantine too rigid for his taste, Inkiostri turned to the "pure and uncorrupted" folk traditions in search for an authentic expression of the "national spirit, freed from the burden of styles."[5] In the spirit of the Secessionist movement, Inkiostri longed for the unrestricted artistic freedom liberated from the nineteenth-century academic disciplines, a new possibility for achieving national architecture equivalent to the new age.

    The rise of methodical research of what was considered Croatian national architecture addressed the vernacular heritage, the peasant dwellings spread through various regions of continental Croatia, including Srem in today's Serbia, after the implementation of Teresian urban reforms following the Ottoman withdrawal from Slavonija and Vojvodina. The initiative coincided with the rising interest in vernacularism among the architectural societies in Central Europe,[6] yet in the Croatian case it was the architectural training of Croatian students at the Academy of Fine Arts under the leadership of Friedrich von Schmidt that more profoundly conveyed the research.[7] The pioneers in field research and recorded drawings were Martin Pilar[8] and Janko Holjac,[9] while still students in Schmidt's studios in 1885. Schmidt insisted on field trips and recording of historical buildings, particularly the Gothic churches, as a compulsory part of architectural training. He was also personally engaged, together with his student Herman Bollé, on the construction and reconstruction of the Gothic churches, taking in consideration the regional qualities of the Gothic. However, the systematic research of Gothic medieval architecture in Croatia never developed into a national project, as was the case with vernacular architecture. Thus, twenty years after the first traveling campaign through the Croatian countryside, Pilar and Holjac produced a series of drawings under the title "Hrvatski građevni oblici" [Croatian building forms], published by the Society of Architects and Engineers. The leading figure in establishing the discipline of art history and museology was Izidor Kršnjavi, the first to obtain a doctoral degree in the discipline from the University of Vienna. As a leader of the Art Society he promoted the ideals of patriotism and nationhood, being not only loyal but supportive of the Habsburg authorities. As was mentioned earlier, he was the founder of the Arts and Crafts Museum, including the school to provide local training to the first generation of Croatian-born builders, as part of the broader network of similar institutions affirming the local cultures within the Habsburg boundaries. The same framework of Viennese-originated art history scholarship traced the roots for investigation, recording and promotion of Dalmatian sacred architecture, since the pre-Romanesque through the Renaissance times, along with the first preservation campaigns of the Ancient Roman heritage. These affairs coincided with the strengthening of Austro-Hungarian rule in Bosnia-Herzegovina and culminated after annexing the region prior to WWI.[10] The first Croat-born architect involved in documenting of Dalmatian heritage was also Viennese-trained, Ćiril Metod Iveković was appointed a member of the central agency for the protection of cultural heritage with the seat in Vienna.[11] During WWI and Italian control over the region, the Italian scholars took over the conceptualization of first comprehensive overviews of Dalmatian heritage. Hence, it would be only the next generation of Croatian scholars trained in Vienna under Max Dvořák, in the first place Ljubo Karaman, to start arguing for explicitly Croatan origins of medieval sacred architecture in Dalmatia, in the 1920s.[12] After Karaman's comprehensive publications on the subject, there were also attempts to synthetize Croatian and Serbian medieval traditions in this area as opposed to addressing their Italian or Byzantine origins, as could be seen in the work of a Serbian scholar born in Croatia, Vojislav Korać.[13]

In contrast to the first attempts at constituting Serbian and Croatian historiography, focusing either on medievalism or vernacularism, establishing the discourse of Yugoslav art and architecture started as an insight into the contemporary production. The previously discussed exhibitions of the Yugoslav art culminating with the foundation of the Council for the Organization of Artistic Affairs of Serbia and Yugoslavism in 1913, with the main objective to establish unified cultural institutions, raised the artistic culture to a higher level and promoted a Yugoslav identity to the international audience.[14] The politically engaged art by Ivan Meštrović culminated with the appearance of the first monograph about him in 1919, and together with the monograph on Plečnik published the following year, traced the future directory of what could be considered the core of a Yugoslav culture. The material for both books was collected by Kosta Strajnić, a prominent art historian and critic, educated in Vienna under the mentorship of Josef Strzygowski. The tone of Strajnić's commentary explicitly defined him as an enthusiastic promoter of a Yugoslav project. The monograph on Meštrović, presenting the model of Vidovdan Tempe on the cover (see Figure 3.1) and the entire list of photographs of the Vidovdan Fragments, was published in 1919. The other on Plečnik occurred a year later after Strajnić's stay in Prague where he had met Plečnik working on the projects for Hradčany. Hence the works by a Croatian sculptor and a Slovenian architect were promoted by a Serbian art historian (since Strajnić was ethnically a Serb from Croatia) as the best examples of what the synthetized Yugoslavia could proudly show to the rest of the world. Yugoslavia was still young, and the three of them obviously considered themselves Yugoslavs at the time of publishing.

What remained considered Yugoslav art and architecture followed the path defined by the concept of Yugoslav exhibitions, and the pre-WWI political engagement of art associations such as the Lada and the Medulić,[15] although the line between Serbian, Croatian, Serbo-Croatian, Croato-Serbian and Yugoslav was never fully elucidated. Since the constitution of the country, various professional associations started operated on the Yugoslav level, including the Association of Yugoslav Engineers and Architects, the UJIA, the first to put emphasis on the attribute of Yugoslav in the title.[16] The inauguration speech delivered at the constitutional ceremony held in Belgrade in 1919 emphasized the unifying role of those who were in charge of building a new nation, literally and symbolically. A similar rhetoric of national unification by architectural means would remain present at most of the mutual gatherings through the late 1930s when the UJIA turned into a decentralized cluster of regional sections in an attempt to please Croatian colleagues, who, in accordance with general Croatian politics, tried to distance themselves from the centralized Yugoslav project. However, the UJIA succeeded in providing a platform for the exchange of ideas among colleagues from the regional sections primarily through its biweekly publication *Tehnički list* [*Technical Bulletin*], published in Zagreb in the so-called Serbo-Croato-Slovenian language. Along with distinguished projects mainly promoting the rising Modernism, *Tehnički list* regularly announced architectural competitions on the state level, followed by the publication of the winning entries. As the paper was printed in the all three languages, using both the Cyrillic-Serbian, Latin-Croatian and Slovenian scripts, it seemed that the ethnic boundaries were about to vanish. A similar play with regional variations of languages and scripts occurred in another two significant architectural periodicals, *Gradevinski vjesnik* [*The Building Herald*], published also in Zagreb from 1932 to 1941 and the already discussed *Arhitektura*, issued in Ljubljana from 1931 to 1934.

In reality, the disagreements among the regional sections had been rising since the foundation of the UJIA. On one side, the Zagreb branch, which had been established and operated independently within the Habsburg network, was discontent about the loss of its Croatian name.[17] On the other, the tensions would culminate after the large competitions, either after the announcement of the competition results or when the winning entries did not materialize. While Croatian architects often participated in the competitions for large-scale public buildings in Belgrade, Serbian architects hardly dared to take part in the similar events taking place in the western provinces of the country. As a sign of political correctness, Croatian architects were often the winners in the competitions in Belgrade; however, very often they would be cut off by the Belgrade professional establishment and the developers wishing to deal with less demanding local firms. Hence, some of the competitions for the key locations such as the Main Post Office and Agrarian Bank flanking the public space around the National Assembly and the Albania Palace at the mouth of the Terazije Square were won by Zagreb architects, but latter redeveloped by Serbian teams. On the other hand, there was no single case of a builder from Serbia to accomplish any kind of significant public structure in Zagreb. Intriguingly, in Ljubljana, with no significant number of Serbian minorities prior to WWI, there was a politically colored attempt to give an architectural homage to the explicitly Serbian identity by the construction of a Serbian-Orthodox church in the Serbo-Byzantine style next to Tivoli Park. After developing the connections with Ljubljana as part of the involvement with the Sokol facilities, its designer, a fervent promoter of the National-Romantic stylization, Momir Korunović, was strongly supported by the municipality to build the Orthodox church at the best location and show the foreigners that "the undividable Yugoslav Kingdom started from White Ljubljana with Serbian and Slovenian brothers being inseparable forever."[18]

A sense of the unified Yugoslav architectural space was promoted through two specifically architectural exhibitions, organized in Belgrade, first in 1931 and then in 1933, to reinforce the synthetizing national program.[19] In contrast to the previously organized Yugoslav art exhibitions, in which architecture was only sporadically presented, these two shows gathered exclusively architectural designs, the representative showcases of the most progressive ideas emerging in the country at the time. Both events took place at the previously discussed Art Pavilion Cvijeta Zuzorić in Belgrade, designed by the leading voices of Modernism, one of the founders of the Group of the Architects of Modern Orientation, Branislav Kojić. Although the post-WWII commentary linked the ideological background of the exhibitions with King Aleksandar's dictatorship, the king's personal role in directing the tone of the show to reinforce the shaken nation seems insignificant. It was rather the architectural profession that finally achieved the level of maturity to be given full credit for the promotion of national unity by means of international Modernism. The new concepts of architectural design and structural engineering based on new technologies and industrially produced materials were spread over the country since 1929 – the year when the dictatorship was established. Yet the king's taste, as it was proved in his initiative to alter Pičman's glass curtain façade of the Main Post Office, was far from being attuned to Modernism. Therefore, it can be assumed that he just stayed away from discouraging the promotion of the avant-garde movements and rebellious participants in the shows. Moreover, the most radical leftist architectural group in the country, Ibler's Zemlja, participated in the show of 1931 with significant publicity. The same group would be banned by a police decree as a political enemy of the regime in 1935, a year after Aleksandar's assassination in Marseilles.

The main role of the exhibitions was to present the so-called contemporary architecture as opposition to previous historical styles – the agenda achieved both through the selection of works as well as the affirmative voices by contemporary critiques who were a part of the same campaign. The positive comments, most of which appeared in the Belgrade press after the first show, noted the accomplishment of organizers in collecting and presenting the best of Yugoslav architecture attuned to the Modern Movement. The supporter of the GAMP, architect and urbanist Branko Maksimović, talked enthusiastically about the exhibit, emphasizing its revolutionary tone and social role of the presented designs.[20] Along with Drago Ibler and his companions from Zemlja, the leading voices of Zagreb Modernism – Lavoslav Horvat, Stjepan Planić, Zlatko Neumann, Vladimir Šterk and Marko Vidaković – set high standards for the first show and inspired their less brave Belgrade colleagues, mainly the members of the GAMP – Milan Zloković, Branislav Kojić, Dragiša Brašovan and the Krstić brothers, among others – to present their Modernist realizations for the first time to a Belgrade audience.

However, some of the Belgrade participants presented older designs, rich in historical references, which were labeled as "Modern-oriented" only because of their affiliation with the GAMP. For that reason, an influential Belgrade-based architectural historian, Đurđe Bošković, saw the exhibition as a promotion of "architecture, which is nothing else but the expression of one new material – reinforced concrete." Yet, Bošković wrote positively about the propagandists of modern architecture. Arguing against the idea that the Modernists were the "Western slaves," he stated that "even if they were slaves, they became that only when they repeated the mistakes of the Western architects. Would they get rid of them, their results would be as much ours, if not even more ours, than any other result brought by the imitation of medieval national heritage."[21] Bošković's definition of "our" architecture landed on the long-lasting discussions about the Western versus the indigenous values imbedded in a specific national genius – the themes already pondered about in the earlier searches of the truly Slavic nature of Meštrović's work as well as on the anti-Western platform of Micić's Zenithism. As a devoted researcher and conservator of medieval heritage, Bošković insisted on the principles of authenticity imported into the preservationist discipline from the theoretical discourse of John Ruskin and Alois Riegl, yet for a specific reason. He was disgusted by the new interpretations of medieval heritage that had just appeared in proposals for new church architecture in Belgrade, namely against the recently approved winning proposal for St. Mark's behind the Main Post Office by the GAMP members Petar and Branko Krstić, conceptualized as a weird replica of the medieval catholicon of Gračanica Monastery in Kosovo.[22] Paradoxically, the project for St. Mark's was presented at the second exhibition of 1933, although was considered neither modern nor Yugoslav.

The second exhibit itself was far less diverse than the first one, with only three participants from Zagreb – Ivan Zemljak, Egon Steinmann and Vjekoslav Muršec – accompanying selected works by the GAMP members. Yet, the reason for a smaller number of participants from Zagreb and Ljubljana than in the previous event seems more prosaic than the later historiography tried to present. Simply, a year after the first Yugoslav exhibition in Belgrade, the Zagreb chapter of the UJIA organized an exhibition with similar contents in Zagreb,[23] thereby the idea of showing the same works all over again in Belgrade motivated no action. Inspired by the Zagreb exhibition, a similar event was organized in Ljubljana the following year. Moreover, the second exhibition exclusively promoted the members of the GAMP so that some of the commentators reviewed it neither as Yugoslav nor Serbian but simply as the group's exhibit.[24] Hence, the agenda of nationalization of architectural internationalism through the Yugoslav exhibits was far less important than the self-promotion in hope for new commissions when the means of modern architecture became appealing for developers and the general public.

These mundane motives were not in conflict with a broader ambition of the organizers, namely the GAMP members, to join the international architectural community under the Yugoslav name. The tensions about the use of the term "Yugoslav" for defining the cultural space of the new nation dated back to the earlier presentations of Serbian and Croatian artists before the international audience and was never fully resolved until the dissolution of Yugoslavia. Yet they were generated by the oscillating political goals reflected on the discourse of art and architectural history and criticism, rather than by architects primarily motivated to explore new design possibilities. The problem of the national identity of the protagonist of the Modern Movement was in fact the same in Yugoslavia as around the globe. While Frank Lloyd Wright, for example, unquestionably symbolizes the American nation, the question remains if the works by Mies van der Rohe in the USA carry on more Americanness than Germanness. In a similar fashion,

212 *Conclusion*

Jože Plečnik was not explicitly Slovenian but also a Yugoslav architect since his arrival in Ljubljana. Yet, the attribute of Yugoslav developed into a politically incorrect term associated with the hegemonistic Serbian aspirations, especially after the federalization of the country during communism in the 1960s and the 1970s. Overburdened with political correctness in the 1980s, the commentator on the Yugoslav exhibitions, architectural historian Zoran Manević, problematized the term "Yugoslav" far beyond its meaning from the 1930s. The same could be said about later attacks on architectural Yugoslavness from the turn of the millennium, a sort of intellectual recuperation – a reaction to the feeling of collective guilt among Serbian intellectuals during the country's dissolution during the 1990s. At the same time, previously Yugoslav architectural heroes such as Jože Plečnik were decontextualized from the Yugoslav cultural space. Since the rediscovery of Plečnik on the international scene in the late 1980s, right before the fall of the Berlin Wall, Plečnik has been considered either a father of the Slovenian national idiom or an epitome of the Central European identity, elaborately discussed among architectural historians focusing on the reaffirmation of Viennese turn of the century legacies.

While the thematically inconsistent Yugoslav exhibitions from Belgrade have been scrutinized for the ideological subtext of a hidden Great Serbian ideology, the attempts by Zagreb architects to define their specific national space during the interwar period has never been discussed from the perspective of separation from the Yugoslav program. The most ambitious among the events of this kind was organized by the Croatian Society of Arts at Zagreb Art Pavilion in 1938, under the title Fifty Years of Croatian Art, 1888–1938. The political background of this show was delicate and its role in strengthening Croatian pride about national culture was tremendous, since soon after, after almost a two-decade-long struggle for defining the national borders, Croatia finally became a specially declared political and administrative unit, Banovina Hrvatska. Thus, the exhibition anticipated and announced the political shift, playing an important role in the further constitution of a way Croatian national architecture was defined and displayed. Stylistically and thematically, it showed a variety of approaches and functions, focusing primarily on the best realizations by almost fifty names included on a list of Croatian architects.[25] The criteria upon which the architects and their buildings were selected reflected the discontent with a secondary role for Croatia in the South Slavic state and the rejection of an assimilation into a centralized state of Yugoslavia under Serbian domination. Croatian political aspirations were concentrated on separate state borders, which would include all Croatian lands; that is, the territory settled by Catholic population speaking Serbo-Croatian and Croato-Serbian. In accord with this idea, the selected architects, besides Croats from today's Croatia, included Croats living in Bosnia or those living in other parts of Yugoslavia, as well as architects of Serbian and Jewish origins settled in Croatia. In terms of the works shown, the exhibition showed what was built by architects considered Croats in cities beyond the Banovina's borders. Thus, the overview presented Hugo Ehrlich's Yugoslav Bank, Branko Bon's Albania Palace and a few projects of smaller scale in Belgrade, also a bunch of realizations from Sarajevo and some other cities in Bosnia. In this way, the selection committee determined the ways of understanding what epitomized the national art and architecture of Croats and created a pattern in which it was to be displayed in the future.

Another layer of defining of an intrinsically Croatian architectural discourse resulted from the further exploration of the vernacular building traditions, rooted in Pilar and Holjac's recordings of peasant architecture and in Antun Radić's turn of the century writings on the national distinctions of Croats. By the late 1930s, Stjepan Planić not only explored the possibilities of linking the Croatian peasant architecture with the contemporary practice but started applying the his theoretical findings on actual designs such as the Villa Fuhrmann, better known as the Round House, built for a glass distributor with walking disabilities in 1935. The circular footprint, laid on a delicately chosen hilly platform, enabled functional connections among all rooms and consequently an easy circulation through the house but also a total openness and visual connection with the surrounding nature. Thus, it was attuned with Planić's discussion about the relationship between the form and the setting of peasant houses "well incorporated into the landscape, standing unpretentiously while perfectly completing the natural scenery."[26] Conceived in the form of the primordial hut, the Round House employed the organic materials – wood, stone and tile – characteristic for its immediate surroundings, also defined as "indigenous building methods" in his treatise about the national style.[27] In this way, Planić tried to literally prove his thesis about the fundamental link between rural and contemporary architecture. Although using the term "national style," he explicitly rejected the importance of ornamentation in achieving an intrinsic national idiom, as Viktor Kovačić had done a few decades earlier. However, Planić went a step further than Kovačić in denying any values of urban architecture for Croatian identity prior to the age of Modernism, in a tradition that could be related to Antun Radić's influence.

Along with Planić, a student of Plečnik, Slovenian-born Dušan Grabrijan, started research on Bosnian vernacularism after settling in Sarajevo in the early 1930s.[28] Together with a younger Zagreb colleague, Juraj Najdhart, Grabrijan explored the traditional Bosnian house as an epitome for the path toward modernity,[29] yet their passion for the vernacular would not converge with the search for a national identity. In Serbia, Branislav Kojić initiated a research of vernacular heritage in Serbia and Macedonia, looking for analogies with the contemporary practice rather than for the origins of a Serbian national style. All their efforts would culminate with a vast interest in rural architecture and its preservation during communist rule, when the highest migration rate from the rural to the urban communities were recorded. At the same time, the new typologies of for housing settlements during communism neglected the nineteenth- and early twentieth-century urban patterns with blocks divided into individual parcels along the regulation lines as the Athens Charter had suggested. Although similar urbanist practices occurred all around Europe from the 1950s to the 1970s, the new city forms were considered here as a particularly communist phenomenon.

The pre-communist city cores of Belgrade, Zagreb and Ljubljana all faced some level of late-Modernist urban transformations attuned to the ideological fight against the petit bourgeois spirit, after the end of WWII. The institutions for protection of cultural heritage – found at first on a centralized Yugoslav level in 1947, and later divided according to the division of country into federative republic – at first took care of either medieval or vernacular sites. Following the Venice Charter of 1964, the preservationists took more care of the late-medieval urban cores such as Ohrid, Kotor and Dubrovnik, but also brought concerns about values of the nineteenth-century urban developments. As Bogdan Nestorović pointed out "all historical research in the sphere of Serbian architecture had started and finished with the middle ages and was mostly concerned with Kosovo."[30] This observation was included into the preface of manuscript "*Architecture of Serbia in the Nineteenth Century*" he studiously worked on until the early 1970s.[31] In a similar fashion, a Croatian art historian, Lelja Dobronić, took a subversive insight into the pre-communist bourgeois past, exploring the early modern, primarily nineteenth-century civic heritage of Zagreb and Croatia. On the other hand, the research of twentieth-century Modernism remained a key national narrative in Croatian architectural historiography. Soon after Strajnić's early attempt to depict Meštrović as a Yugoslav artist, the first collection of plans and drawings by Viktor Kovačić, edited and annotated by Vienna-trained Edo Schön, were published as the first monographically conceived homage to the father of Croatian architecture. A similar national endeavor was noticed in Slovenian historiography. The leading figure in elevating the discipline at the national level was France Stelè, trained under Mark Dvořak and influenced by Josef Strzygowski's legacy, who edited the three-volume publication of the drawings and texts by Jože Plečnik titled *Napori* at the outbreak of WWII. In contrast to Croatia and Slovenia, Serbian researchers stayed detached from Vienna at the turn of the century, so that the passion and knowledge for the promotion of Modernist discourse did not emerge in Serbia in the same way. Moreover, the first monographs on Serbian Modernist architects were published only in the 1980s.[32] Luckily, the interest in civic architecture and the age of modernity among the historiographers has been growing, although Serbia has been experiencing a growth of populist politics ever since the breakup of Yugoslavia. Interestingly, despite the nationalist and populist political tone in recent decades, research regarding medieval and vernacular heritage tends to disappear.

Conclusion 215

The importance of urbanization and the rise of civic societies, and consequently the urban architecture, has been vital for the constitution of nation-states in modern Europe. This is especially applicable on the architecture of capital cities – the key carriers of modern national identities. One may scrutinize their architectures through the lens of urban and architectural programs, typologies, stylization, patronage etc., however, the same issue could be the carrier of various national narratives. What defines these narratives is the political subtext of the writer and the writing rather than the urban and architectural form itself. Although research regarding Zagreb and Ljubljana re-established their broken ties with Vienna after the fall of the Berlin Wall in discussions of their architectures, this does not mean the that their natural ties with Belgrade can be neglected. This is of critical importance at the moment when Slovenian and Croatian citizens experience themselves as second-tier members among the European nations, and, even worse, when Serbian citizens feel that their national politics push them toward the camp of non-European countries of the Third World.

Notes

1 Prince Miloš Obrenović sent one of the most educated men in Serbia, writer and dramaturg Joakim Vujić, to travel and describe medieval churches in the areas liberated from the Ottomans after the Second Uprising. In the 1840s, this concern about national heritage was officially included into the affairs of the Ministry of Education and Culture.
2 Mihailo Valtrović (1839–1915) was born in a Serbianized family of German origins. After graduating from Karlsruhe Polytechnic, he returned to Serbia and started research on medieval architecture, later becoming the first director of the National Museum and the founder of Archeological Society. Discussed in Ivan Stevović, "Od terenske skice do skice celine: Mihailo Valtrović i srpska srednjovekovna arhitektura" [From the Field Sketches to a Sketch of the Whole: Mihailo Valtrović and Serbian Medieval Architecture], *Zbornik Narodnog muzeja*, vol. 22, no. 2. (2016): 9–46.
3 Dragutin Milutinović (1840–1900) graduated from Karlsruhe Polytechnic, after which he returned to Serbia to work for the Ministry of Buildings and later was professor of architecture at the Technical Faculty in Belgrade. Together with Mihailo Valtrović, Milutinović researched and recorded medieval churches in Serbia.
4 Valtrović and Milutinović traveled and documented medieval church architecture together. Their original drawings and texts are published in Tanja Damljanović (ed.), *Valtrović and Milutinović: Documents 1–3*, Belgrade: Historical Museum of Serbia, 2006–2009. Their role is discussed in Sonja Bogdanović, *Mihailo Valtrović i Dragutin Milutinović kao istraživači srpskih starina*, Belgrade: SANU, 1978.
5 Dragutin Inkiostri (1866–1942) was "an artist and theorist who ventured into architecture as a designer of facades. In his words, 'we should seek our style among peasants and shepherds'." Bratislav Pantelić, "Nationalism and Architecture: The Creation of the National Style and Its Political Implications," *JSAH*, vol. 56, 1997: 30.

216 Conclusion

6 Vesna Dubovečak, "Društvo inžinira i arhitekata i izdavanje atlasa Hrvatski građevni oblici," *Časopis za suvremenu povjest*, no. 1 (2017): 123–154.
7 Dragan Damjanović, "Radovi hrvatskih arhitekata u časopisu Wiener Bauhütte" [The Works of Croatian Architects and the Journal Wiener Bauhütte], *Radovi instituta za povjest umjetnosti*, vol. 30 (2006): 229–240.
8 Martin Pilar (1861–1942) graduated from the Academy of Fine Arts in Vienna and after returning to Zagreb worked first with Bollé and later opened his own studio. He was one of the first Croatian architects to compete with the foreign builders.
9 Janko Holjac (1865–1939) studied in Vienna and upon settling back in Croatia worked on the design and reconstruction of churches. He served as a mayor of Zagreb from 1910 to 1917.
10 The political background is discussed in Matthew Rampley, *The Vienna School of Art History: Empire and the Politics of Scholarship, 1847–1918*, University Park, PA: Pennsylvania State University Press, 2013.
11 Joško Belamarić, "Dalmatia in the Visual Narrative: Georg Kowalczyk and Cornelius Gurlitt: An Atlas of Photographs of Dalmatian Monuments" in Costanza Caraffa and Tiziana Serena (eds.), *Photo Archives and the Idea of Nation*, Berlin: Walter de Gruyter, 2015: 95–118.
12 The early studies include: Ljubo Karaman, "Kulturni spomenici na našem Jadranu" [Cultural Monumentn in Our Jadran], *Almanah Jadranska straža* (1925) and "Spomenici u Dalmaciji u doba hrvatske narodne dinastije i vlast Bizanta na istočnom Jadranu u to doba " [Monuments in Dalmatia at the Time of Croatian National Dynasty and the Rule of Byzantium at the Same Time], *Šišićev zbornik* (1929). The post-WWII comprehensive synthesis is Ljubo Karaman, *Pregled umjetnosti u Dalmaciji* [*The Survey of Art in Dalmatia*], Zagreb: Matica hrvatska, 1952.
13 Vojislav Korać, *Graditeljska škola Primorja*, Belgrade: Naučno delo SANU, 1965.
14 Dejan Medaković, "Principi i program 'Odbora za organizaciju umetničkih poslova Srbije i Jugoslovenstva' iz 1913 godine" [Principles and Program of the Council for the Organization of Artistic Affairs of Serbia and Yugoslavness], in *Zbornik Filozofskog fakulteta*, Belgrade: Filozofski fakultet, 1970: 671–682.
15 The contradiction of naming is explained in Sandi Bulimbašić, *Društvo hrvatskih umjetnika Medulić, 1908–1919 umjetnost i politika*, Zagreb: DPUH, 2016. Although the Medulić society was explicitly pro-Yugoslav in its strong politicly colored program, its official name emphasized that it was an association of Croatian artists.
16 Discussed in Aleksandar Ignjatović, "Dom Udruženja jugoslovenskih inženjera i arhitekata u Beogradu," *Nasleđe- Heritage*, vol. 7 (2006): 87–118.
17 The Club of Croatian Engineers and Architects was found in March 1878 and developed into the Society of Engineers and Architect in 1895. Since its foundation it published the bulletin *Viesti Kluba inžinirah i arhitektah* [*News of the Club of Engineers and Architects*]. When the Slovenian Club was founded in 1911, *Viesti* as a conjoined journal started in Ljubljana. *Srpski tehnički list* [*Serbian Technical Bulletin*] was published separately in Belgrade from 1900 to 1918, and was fused with the *Tehnički list* after unification.
18 Anonymous, "The Construction of the Orthodox Church in Ljubljana," *Vreme* (August 7, 1930). Quoted in Aleksandar Kadijević, *Momir Korunović*, Belgrade: RZZSK, 1996: 72.

Conclusion   217

19 The thesis put forward by Zoran Manević," Izložbe jugoslovenske savremene arhitekture u Beogradu (1931,1933)" [Exhibitions of Yugoslav Contemporary Architecture in Belgrade], *Godišnjak grada Beograda*, vol. 27 (1980): 271–278.
20 Branko Maksimović, "Prva izložba savremene jugoslovenske arhitekture" [The first Exhibition of Contemporary Yugoslav Architecture], *Politika* (February 22, 1931): 5.
21 Djurdje Bošković, "Izložba savremene jugoslovenske arhitekture" [The Exhibition of Contemporary Yugoslav Architecture], *Vreme* (February 27, 1931): 7–8.
22 He bitterly criticized this design in Djurdje Bošković, "Crkva Sv. Marka u Beogradu kao karikature Gračanice" [The Church of St. Mark in Belgrade as a Caricature of Gračanica], *Srpski književni glasnik*, no. 35 (1932): 302–304.
23 Tamara Bjažić-Klarin, "Internacionalni stil – Izložbe međuratnog Zagreba 1928–1941" [The International Style – the Exhibitions of Interwar Zagreb 1928–1941], *Radovi Instituta za povjest umjetnosti*, vol. 31 (2007): 313–326.
24 Branko Maksimović, "Izložba Grupe arhitekata modernog pravca u Beogradu" [The Exhibition of the Group for Modern Orientation in Belgrade], *Beogradske opštinske novine – BON*, no. 3 (1933): 228–230.
25 The exhibition was accompanied with the catalog with the list of presented works and architects in alphabetical order. It also included short biographies and photographs of the works. See *Pola vijeka hrvatske umjetnosti*, exhibition catalog, Zagreb: Hrvatsko društvo umjetnosti, 1938. Besides the exhibition catalog a few more overviews accompanied the exhibit: Stjepan Planić, "Pedeset godina arhitekture u Hrvatskoj" [Fifty Years of Architecture in Croatia], *Književnik – hrvatski književni mjesečnik*, no. 12 (1939): 49–64; Vladimir Potočnjak, "Arhitektura u Hrvatskoj 1888–1938," *Građevinski vjesnik*, vol. 8, no. 4–5 (1939): 49–79.
26 Stjepan Planić, "O nacionalnom stilu u graditeljstvu" [About a National Style in Architecture], *Hrvatski narodni kalendar – Napredak* (1937): 205.
27 Ibid., 204.
28 Dušan Grabrijan (1899–1952) was one of the first three students of Plečnik to graduate in 1924. He received a scholarship to study in Paris in 1925/1926 where he became acquainted with Le Corbusier's teaching and possibly his understanding of a link between the modern and vernacular. See Zupančič, *Plečnikovi student i drugi jugoslovanski arhitekti v Le Corbusierovom ateljeju*: 164–168.
29 Dušan Grabrijan and Juraj Neidhardt, *Arhitektura Bosne i put u suvremeno* [*Architecture of Bosnia and the Path Towards Modernity*], Ljubljana: Državna založba Slovenije, 1957.
30 Nestorović, *Arhitektura Srbije u 19. veku*: 554.
31 Published for the first time only recently. See Chapter 1, endnote 39 for a more elaborate list of references by Bogdan Nestorović.
32 The first collection of text and drawings on Nikola Dobrović was published in 1980 followed by the monograph on Milan Zloković in 1989.

Index

Note: Page locators in *italics* refer to figures.

Agricultural Faculty, Zagreb University 147–150, *148*
Air Force Headquarters, Belgrade 104–106, *105*
Albania Palace, Belgrade 115–116, 120, *121*
Aleksandar, King 9, 73, 76, 96, 99, 102, 103, 210
Anastasijević, M. 26–27
Ante Starčević Square, Zagreb 52
Arhitektura 111, 112, 115, 192
Art Pavilion, Belgrade 113–114, *114*, 209–210
Art Pavilion, Zagreb 50, 212–213
art, Yugoslav 65–67; Exhibition of Yugoslav Artists, Paris 72; Exhibitions of Yugoslav Art 65–66, 68, 75; International Exposition 1911 69–70
Association of Yugoslav Engineers and Architects (UJIA) 208–209, 211
Astronomic Observatory, Belgrade 100–101, *100*

Babić, L. 55
Bajalović, P. 69, 82n17, 115
Bamberg House, Ljubljana 171
Banski Dvori (Ban's Palace), Zagreb 41–42
Bastl, V. 51
Batal Mosque 32, 40n59
Belgrade: Airport 106; apartment scheme 109; architectural exhibitions 1931 and 1933 209–211; architectural statehood 25–35; attempts to homogenize appearance of buildings 21, 23; Building Department 25; building industry 89–90; Building Law, 1896 21; church projects 31; commercial and business area 115–121; cultural projects 113–115; Cvijeta Zuzorić 113–114, *114*, 209–210; differing concepts of nationhood in 25; economy at start of 20th century 23; electric power 23; "Europeanized" Bešlić 21, *22*; growth and development after Great War 89–93; housing apartment scheme 109; housing for poor 108–109; housing for wealthy 111–112, *112*; housing, new build 89–90, 109; housing shortage 23–24, 91, 107–108; as imperial capital 89–93; Law for the Construction of Public Buildings, 1865 26; Master Plan, 1912 24–25; Master Plan, 1923 90–91, *91*, 98, 108, 117; modernization process and new technologies 91–92; monumental state buildings 93–106; nationalizing urban fabric 17–25; parks 20, 90; poverty 107–108; public buildings for Serbian institutions 18–19, 20, 25–35; Regulatory Plan for Belgrade within the Moat 19–21; removal of Muslims 17, 18, 19–20, 28; resurfacing streets 23; sewage system 23, 24; slow modernisation pace 25; "state-axis" development 93–96; tensions with periphery 107; Terazije area development 115–121; transport system 20–21; University area 23, 96–99; urban growth 23; vernacular traditions in shop buildings 19; vying

with Zagreb for supremacy 9; water supply 23; Western-looking first urban transformation in autonomous 17, 18–21, 24; withdrawal of Ottoman army 19–20
Belgrade architectural projects: Air Force Headquarters 104–106, *105*; Albania Palace 115–116, 120, *121*; Anastasijević palazzo 26–27; Astronomic Observatory 100–101, *100*; Batal Mosque 32, 40n59; Financial Park 93–96; Hotel Moscow 56–57; Igumanov Endowment *116*, 118–119; Istanbul Gate 29; Kapetan Miša's Endowment 27, *27*; Kolarac Endowment 114; Main Post Office and Postal Saving Bank 102–103; Ministry of Agriculture 94–95, *95*; Ministry of Buildings 25–26; Ministry of Finances 95, *95*; Ministry of Justice 30–31; Mortgage Merchandise Bank 119–120; National Assembly 32–33, *32*, 34; National Bank 31–32; National Theater 27–29, *28*, 113; Prizenska Street 110–111, *111*; Royal Court 29–30, 33; Russia Palace 130; St. Mark's Church 211; St. Sava Cathedral 20, 33–34, 76; Stari konak (Old Palace) 29; State Archive 98; State Printing Plant 103–104, 106; Terazije Terrace 99; University Library 96–97, *97*; University Student Dormitory 98–99; University Technical Faculty 97–98, *97*; Villa Milićević 111–112, *112*; *Vreme* Headquarters 116, *116*; Worker Insurance 142; Yugoslav Agrarian Bank 117; Yugoslav Union Bank 102
Berlin Congress, 1878 5, 20
Bollé, H. 53–55, 62–63n37
Bošković, D. 210–211
Botanical Garden, Zagreb 51–52
Brašovan, D. 94–95, 103, 122n11
Bugarski, A. 28–29, 30, 38n45
Building Code, 1857 43
Building Department, Belgrade 25

Car, M. 69
Cathedral of Freedom, Ljubljana 178–179, *178*, 202n48
Chambon, A. 24–25
Chemical Institute, Zagreb 51

Chronicle of the Priest of Dioclea 4
church architecture 31; Church of St. Blaise, Zagreb 57–59, *57*; Serbian-Orthodox church, Ljubljana 209; St. Mark's Church, Belgrade 211; St. Sava Cathedral 20, 33–34, 76; Zagreb Cathedral 53–54, *55*
Church of St. Blaise, Zagreb 57–59, *57*
CIAM 158, 159, 160
Club of Architects 192
Cologne Cathedral 53, 54, 63n40
Communal Municipal Services Headquarters, Zagreb 151
Congress Square, Ljubljana 175–176, *175*
Cooperative Bank, Ljubljana 186–187
cultural projects, Belgrade 113–115
Cvijeta Zuzorić 113–114, *114*, 209–210
Czech Rondocubism 146, 187, 189, 197

Davidović, D. 8
Denzler, J. 151, 163n55
Dobrović, N. 99, 103–104, 123n28
Dolinar, L. 197
Đorđević, D. 97
Dragotin Fatur 192
Dubový, J. 100–101, 108
Dubronić, L. 214
Duklja, Kingdom of 4–5

Ehrlich, H. 102, 130, 150, 151
Elementary School Jordanovac, Zagreb 152–153, *152*
ethnic nationalism 2
exhibitions: Belgrade 1931 and 1933 209–211; Exhibition of Czech Architecture 102, 115, 124n36, 130, 139; Exhibition of Yugoslav Artists, Paris 72; Exhibitions of Yugoslav Art 65–66, 68, 75; "Fifty Years of Croatian Art," Zagreb 1938 212–213; International Exposition 1911 69–70; UJIA, 1932 211; World Exposition Paris, 1937 78–80

Fabiani, M. 169, 170, 171, 174, 176, 186, 200n15
Felbinger, B. 42
Fellner & Helmer 48, 49
Ferenček, M. 92
First Men's High School, Zagreb 155–156
Foundation Hospital, Zagreb 145, 148

Franz Joseph Square, Zagreb 49–50
French Revolution Square, Ljubljana 176
GAMP (Group of Architects of Modern Orientation) 101, 103, 110, 118, 210, 211
Garašanin, I. 8
Genius, statue of 197
Gočár, J. 139, 187
Grabrijan, D. 213, 217n28
Green Horseshoe program, Zagreb 44–53, *44*, 156
Gropius, W. 160

Halm House, Zagreb 45
Harmica, Zagreb 42–43
HAŠK (Croatian Academic Sport Society) 146
higher education institutions, Belgrade 23
historical background 1–10
Historicism 26, 30, 75, 93, 119, 206; criticism of 49, 54, 55, 56; in housing developments 109, 110; shift to Modernism from 102, 103
historiography, role of architectural 205–217
Holjac, J. 207, 216n9
Hönigsberg & Deutsch 52, 62n35
Horseshoe program, Zagreb 44–53, *44*, 156
Horvat, L. 142, 163n47, 163n48
Hotel Esplanade, Zagreb 52, 62n34
Hotel Moscow, Belgrade 56–57
Hotel Slon, Ljubljana 193
housing: Belgrade apartment scheme 109; garden-city suburbs, Zagreb 138–141, *138*; interpolated rental buildings 135; Meksika housing project, Ljubljana 193–194; mixed-use projects, Zagreb 135–137, 137–138; new build, Belgrade 89–90, 109; for poor, Belgrade 108–109; shortage, Belgrade 23–24, 91, 107–108; Svetokrižki okraj, Ljubljana 176–177, *177*; for wealthy, Belgrade 111–112, *112*; workers, Ljubljana 189–190
Howard, E. 176
Hribar, R. 172, 201n22

Ibler, D. 131, 135–136, 141–143, 144, 161n10
Igumanov Endowment, Belgrade *116*, 118–119
Ilica Street, Zagreb 42
Ilkić, J. 30, 34
Illyria 1–2, 168; monument to French 176
Illyrian Movement 7–8, 42, 47, 50, 60n1, 66, 168
Inkiostri, D. 206, 215n5
Institute of Hygiene (Public Health Palace), Zagreb 143–144
Institute of Physics, Zagreb 51
International Exposition, Rome 1911 69–70
International Style 139, 142, 144, 153
Istanbul Gate, Belgrade 28
Ivačković, S. 30–31, 39n52, 39n55

Janke, F. 18–19, 25
Jaržabek, F. 50
Jewish Hospital, Zagreb 144–145
Josimović, E. 19–21, 36n12
Jovanović, K.A. 31–34

Kapetan Miša's Endowment 27, *27*
Karadžić, V.S. 3
Khuen-Héderváry, K. 50
King Peter Krešimir Square, Zagreb 156–157
Kingdom of Serbs, Croats and Slovenes 9
Klek, J. 78
Koch, C.M. 170, 171, 200n13
Kojić, B. 110–111, 113–114, 115–116, 125n61, 209, 213
Kolarac Endowment, Belgrade 114
Kopitar, J. 3
Korb & Giergl 50
Korka-Kiverov-Krekić 157
Korunović, M. 188–189, 209
Kosovo myth 67
Kovačević, M. 151, 164n70
Kovačić, V. 55–60, 63n42, 63n44, 63n45, 127–130
Kovalevsky, G. 98–99
Krasnov, N. 95, 98, 122n16
Krečić, P. 179, 182–183
Krleža, M. 141, 142, 163n44
Kršnjavi, I. 54, 57, 207
Krstić brothers 103, 109, 111–112, *112*, 117–119, 211
Kulturnation 2, 3, 27, 169

Labor Exchange, Zagreb 156
Lada Society 66

language: Slavic 2, 3, 4, 7; Slovenian 6, 7, 168, 169
Law for the Construction of Public Buildings, 1865 26
Lazarević, Ð. 119
Le Corbusier 78, 113, 136, 158, 159, 189, 198
Legio Bank, Prague 187
Leko, D.T. 33, 94
Lenuci, M. 44, 47, 50, 61n23, 156
Ljubljana: cultural societies 169; history 166–168; interwar development 171–199; micro-urban designs 172, 175–181; pedestrian routes 179–181; post-earthquake planning and reconstruction 169–171, 176; railway 168; Regulatory Plan 1888 168; riverbanks 180, *180*; transformation to an economic hub 168–169; urban plan, 1928 172; workers' housing colony 189–190
Ljubljana architectural projects: Bamberg House 171; Bežigrad 176; Cathedral of Freedom 178–179, *178*, 202n48; Congress Square 175–176, *175*; Cooperative Bank 186–187; French Revolution Square 176; Hotel Slon 193; Meksika housing project 193–194; Miklošić Square 170–171; Modern Gallery 198; Narodni Dom (People's House) 169; National and University Library 181–184, *182*; Nebotičnik (Skyscraper) 194–197, *196*; Serbian-Orthodox church 209; Slovenian Pantheon 178; Slovenian Philharmonics 168–169; Slovenian Square 170–171; Sokol Hall 187–188, *187*; Svetokrižki okraj (Holy Cross District) 176–177, *177*; University Faculty of Architecture 172, 174, 186, 189, 190, 198; University Library, National and 181–184, *182*; Villa Oblak 190–192, *191*; Workers' Chamber 194, *195*; Zacherl House 173, 201n29
Loos, A. 55, 56, 63n45, 102, 129, 130, 151, 173
Löwy, S. 134
Lubynski, R. 51, 61–62n25, 137, 141

Macura, Z. 92
Main Post Office and Postal Saving Bank, Belgrade 102–103

Maksimović, B. 108, 210
Marić Passage, Zagreb 137, 162n30
Marulić Square, Zagreb 51–52
Marxism 158–160
Maskimir Park, Zagreb 146
medical facilities, Zagreb 143–145
Medulić 66–67, 68
Meksika housing project, Ljubljana 193–194
Meštrović, I. 66–75, 77, 81n2, 142, 208; emigrates to USA 72–73; in exile 71; International Exposition 1911 69–70; Tomb of the Unknown Soldier 73–75, *73*, 77, 84n44, 84n57; V&A show 71; Vidovdan Fragments 67–68, 69–70, 71, 72; Vidovdan (St. Vitus Day) Temple 67–69, *68*, 70–72, 74, 81n6, 83n40
Michel, A. 72
Micić, L. 77, 78
micro-urban designs, Ljubljana 172, 175–181
Mihailo, Prince 27, 28, 29
Miklošić Square, Ljubljana 170–171
Milan, King 29, 30, 31
Miloš, Prince 17, 18
Milunović, M. 80
Milutinović, D. 206, 215n3
Ministry of Agriculture, Belgrade 94–95, *95*
Ministry of Buildings, Belgrade 25–26
Ministry of Finances, Belgrade 95, *95*
Ministry of Justice, Belgrade 30–31
Mitrinović, D. 69–70, 82n19
mixed-use developments 130–137, 137–138
Modern Gallery, Ljubljana 198
Modernism 11, 99–106, 130–137, 210; high-rise blocks 131–135; medical facilities 143–144; residential developments 109, 110, 111–112, *112*, 138–141, *138*; Slovenian 190–199
monumentality, interwar 79, 93–106, 108, 110, 114, 118, 120, 150, 184
monuments and shrines, national 10; Cathedral of Freedom 178–179, *178*, 202n48; mausoleums 33, 34, 59; Monument to French Illyria 176; Slovenian Pantheon 178; Tomb of the Unknown Soldier 73–75, *73*, 77, 84n44, 84n57; Vidovdan Temple 67–69, *68*, 70–72, 74, 81n6, 83n40

Index

Mortgage Merchandise Bank, Belgrade 119–120
mosques, destruction of 20, 36n15
movie theaters 92
Muslims, removal from Belgrade 17, 18, 19–20, 28

Načić, J. 23–24, 37n27
Nagodba 43
Najdhart, J. 213
Napredak (Progress), Zagreb 131–133, *132*
Narodni Dom (People's House), Ljubljana 169
Narodni Dom (People's House), Zagreb 42
National and University Library, Ljubljana 181–184, *182*
National Assembly, Belgrade 32–33, *32*, 34
National Bank, Belgrade 31–32
national style, architectural 10–12, 34–35, 186–187, 213
National Theater, Belgrade 27–29, *28*, 113
National Theater, Zagreb 47–49, *48*, 61n19
nationalism 2–3
Nebotičnik (Skyscraper) 194–197, *196*
Nestorović, B. 26, 94, 99, 214
Nestorović, N. 94, 97–98
Nevole J. 25, 27
Novakova Street, Zagreb 139–141

Obrenović, Mihailo 27, 28, 29
Obrenović, Milan 29, 30, 31
Obrenović, Milos 17, 18
Ottoman Empire 5

Palace of Labor, Zagreb 156
Pfaff, F. 49
Pičman, J. 102, 149, 150
Pilar, M. 207, 216n8
Planić, S. 131–133, 146, 161n13, 213
Plečnik, J. 172, 173–185, 186, 190, 194, 195, 197, 198, 199, 208, 212
Podrecca, B. 58–59
post-Academism 93–99
poverty 24, 91, 107–108
Prelovšek, D. 174–175
Prizenska Street, Belgrade 110–111, *111*
Progressive Youth 65
Public Health Palace, Zagreb 143–144

Radna Grupa Zagreb (RGZ) 147–149, 156, 159
Radovan, Zagreb 133–135, *133*
Ravnikar, E. 198–199
Rittig House, Zagreb 135
Rohrman, S. 193
Rondocubism 146, 187, 189, 197
Rosandić, T. 80
Rosinger & Jungwirth building, Zagreb 138
Round House, Zagreb 213
Royal Court, Belgrade 29–30, 33
Russia Palace, Belgrade 130
Russian architects 35, 93, 95–96, 98–99

Schmidt, F. von 45, 53, 54, 58, 207
Schön, E. 56, 117, 147, 150, 151, 164n64, 214
schools, Zagreb 151–156
Secessionism 56, 171, 173, 174
Second High School, Zagreb 154–155, *154*
Seissel, J. 77–78, 78–80, 85n64, 85n72, 149, 150
Semper, G. 31, 33, 56, 174, 184
Serbian Academy of Sciences and Arts 47, 98
sewage system 23, 24
Shell Company building, Zagreb 137
Siebeck, R. 45, 61n11
Sitte, C. 169, 170, 179, 185
skyscrapers 197–198; Albania Tower 115–116; Napredak 131–133, *132*; Nebotičnik 194–197, *196*; Radovan 133–135, *133*
Slovenian Pantheon, Ljubljana 178
Slovenian Philharmonics, Ljubljana 168–169
Slovenian Square, Ljubljana 170–171
social role of architecture 142–143, 157–160
social welfare, capital of 141–160
Socialist Federative Republic of Yugoslavia 9–10
Sokol Hall, Ljubljana 187–188, *187*
Sokol Movement 145–146, 188
Sokol Velodrome, Zagreb 146
Sokol Stadium, Zagreb 146
sports facilities, Zagreb 145–147
St. Mark's Church, Belgrade 211
St. Sava Cathedral 20, 33–34, 76

Index 223

St. Vitus Day (Vidovdan) Štampar, A. 143, 145
Starčevićev Dom, Zagreb 52
Stari konak (Old Palace), Belgrade 29
"state architects" 25–35
State Archive, Belgrade 98
State Printing Plant, Belgrade 103–104, 106
Steinmann, E. 51, 154–156, 165n75, 211
Stelè, F. 171, 182, 214
Šterk, V. 138
Stock Exchange, Zagreb 57, 127–130, *128*
Strajnić, K. 76, 208
street surfaces 23
Strossmayer Art Society 129
Strossmayer, Bishop Josip Joraj 7, 45, 47, 53, 54
Strossmayer Gallery, Zagreb 66
Strzygowski, J. 68, 208, 214
Student Dormitory, Belgrade 98–99
Šubic, V. 112, 193–197, 204n88
Sunko, D. 52, 62n33
Svetokrižki okraj (Holy Cross District), Ljubljana 176–177, *177*

The Tablet 74
Tanzimat reforms 21
Tehnički list (Technical Bulletin) 208–209
Terazije Terrace, Belgrade 99
Temple 67–69, *68*, 70–72, 74, 81n6, 83n40
Tomažič, F. 190–192, 204n82
Tomb of the Unknown Soldier 73–75, *73*, 77, 84n44, 84n57
Tomislav, King 4
Trešnjevka Elementary School, Zagreb 153

UJIA (Association of Yugoslav Engineers and Architects) 208–209, 211
Ulrich, A. 146–147, 164n62
University of Belgrade 96–99; Library 96–97, *97*; Student Dormitory 98–99; Technical Faculty 97–98, *97*
University of Ljubljana: Faculty of Architecture 172, 174, 186, 189, 190, 198; National and University Library 181–184, *182*
University of Zagreb 147–151; Agricultural Faculty 147–150, *148*;

Library 51; Technical Faculty 150–151; Veterinary Faculty 150
Uskok rowing club, Zagreb 146–147

Valtrović, M. 206, 215n2
Vancaš, J. 57, 62n36, 171
vernacular architecture 10, 19, 70, 78, 90, 92, 113–114, 206–207, 213
Victoria and Albert Museum, London 71
Vidaković, M. 112, 139
Vidovdan Fragments 67–68, 69–70, 71, 72
Vidovdan (St. Vitus Day) Temple 67–69, *68*, 70–72, 74, 81n6, 83n40
Villa Fuhrmann (Round House), Zagreb 213
Villa Karma, Lake Geneva 130
Villa Milićević, Belgrade 111–112, *112*
Villa Oblak, Ljubljana 190–192, *191*
Villa Pfeffermann, Zagreb 112, 138–139, *138*
Vitezović, P.R. 7–8
Volksgeist 2, 3, 10
Vreme Headquarters, Belgrade 116, *116*
Vrkljan, Z. 150, 157, 164n68
Vurnik, I. 174, 185–188, 189–190, 203n67

Wagner, O. 11, 56, 130, 173, 174, 183, 184, 185
Weissmann, E. 145, 147–148, 158–159, 160, 163n58
Wellisch House, Zagreb 135–137, *136*
Workers' Chamber, Ljubljana 194, *195*
Workers' House, Zagreb 156, 157, *157*
Workers' Insurance, Belgrade 142
Workers' Insurance, Zagreb 141–142
World Exposition Paris, 1937 78–80

Yugoslav Academy of Science and Arts 7, 45–47, *46*, 52–53, 129
Yugoslav Agrarian Bank, Belgrade 117
Yugoslav Art Colony 66
Yugoslav Committee 71
Yugoslav Pavilion at World Exposition 1937 78–80
"Yugoslav," term 211–212
Yugoslav Union Bank, Belgrade 102
Yugoslavism, quest for 7–9, 47, 65–67, 68–69, 75; and Yugoslav Pantheon 75–80

Zach, F. 8
Zacherl House, Ljubljana 173, 201n29

224   Index

Zagreb: economic development, interwar 143; "Fifty Years of Croatian Art" 212–213; history of a modern Croatian capital 41–43; housing, garden-city suburbs 138–141, *138*; housing, mixed-use projects 135–137, 137–138; industrial development 43; interpolated rental buildings 135; interwar development 127–160; Kapitol development 59; Kapitol, Gradec and Lower City united 43; medical facilities 143–145; mixed-use developments 130–137, 137–138; modern and national architecture 53–60; office buildings 137; parks 146, 156; railway 49, 52; Regulatory Plan 1932 *158*; Regulatory Plans 1865 and 1888 43, 44, 45; School of Arts and Crafts 53; schools 151–156; skyscrapers 131–135; social welfare 141–160; sports facilities 145–147; vying with Belgrade for supremacy 9; Zemlja art group 130, 142–143, 149, 159, 210

Zagreb architectural projects: Ante Starčević Square 52; Art Pavilion 50, 212–213; Banski Dvori (Ban's Palace) 41–42; Botanical Garden 51–52; Building Code, 1857 43; Cathedral 53–54, *55*; Chemical Institute 51; Church of St. Blaise 57–59, *57*; Communal Municipal Services Headquarters 151; Elementary School Jordanovac 152–153, *152*; First Men's High School 155–156; Foundation Hospital 145, *148*; Franz Joseph Square 49–50; Green Horseshoe program 44–53, *44*, 156; Halm House 45; Harmica 42–43; Hotel Esplanade 52, 62n34; Ilica Street 42; Institute of Physics 51; Jewish Hospital 144–145; King Peter Krešimir Square 156–157; Labor Exchange 156; Marić Passage 137, 162n30; Marulić Square 51–52; Maskimir Park 146; Napredak (Progress) 131–133, *132*; Narodni Dom (People's House) 42; national memorial 59; National Theater 47–49, *48*, 61n19; Novakova Street 139–141; Palace of Labor 156; Public Health Palace 143–144; Radovan 133–135, *133*; railway station, main 49; Rittig House 135; Rosinger & Jungwirth building 138; Round House 213; Second High School 154–155, *154*; Shell Company building 137; Sokol Stadium 146; Sokol Velodrome 146; Starčevićev Dom 52; Stock Exchange 57, 127–130, *128*; Strossmayer Gallery 66; Trešnjevka Elementary School 153; University Agricultural Faculty 147–150, *148*; University Library 51; University Technical Faculty 150–151; University Veterinary Faculty 150; Uskok rowing club 146–147; Villa Pfeffermann 112, 138–139, *138*; Wellisch House 135–137, *136*; Workers' House 156, 157, *157*; Workers Insurance Headquarters 141–142; Yugoslav Academy of Science and Arts 45–47, *46*, 53–54; Zakladni blok (Foundation Block) 130–133; Zrinjski Square 45

Zakladni blok (Foundation Block), Zagreb 130–133

Zdravković, I. 120

Zemlja art group 130, 142–143, 149, 159, 210

Zemljak, I. 151–153, 164n72

Zenit 77, 78

Zenitism 77–78

Zrinjski Square, Zagreb 45

Zrinski, P. 59

Žrnov Fortification 73, 84n46

Zvonimir, King Dmitar 4